5

# Kids as Customers

*A Handbook of Marketing
to Children*

James U. McNeal

Lexington Books

*An Imprint of Macmillan, Inc.*
NEW YORK
Maxwell Macmillan Canada
TORONTO
Maxwell Macmillan International
NEW YORK • OXFORD • SINGAPORE • SYDNEY

*Library of Congress Cataloging-in-Publication Data*

McNeal, James U.
Kids as customers : a handbook of marketing to children/
James U. McNeal.

p. cm.
Includes bibliographical references and index.
ISBN 0–669–27627–8
1. Youth as consumers—United States. 2. Marketing research—
United States. I. Title.
HF5415.33.U6N36   1992
658.8′ 348—dc20                                    91–46537
                                                    CIP

Lexington Books
An Imprint of Macmillan, Inc.
866 Third Avenue, New York, N.Y. 10022

Maxwell Macmillan Canada, Inc.
1200 Eglinton Avenue East
Suite 200
Don Mills, Ontario M3C 3N1

Macmillan, Inc. is part of the Maxwell Communication
Group of Companies.

Printed in the United States of America

printing number

1  2  3  4  5  6  7  8  9  10

*Being a consumer in our nation is a right.*
*Being a marketer is a privilege.*

*From* Children as Consumers:
Insights and Implications

# Contents

*Preface*   *ix*

**PART ONE**

## Introduction

**1**  The Emergence of Children as Customers                    2

*A Historical Perspective   4*
*A Sociological Explanation   6*
*Children's Development as Consumers   8*
*The Role of the Marketer   13*
*Children as a Multidimensional Market   14*
*Summary: A Vote for Kid Kustomer   17*
*A Couple of Warnings   18*
*Later Chapters   20*
*References   20*

**PART TWO**

## Children Are Three Markets

**2**  Children as a Primary Market: Their Income,
Spending, and Saving                                           22

*Children's Income   23*
*Children's Savings   29*
*Children's Expenditures   31*
*Overprivileged Children   32*
*Marketing Implications of Kids with Money   34*
*Summary and Conclusions   35*
*References   37*

**3** Children as a Primary Market: Their Spending
and Shopping                                              *38*

*Products Purchased by Children   39*
*Children's Preferred Stores   42*
*Children's Independent Purchase-Visits   44*
*What Shopping and Spending Mean to Children   46*
*References   61*

**4** Children as a Market of Influencers                    *62*

*Reasons for Children's Influence   64*
*Extent of Children's Consumer Influence   65*
*Information Sources Underlying Children's Requests   70*
*Children's Requesting Styles and Appeals   72*
*Location of Children's Requests to Parents   74*
*Influence of Kids on Parents' Choice of Retail Outlets   76*
*Parental Response to Children's Requests   77*
*Marketers' Perceptions of Kids' Influence*
  *on Parental Purchases   81*
*Marketing to Children as Influencers   84*
*References   87*

**5** Kids as a Future Market: Reaching Them Through
a Multidimensional Segmentation Strategy                 *88*

*Children as a Source of Future Customers   91*
*The Importance of Loyalty in Cultivating Kids*
  *as Future Customers   92*
*Building a Loyal Relationship with Children*
  *as Future Customers   95*
*Marketing to Kids Using a Multidimensional*
  *Segmentation Strategy   101*
*Managerial Suggestions   102*
*References   104*

**PART THREE**

# Marketing to Kids as Customers

**6** Retailing to Children                                  *106*

*Reasons for Retailers to Target Children as Consumers   107*
*Retailers' Responses to Kids as Customers   111*

*Some Retailers Target Children, Some Don't* 115
*Nonstore Retailing* 122
*Service Retailers* 124
*Conclusions and Recommendations* 126
*References* 129

**7** Advertising to Children      *130*
*Advertising as Part of the Marketing
    Communications Mix* 131
*Changes in Advertising Media Targeted to Children* 136
*Effects of Advertising to Children* 144
*Encoding/Decoding Problems in Advertising to
 Children* 147
*Observations and Recommendations* 153
*References* 157

**8** Targeting Promotion and Publicity to Children    *158*
*Targeting Promotion to the Children's Market* 160
*Children-Targeted Public Relations* 168
*Kids Clubs: A New Channel of Communications* 173
*Summary and Suggestions* 177
*References* 179

**9** Planning and Developing New Products for Children *180*
*Strategies for New Products for Kids* 182
*Remember, the Package Is for Kids, Too* 193
*Needed: New, New Product Strategies That Really
    Target Kids* 197
*References* 201

**10** Marketing Research Among Children: Purposes,
Procedures, Problems      *202*
*Purposes of Researching Young Consumers* 204
*Techniques and Procedures for Researching Children* 209
*Problems in Researching Kids as Customers* 220
*Using Parents as Surrogates for Children
    in Marketing Research* 223
*References* 225

**PART FOUR**
# Kids as Customers Tomorrow

**11** Children as Global Consumers                                       *228*

   *Reasons to Consider Children as Worldwide Consumers   230*
   *Reasons to Study Children as Global Consumers   234*
   *Children's Consumer Behavior in Other Parts of the World:*
      *The Case of the Pacific Rim   235*
   *Multinational Marketing Strategy to Kids: Standardize*
      *or Localize?   248*
   *References   250*

*Name Index   251*

*Subject Index   254*

# Preface

This book is about the market potential of children, ages 4 to 12, and marketers' responses to them. Not as one market, but as three rolled into one—primary, influence, and future markets. Chapter 1 describes the emergence of children as these three markets and shows that they have the greatest potential of any market. This is why so much marketing attention is focused on them. As a *primary* market, children have around $9 billion in income from their families, their household responsibilities, and work, and they spend a major portion of it on a wide variety of items to please themselves. They also save some of it, which is beginning to please bankers who now acknowledge them as three markets. Chapters 2 and 3 describe this primary market of young spenders—their income, savings, spending, where they spend, how often they spend, what they buy, and why they buy. Chapter 2 also reports on an initial research effort to identify and describe the consumer behavior of overprivileged children. A new study reported in Chapter 3 ascertains children's perceptions of the marketplace through drawings. Some of these drawings are displayed throughout the book.

Children also are a market of *influencers* giving directions to at least $130 billion of parental purchases. We are not speaking here of passive influence where Mom sees Wrangler jeans on sale when she is at the department store and decides to get Robert some because he likes that brand. We are referring to Robert and around 37 million other kids requesting, suggesting, demanding Wrangler jeans and hundreds of other items. Chapter 4 describes this market and shows, for the first time, the extent to which children directly influence 62 lines of products. And it describes how they go about it.

Children are a *future* market for *all* goods and services. They will eventually buy all the food for their own families, as well as clothing, autos, and everything else and, as Chapter 5 reveals, they are planning on it. We often hear them saying such things as, "When I get big, I'm gonna buy a Lamborghini." This chapter demonstrates how children's future market potential causes business firms to seek them out now with new marketing programs, so that when the children reach market age for a specific firm, they can more easily be converted into loyal customers. The chapter also explains a multidimensional segmentation strategy used by businesses to appeal to all three of these markets of children.

Chapters 6 through 10 describe the various marketing efforts directed to children as three markets, including the mistakes that are made, problems encountered, and suggestions and guidelines for marketing ethically and effectively. Chapter 6 describes, with some new research, specific marketing practices targeted to children by various segments of retailing. It also discusses the rapid growth of nonstore retailing to kids through such means as catalogs and clubs.

Chapter 7 gives an overview of the marketing communications mix that is targeted to children—advertising, promotion, publicity. For the first time, there is an estimate of total marketing communications dollars spent on the children's market in order to provide an idea of how much money the business community spends to attract children as consumers. The lion's share of this chapter is devoted to advertising as a major part of the marketing communications mix and its impact on children as consumers. Various media are discussed: television, radio, newspapers, magazines, movies, and videos.

Chapter 8 focuses on promotion—premiums, coupons, contests, sweepstakes—and public relations and publicity. Special consideration is given to marketing to children through schools, clubs, and special events.

New products strategies that target children are the topic of Chapter 9. Various strategies are described, their strengths and weaknesses, and how to effectively plan and develop products for kids. A key ingredient, "kid-ness," is explained. Also, effective and ineffective packaging of children's products is discussed.

Conducting marketing research among child consumers is discussed in Chapter 10 by explaining its purposes and describing some major techniques and procedures. The use of drawings as a research technique to circumvent the language difficulties encountered when working with children is discussed. Included, also, is a treatment of marketing research among parents in order to understand kids better and to market to them with parental approval.

The last chapter, Chapter 11, discusses children as a potential worldwide market. Reasons for considering children as a global market are explained. Actual research results of children's consumer behavior in the Pacific Rim are reported and compared with that of U.S. children.

This book is really the outgrowth of my earlier book, *Children as Consumers: Insights and Implications*, published in 1987 by Lexington Books. The purpose of that book was to describe for the first time children as a legitimate market of consumers using all the available published research. It was a book whose time had come, according to one business journalist. Response to it by the business community was overwhelming. This new book in some ways updates that one, by expanding the understanding of children as consumers with new research and new research techniques, and by describing, in detail, marketing efforts directed to them as three separate but interrelated markets. It relies on new data for these efforts, much from my own research, but also it relies on my consulting experiences in a number of industries, and of course, the many business articles that have been written about this topic.

The reader will notice the use of a number of headlines throughout the book that herald children as a major market. These were chosen from *Advertising Age, Adweek, Business Week, Food & Beverage Marketing, Fortune, Marketing News,* and the *Wall Street Journal.* Also, some come from regional newspapers including the *Boston Globe, Houston Chronicle, Los Angeles Times, Philadelphia Inquirer,* and the *Washington Post.*

No topic attracts the attention of the public more than children. This is logical; they are our most prized possessions. Consequently, the subject of children as consumers is no exception. There are many ethical questions that arise when discussing children as consumers and the marketing practices directed to them. *Children as Consumers* attempted to address these. They are noted in this book, also, but in less detail. On the other hand, there is more emphasis in this book on how to do it right—how to market to children ethically and profitably. This is summarized in Chapter 5's caveat, "When marketing to kids, wear kid gloves."

As a result of my twenty-five years of interest and work in this area of children's consumer behavior, I have accumulated an office-full of information about the subject. Rather than burdening this book with footnotes and references, I have accumulated over six hundred of them, annotated them, and placed them in a separate volume entitled *A Bibliography of Research and Writings on Marketing and Advertising to Children* that is published by Lexington Books. The first chapter of this bibliography also chronicles the history of news and research related to the consumer behavior of children.

I have had a lot of help in my work with children as consumers and the preparation of the resulting information for this book. I know that it has been frustrating sometimes for the people working on the project because of the changes that take place so rapidly in this relatively new market. I thank them all for their help and patience. I want to thank Dr. Larry Gresham, in his association with the Center for Retailing Studies at Texas A&M University, for his substantial contribution to the chapter on retailing. I particularly wish to acknowledge the assistance of David Boyd and Chyon-Hwa Yeh. The latter gave life to facts and figures; the former gave body.

# PART ONE

# Introduction

Kids catching marketers' eye

Kids are consumers, too

Recent Survey Shows
Today's Children Have
Deep Pockets

Children Are Spending More at Retail

kids'
market

Sugary Pitches
to Kids Capture
a Sweet Market

Planning Priorities for Marketing to Children

Marketers See
Future in Kids

Kids Buy the Darndest Things

Children come of age as consumers

Building Brand Loyalty
With Kids

The Influencing Role of the Child in Family
Decision Making

Children: The powerful new consumers

Children wield power
at the cash register

Children and
Shopping

The
Children's Market

FIGURE 1–1

# 1

# The Emergence of Children as Customers

The headlines from business magazines and newspapers shown on the opposite page (Figure 1–1) pretty much summarize this book. Kids today are customers, buyers, spenders, shoppers, consumers. All these terms are used to describe them. In fact, they are not just one market, they are three markets, as we will describe shortly. These headlines also imply the wide range of marketing activities that may be targeted to kids as customers. No longer is there just television advertising targeted to kids in order to get them to make purchase requests to their parents. There is still plenty of that; some critics say too much. But now a total, integrated marketing mix has been developed specifically for informing, persuading, selling, and satisfying children as consumers.

All of this economic activity at the junior ranks is relatively new—really a phenomenon of the 1980s—and it is big. As we will learn in later chapters, over a billion dollars a year is being spent just on marketing communications to children—advertising, promotion, publicity, and packaging—and these expenditures are backed by millions more invested in marketing research. All this and more because today's kid is an increasingly self-reliant youngster, pretty savvy as a consumer, with money of his or her own to spend, materialistic, willing to sub for the parents as a shopper, soon to be master of the marketplace. In boxing terms, a lightweight with an economic power punch whom we might nickname Kid Kustomer. This surprising new power punch is the focus of this book.

## A Historical Perspective

Thinking of kids as customers is a postwar phenomenon. Some retail executives over 50 still have trouble with the idea. For them, referring to children as customers often conjures up an image of a little kid's nose pressed against the glass of a candy counter. Today, because of the Kid Kustomers, there is no glass around the candy counter. It is open, extends to the floor, and covers, perhaps, six linear feet in a Circle-K or 7-Eleven store. And most likely the nose that is pressed against the glass today belongs to a kid who is peering anxiously into the glassed-in case of jewelry or cameras at a K mart or Wal-Mart store. One of these days those glass barriers will come down, too.

When did all this start? When did children become customers instead of being the sons and daughters of customers? With the baby boom, of course.

For children to be considered consumers, at least from a marketer's standpoint, they must have wants, money to spend, and there must be enough of them to make marketing efforts worthwhile. This was not the case prior to World War II. At most there was the same number of children then as there was at the turn of the century—around 10 million. But when the war was over in 1946 the baby boom began. Within a five-year period the number of kids increased over 50 percent! Now, *that's* a baby boom (to paraphrase Crocodile Dundee).

All that was needed to go with the numbers was the money and the wants to spend it on. Both came quickly. The war years somehow made everyone older, gave them a short-run attitude ("Have fun and die young," was often heard), and produced a self-centeredness the world had never seen. (It was apparent in advertisements that emphasized the key words, "I," "me," "my," and "mine" to feed this solipsism, for example, "My painting and Miss Clairol. This I do for me!") This "look-out-for-number-one" extended from the parents to their children who, growing in numbers, were given more money of their own to spend on themselves ("because they deserve it"). It was at least as much a new way of thinking as it was an increase in children-centeredness.

With their numbers and their dollars going up, kids began to attract the attention of marketers. And through that 1950s innovation called television, children were presented with things to want—Barbie dolls and Big Wheels, Sugar Pops and Frosted Flakes, to name a few.[1] TV advertising to children was used and even abused, so much in fact that by the 1970s there was a strong movement among consumer advocates and business regulators to get rid of it. And the Federal Trade Commission almost did in 1978.[2] Probably this one action symbolized more vividly than any other the unbelievably rapid growth of children as consumers and the concurrent marketing efforts aimed at them.

By the last half of the 1960s kids were spending over $2 billion a year of their own money for whatever they wanted, and they were influencing billions more of parental spending. It was about this time that the first publication declaring children to be a market appeared.[3] Their dollar power had finally gained them notoriety.

The '70s were affirmation years for kids as consumers. As the first generation of kids from the baby boomers, the children of the '70s received the blessings of their parents to be consumers. Marketers acknowledged them as buyers in their own right, as well as a market of influencers, by bombarding them with new products to buy or to get their parents to buy. Ronald McDonald, born in the '60s, became the standard bearer for McDonald's in the '70s and did battle with Burger King's King for the rights to kids' tummies—and the right to fill them with restaurant foods designed just for them. Meantime Geoffrey the giraffe introduced the kids to a whole new concept in toy merchandising—Toys "R" Us—that permitted kids and their parents to shop for toys just as they shopped for food. And ordinary bubble gum was practically replaced by Bubble Yum and similar, not-so-ordinary gums that provided kids with much more than just flavorful chewing. It provided them with fun, fantasy, and escape.

Consumer advocates of the 1970s saw children as consumers too, but more as consumers-in-training, and sought consumer education to direct them and regulations to protect them. The results were a mass of children-oriented consumer education programs originating from many sources—even the President's office—and a flurry of public policy efforts spearheaded by the Federal Trade Commission.

The academic community began to publish research regularly on the subject of children as consumers—a trickle in the early '70s, a stream in the late '70s. Of the approximately 300 papers written on the topic during the 1970s (250 more than were written in the 1960s), academicians produced over 75 percent of them.[4]

Surely, though, the 1980s will be recorded as the decade of the child consumer. Looking back through marketers' eyes, the '50s provided children in large numbers, the '60s gave them increased incomes to spend, the '70s developed and produced many new products and services for the children to want and buy, and the '80s gave the children legitimacy, or equality of sorts with adult consumers. The 1980s witnessed an explosion in media for kids. They got their own television networks (e.g., Nickelodeon), radio networks (Kids Choice Broadcasting Network), a number of new magazines (*Sports Illustrated for Kids*), and newspapers (*Young American*). Kids clubs sprang up among these media (Fox Kids' Club from Fox Network), and also among retailers (Burger King Kids' Club) and producers (Kraft's Cheese and Macaroni Club). The 1980s saw children-based retailing flourish, and not just toy and fast food retailers, but also clothing (GapKids), books (WaldenKids), banking (First Children's Bank), and hospitality (Camp Hyatt). And the 1980s witnessed many new high-ticket items for children offered by these retailers—designer brand shoes and clothing, cameras, telephones, and camcorders, to name a few—that only a decade ago would have been seen as major buys for adults.

As the decade of the '90s gets under way we can expect marketers to treat the children's market as a major market to be segmented into smaller, more profitable ones—just as they do for adults. Recently children as a primary market have been segmented by age into young (4–6), school age (7–9), and tweens (10–12). Segmentation according to household income, media habits, and culture can be anticipated.

## A Sociological Explanation

Some sociological changes in the 1980s appear to offer at least a partial explanation for children's newfound economic status. In no particular order and with lots of overlapping these changes can be described as follows.

**FEWER CHILDREN PER PARENT.** Busy schedules, career mindedness, economic pressures, and "'70s sensibility" caused families to begin reducing their number of children. The 1980s experienced a "Chinese syndrome" of sorts where "one is enough" became more common thinking among new parents. Whereas baby boom parents averaged over three children per family, the baby boomers' married children average less than two. The impact of this thinking has been the ability and desire to shower those fewer children per family with more—with more to have and more to spend. Thus, the growth in the population of children is flattening, but marketers need not fret because children's consumer clout continues to grow.

**FEWER PARENTS PER CHILD.** A combination of divorces and mothers not getting married has produced a large number of single-parent families. In these single-parent homes children are expected to assume more of the role of partner and to perform some of the consumer-related tasks that the missing parent might ordinarily do—shopping, preparing meals, feeding pets, cleaning house. The net result is that kids handle more money, often at an earlier age, buy more for themselves, and buy more for the household.

**POSTPONEMENT OF HAVING CHILDREN.** The increased importance of careers—often for both spouses—combined with the desire to develop a nest egg, has caused many adults to postpone having children (and also to have fewer of them). Therefore, when children are born to older parents (perhaps 30 plus), they are treasured more. The anticipation seems to make the child more valued. The growth in financial ability during postponement allows the parents to demonstrate this worth by providing the kids with more. When the kids reach the wanting age, these parents tend to be more responsive.

**DUAL-WORKING FAMILIES.** With Mom and Dad both working they are able to spend more money on their kids but they have less time with them. They often feel guilty about not spending more time with their children and therefore use the extra income to buy them more and give them more. Dual-working parents also tend to ask their kids to do more around the house and to be more self-reliant. This, in turn, requires the youngsters to assume the consumer role more frequently and probably at an earlier age.

When all of these social forces occur together, as they did during the '80s, the result is a better heeled, more self-reliant, more market-mature child. She or he is not only better off financially than the '70s kid, but knows a lot more about being a consumer and knows it at an earlier age. Mom and Dad have seen to it. But so have marketers. While the 1980s parents were pushing the child into the consumer role, marketers were pulling with more and varying promotion efforts that provided children additional marketplace knowledge. The result: Kid Kustomer with a stronger, one-two punch—one, as a market of primary consumers, and two, as a market of influencers.

## Children's Development as Consumers

To gain a better understanding of how children develop into consumers, let's look at it in its earliest stages. Children learn their consumer behavior mainly from parents and marketers. Parents are children's primary socialization agents who introduce and indoctrinate them into the consumer role. But marketers play an important part in children's consumer socialization, and their influence continues to grow as parents have less time and marketers have more interest.

An important point, in fact, should be made now about the nature of children's learning to be consumers before we continue our examination of it. Although being a consumer is as fundamental in our society as being a worker, faith worshipper, or student, it is not something that is carefully and deliberately taught—by anyone. It is taught by everyone, so to speak, with no one claiming primary responsibility. Most parents try to teach their kids some of the ins and outs, pros and cons, dos and don'ts of being a consumer, but rarely do the parents have an agenda in mind. It tends to be more of a watch-what-I-do, listen-to-what-I-say kind of teaching. Parents are not quick to admit this for fear of being thought irresponsible. Yet, when marketers bombard their kids with informative and persuasive messages, some parents get incensed, feeling that the marketers are usurping their responsibility for teaching their children about marketplace matters.

Some parents, educators, and lawmakers feel that the education system must assume more of the responsibility for teaching children to be consumers. Today, therefore consumer education is often taught in kindergarten and throughout the primary and secondary grades. But it is often done much like parental instruction—on a hit-or-miss basis. Some states—Illinois, Michigan, and Hawaii, for instance—have some mandatory consumer education, others have encouraged it through legislative resolutions, and some just teach it because it seems right. Usually it is not systematic, as was recommended by the White House's Special Assistant for Consumer Affairs in the 1970s, it is not consistent from school to school, and it is not seen as important by a large number of school officials or parents. There is, in fact, little teacher preparation for it. More will be said about consumer education throughout the chapters of this book. For now, as we discuss how children learn to be consumers, it is important to point out that their learning is more incidental than intentional even though becoming a consumer is basic to our way of life.

Interviews with several thousand households over the years suggest some generalized stages in the development of children's consumer behavior patterns. (While the stages are numbered for purposes of presentation, these numbers also roughly correspond to the age of the child at the beginning of that stage.)

1. *Accompanying Parents and Observing.* By the time a child can sit erect, he or she is placed in his or her culturally defined observation post high atop a shopping cart. From this vantage point the child stays safely in proximity to parents but also can see for the first time the wonderland of marketing. The youngster soon discovers that such outlets as the supermarket, hypermart, and discount house are stocked with good things to eat and fun things to play with—in fact, all those things used by the parents to reward and to show love. By age 2, a few connections between TV advertising and store contents are probably being made by the child along with connections between certain stores and certain satisfying products.

2. *Accompanying Parents and Requesting.* Starting around age 2 the youngsters begin making requests while shopping with Mom and Dad. Repeated store visits, more frequent consumption of cer-

tain items (foods, toys), and greater attention to advertising messages during television programming produce an increasing list of things for kids to want. At the same time, the youngster is learning how to get parents to respond to his or her wishes and wants. This may take the form of a grunt, whine, scream, or gesture—indeed some tears may be necessary—but eventually almost all children are able on a regular basis to persuade Mom or Dad to buy something for them. Whether their recommendations take the form of a tiny finger pointing at a certain box of cereal on the supermarket shelf or a big tantrum in front of the frozen desserts display, child influence on the consumer behavior of parents has begun and will intensify. How it is handled depends on parenting style. But for all parents it sometimes can be embarrassing. Such in-store embarrassments may trigger or amplify anti-marketing sentiments by parents toward marketers who target children, and these viewpoints may be learned by the children, too.

Requesting a product, such as a certain brand of cereal, and receiving it—perhaps to hold it while sitting in the shopping cart—adds another layer to the child's understanding of what being a consumer means. It also gives greater significance to the consumer role—it is recognized as a legitimate way to get things. This asking and receiving also lends importance to certain products and/or brands—"You can have this one, not that one," "That one is better," or "That one is not good for you." Moreover, the process of asking and receiving produces mental scripts that emphasize certain stores as sources of certain things. For example, one script might read that a supermarket is where you get breakfast food, except for fruit, which is obtained from the fruit and vegetable market.

3. *Accompanying Parents and Selecting with Permission.* By age 3 or 4 children are climbing down from the shopping cart, walking beside it, and asking to make some selections on their own. By now they probably recognize most brands of children's cereal, toaster treats, frozen desserts, candies, and salty snacks, and know their locations in the stores. (The role of a memorable package is very important here.) Moreover, at this stage children seem to have some favorite brands, although these change frequently. Some favorite stores even become favorites based on the children's knowledge of the merchandise and their comfort level in the stores. (This is not an insignificant fact to supermarkets and mass merchandisers, for

instance, but it is just now being taken into serious consideration by the management of these stores.)

Parents at this stage may begin allowing their kids to make some selections of favorite products. Sometimes the purpose is to keep the children busy; sometimes it is to teach them some rudiments of shopping. In the latter case the concerned parent uses these moments to talk about such matters as product and/or brand comparisons, prices, nutrition, and safety. In any case, for the first time children react to the store setting on their own and retrieve a product from it. Fingers that have been clenching the steel mesh of the shopping cart are unhooked, and the youngsters take their first steps toward developing their own consumer legs.

At this point the child has completed many connections, from advertisements to wants, to stores, to displays, to packages, to retrieval of want-satisfying products. For many parents this is a pleasing experience. Ditto for the marketers, for it signals the beginning of the child's understanding of the want-satisfaction process in a market-driven society.

4. *Accompanying Parents and Making Independent Purchases.* There is just one more step in the consumer cycle from wants to want-satisfying goods. That is, paying for them. This is a complex undertaking for children, even though they have seen their parents do it many times. Initially this act is an interference to children who are trying to obtain a particular product because they cannot yet conceptualize the exchange system. It also is frustrating and confusing because of the mathematics of money. These emotions are compounded by often having to wait in line, waiting in line with adults, and then often being received with indifference or worse by store personnel. Once the procedure is performed a few times, however, it gets simpler and has a more rewarding dimension to it as the child recognizes that handling money and paying for things not only produce satisfying goods and services, they are very adult. The problems with the mathematics of money and the basic requirement of having to pay for want-satisfying items tend to encourage children to try to understand money and the ways to obtain it. In fact, it is precisely this exchange process that is used by some kindergarten and elementary school teachers to teach arithmetic and some parents to teach money management.

A child's first independent purchase with parents is usually in a supermarket, convenience store, or discount department store. The activity usually leaves an indelible impression on the youngster, and the stores associated with early purchases tend to have a special place in the heart that may continue throughout life. The role of the retailer is probably more important at this stage of the child's consumer development than at any other. The retailer can help make the activity a very satisfying one for the child, and at the same time begin the development of the child as a lifetime customer. Opposite and negative results can occur, too, and often do. The actual impact of the retailer on the child's consumer socialization will be discussed in Chapter 4.

This step in which the item is actually purchased does not change the direction and flow of the want-satisfaction process learned in step three. It simply makes it more complex. One of the reasons for this complexity is the interaction with store personnel that is required in order to make the exchange. The children with their attitudes, emotions, and wants must interact and cooperate with strangers who may hold conflicting attitudes and emotions and wants—children, their satisfaction, and their purchases may or may not be important to the retail people.

5. *Going to the Store Alone and Making Independent Purchases.* Prior to or upon entering the first grade, usually between the ages of 5 and 7, the child solos as a consumer. The first independent store visit is usually to a convenience store but it may be to any nearby retail outlet—to a supermarket for a candy bar, to a fast food restaurant for a soft drink. The purpose is probably self-serving, although an increasing number of parents are encouraging their kids to make bread-and-milk runs in order to speed up activities in the household. Later, when children relate this first independent store trip, they often do it with all the excitement of a pilot who just made his first solo flight.[5] The specific store, what they bought there, when and how they consumed it, seem to be all-important matters to the youngsters. They may sense that they have opened the door not just to a store but to a world of want-satisfying things. Perhaps this explains why young children particularly think highly of convenience stores. If convenience store management, or management of any store involved in this first independent visit, understood the real reasons behind these feelings, it could better please the child then, and in the future.

In the process of accompanying parents to stores, which continues into the teen years, and going to stores on their own, which will continue throughout life, the children learn much about stores and their offerings. In fact, by the time children are in the third and fourth grades, they can provide detailed descriptions of a K mart or Kroger store, including store layouts, product and brand offerings of items for children and their households, and names and characteristics of some people who work in the stores. They also can describe the packages for many products and the advertisements for many more. Thus, becoming a consumer is neither a simple experience nor a programmed one. It is a combination of successes and failures, of increasing complexities and increasing satisfaction.

## The Role of the Marketer

The importance of parents, marketers, and educators cannot be overstated in children's consumer socialization, but the pivotal role of the marketer should be underlined. It is the marketer who provides the specific mix of products, describes them in advertisements, then packages, prices, and displays them. It is the marketer who lays out the store, determines its operating hours, the degree of light, noise, traffic. It is the marketer who decides the number of checkout stations in a store. All of these efforts and activities, and many more, also determine in great part what the child consumer will learn, feel, think, want, and how he or she will behave toward the marketplace. Marketers have discovered through research that a significant portion of adults, perhaps 20 percent, are anti-shoppers. That is, one person in five does not like shopping and would not do it if it weren't necessary. It is not known how early in life this negative attitude toward the marketplace starts, but it may have its genesis in childhood just as positive attitudes toward shopping do. Marketers who show sensitivity and provide assistance to these consumer-trainees can help assure that negative attitudes toward the marketplace do not develop, and that children get the most satisfaction from it. By doing this the marketer will be making an important contribution to our economic system as well as to the kids and their parents, and at the same time will begin an alliance with these new customers that can last a lifetime. The marketer who targets kids as customers is often described in any but positive terms by some parents, consumer advocates, and cause seekers. This negative characterizing often is deserved as a result of unethical practices toward kids. Such charges, true or false, only highlight the very basic role that marketers play in children's development of economic behavior.

## Children as a Multidimensional Market

Today's children are not just a group of blossoming young customers or just one market of 37 million potential buyers. They constitute market segments, in fact, relatively complex market segments. It is true that some cereal brand managers, for example, may see kids as a mass market, ages 2–11, but others see them as a multidimensional market as illustrated in Figure 1–2.

The vertical layers in Figure 1–2 show that all children are a primary (current) market of consumers, a market of influencers, and a future market. The horizontal layers show the children additionally as markets according to demographics, life-styles, benefits, and

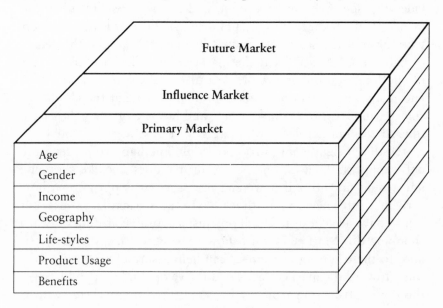

**FIGURE 1–2**
*Children Constitute Many Markets.*

product usage rates. Children as markets will be discussed throughout the book, but let us put the concept in perspective now. The vertical layers in Figure 1–2 are best termed markets since each potentially includes all children. That is, all children are considered a current market, a market of influencers, and all certainly are viewed as future consumers. Thus, children are *three markets in one*. This is much less true of adults who are viewed by marketers mainly as primary or current consumers, and less often as a future market or as a market of influencers. But each of these major types of children's market is segmented as shown in the horizontal layers—by age or gender, for example. Briefly, then, the elements of the children's market (according to marketing practices) are as follows.

- *Primary Market*. Children are a primary market—a market in their own right—in the sense that they have money of their own, needs and wants, and authority and willingness to spend the money on those needs and wants. In a later chapter we will learn that they have well over $8 billion of their own to spend, spend around $6 billion of it on toys, sweets, clothing, and many other items, and save the rest. Their $2-plus billion in savings suggest they are a primary market for the financial industry, also.
- *Influence Market*. Children directly influence over $130 billion in household purchases and indirectly influence that much again. For this reason the influence market shown in Figure 1–2 is larger than the primary market of children. Direct influence refers to children making requests for goods and services such as suggesting where to eat out, telling mom to buy a certain brand or flavor of ice cream, or making the selection when the family is shopping. Indirect influence means that the children's preferences are given consideration when parents make purchases.
- *Future Market*. Children will obviously become the consumers of *all* products and services as they grow older. This statement should not elicit a "so-what" response, however. Of the three dimensions of the children's market, this has by far the greatest potential. That is why it is shown as the largest market in Figure 1–2. Many companies

and trade associations invest in this market of children for ten to twenty years so that when the children reach market age they will be more easily converted into customers.

- *Demographic Segments.* We know that children are viewed as male and female segments, for example, by doll manufacturers. They may also be segmented according to their income, age, and geography. High-income children—they will be referred to as overprivileged children in a later chapter—are targeted as important customers of designer brand clothing, for example, as compared to children in general. As for age, children, like adults, may be considered young, middle-aged, and old. The three groups are also called preschoolers, school children, and tweens (not kids, not teens, but in be*tween*). Preschoolers are a great coloring book market, school children influence or buy jeans, and tweens buy jewelry, fragrances, and video game software. Bear in mind that these demographic segments may be current, future, or influence markets—for example, girls may be viewed as a future market for fur coats, boys as a future market for motorcycles.
- *Life-style Segments.* Children may be segmented according to their life-styles or those of their parents. Children can be seen as active, fitness-oriented, outdoor types, learning-centered, or fashion-conscious, just to name a few life-styles. All these terms and more may be used to describe children's parents, whose own life-styles cause the children to want to consume in ways consistent with theirs. The outdoor child, for example, belongs to a primary and influence market for sporting goods that might be reached through such magazines as *Boys' Life* or *Sports Illustrated for Kids.* A fitness-oriented youngster who wants exercise equipment and clothing might be targeted through these magazines, also. If the parents are, for instance, outdoor types, marketers of vacations might target children as influencers.
- *Benefits Segment.* There are no limits to the number and kinds of benefits children seek, and in some cases these benefits become significant enough to constitute a segmentation variable. Free or low-cost items are perceived as a benefit by many children because they believe that it

will be easier to convince their parents to obtain them. For example, a premium offer that states "Free with two proofs of purchase" often is interpreted positively by children as, "Mom can't complain or refuse if it's free." This is no less true for educational benefits. Being able to say, "You want me to learn, don't you," to parents about a desired product is an important benefit. Adult-likeness is another important benefit to children. Products that promise super powers, performance just like Dad, or increased physical dimensions, are very appealing to children. One other benefit should be mentioned, although there are many. That is, the benefit of long-lastingness. If a candy bar or soft drink lasts a long time or the flavor does, that is good according to a kid. *Product Usage-Rate Segment.* Children may be heavy or light users of products and respond favorably to products or services in these categories. For instance, children often are heavy users of video arcades and respond to advertisements of "ten extra tokens with a five dollar purchase." At least one manufacturer of toy cars sells them several to a package for the youngster who needs a fleet. Children may respond also to offers of smaller quantities such as a "child's plate" or "snack size" particularly in cases where products are preferred by their parents but not so well liked by the kids, such as liver, spinach, or grapefruit juice.

## Summary: A Vote for Kid Kustomer

These introductory remarks have attempted to show that kids are no longer the penny-candy purchasers of the 1950s and before. Due to many changes in our social and economic fabrics, kids have become a potent force in the marketplace, and not as one market but as three markets. They know more, they do more as consumers than their counterparts of earlier years. Astute marketers can no longer ignore them, regardless of the marketers' business. There can be no more "Go away kid, you're bothering me."

To symbolize this new consumer, the concept of Kid Kustomer was developed. In effect, today's kids really pack a punch—an economic punch—and they're not just one-punch sluggers either. They pack a one-two-three punch as current, future, and influence markets. As our research group sorted through the many drawings that children have done for our research, we took an informal poll to see whom we might choose as Kid Kustomer. Our choice is shown in Figure 1–3. She is a confident 9-year-old with a cute little nose and arms full of shopping bags, emerging from a department store. This combination of characteristics—confident, a big spender, able to cope in the marketplace—seems to summarize well this new economic force. Keep her in mind as we continue to talk about children as consumers in the following chapters.

## A Couple of Warnings

This is a good place to preface the remaining chapters with a few words of warning. Marketing to children may be practiced by anybody, but *successful* marketing to children is done by very few. It is common practice to try to capitalize on the potential of the children's market by producing adult products in kid form—scale them down, make them smaller, lighter, simpler, more fun. Such a strategy usually is not successful. It is also not uncommon for marketers to see kids through their own childhood experiences—"When I was a kid I always wanted a _____, and now I'm going to produce one and make a killing." Probably the only killing will be of the profits of the company that underwrites such thinking. Finally, there are those marketers who produce a certain product in a certain form because they believe they have a special understanding of kids. "I ought to know a lot about kids, I had four of my own," we may hear them say. This is likely to be a very expensive way for a marketing executive to discover the uniqueness of his children.

The pages of this book will reveal clearly the enormous market potential of the children's market and some major successes in marketing to it. This may be misleading if in the process they suggest that marketing to children is a snap. It isn't. It is not "a piece of cake," or "child's play," and it is not like "taking candy from a baby." It depends on some luck and most of all a lot of trial and error because *children are the most difficult of all markets to understand.* If they are difficult to understand, they are difficult to satisfy, and if they are difficult to satisfy, they are difficult to market to profitably. The only successes come from well thought out, well tested marketing strategies that have been designed by people who

## Kid Kustomer

**FIGURE 1-3**

acknowledge that kids are not mini-adults but special people in their own right.

This brings up one more warning of sorts. Kids are the most unsophisticated of all consumers; they have the least and therefore want the most. Consequently, they are in a perfect position to be taken. While it is difficult to market to them successfully, as observed above, it is equally difficult to market to them ethically. Safeguards must be in place every step of the way.

## Later Chapters

In this introduction I have shown that children are potential customers, described how this phenomenon came about, and identified some of the concerns about it. I have also described briefly what kinds of customers or markets children are, according to marketing practices.

In the remainder of the book I want to explain in detail what has been introduced here. Future chapters will reveal the nature of children acting as a variety of markets, and a wide range of marketing strategies and tactics related to children will be described. I will support these two flows of information with some marketing how-tos and do-nots. Also, I will introduce the concerns and activities of others, namely, parents, consumer advocates, and regulators. Altogether, the result should be interesting and useful to everybody concerned about children as consumers.

## References

1. For a good description of televised products for kids in the 1950s see Jim Hall, *Mighty Minutes: An Illustrated History of Television's Best Commercials* (New York: Harmony Books, 1984), Chapter 5.
2. The FTC rule that almost passed was described in "FTC Staff Report on TV Advertising to Children," *Advertising Age*, February 27, 1978, pp. 73–77.
3. James U. McNeal, "The Child Consumer: A New Market," *Journal of Retailing*, Summer 1969, pp. 15–22, 84.
4. James U. McNeal, *A Bibliography of Research and Writings on Marketing and Advertising to Children* (New York: Lexington Books, 1991).
5. James U. McNeal, *Children as Consumers* (Austin: Bureau of Business Research, The University of Texas, 1964).

# PART TWO

# Children Are Three Markets

**FIGURE 2–1**

# 2

# Children as a Primary Market:

## Their Income, Spending, and Saving

Stephanie, a fourth grader, drew the picture of the shopper in the music store in Figure 2–1. The shopper is Stephanie. She portrays herself as she really is—a shopper and buyer of cassettes of rock music and many other items. In an interview after she made the drawing she told us, "I go to the Music Bar [music store] every week and sometimes every day." She explained that she often goes to a shopping mall after school along with one or two friends, looks and listens to music, and buys at least one cassette a month with her own money. She also related other shopping experiences at the mall in which the music store is located.

Stephanie is part of a primary market of children in the United States that spends over $6 billion a year on a variety of goods and services. The term "primary market" is distinguished here from "secondary market," a term that often is used to describe children as receivers or users of goods and services purchased by others, usually parents. As a primary market, children spend their own money on their own wants. Parents, in fact, are sometimes described as a secondary market when discussing children as consumers because children buy them gifts for various occasions.

In this chapter and in the following chapter we will discuss children as a primary market. Here we will describe and explain their income, spending, and savings—their receiving and handling money—while Chapter 3 will focus on their store behavior as customers.

## Children's Income

I conducted a study during the fall of 1988 and the beginning of 1989 to determine the income, spending, and savings of children.

It was conducted in the southeastern and south central portion of Texas in a manner that attempted to produce a demographically representative sample of the nation as a whole. It consisted of a cluster sample of 1,018 households containing 1,330 children ages 4 through 12. The sample was obtained by taking a random sample of blocks from street maps, randomly selecting a household from each block, and conducting a qualifying interview with that household to determine if it housed any children ages 4–12. The qualified household was used as a reference for determining other households with children, and this procedure was continued until all target households in the block had been interviewed. One or both parents were interviewed in person for a period of around 25 minutes. Children were often involved although information from the parents was the primary focus. This study, herein called the 1989 study, is the basis for most of the economic data presented here, and is compared with 1984 data produced in the same region.[1]

Table 2–1 presents a summary of children's income, spending and saving based on the data from the 1989 study and compares it with similar data for 1984. It shows that children receive an average income of $4.42 per week, $229.84 per year, which if extended to a national basis amounts to $8,641,984,000. (The actual number of children aged 4 through 12 nationwide was not available but was estimated on the basis of Census Bureau forecasts at a maximum of 37,600,000, the number used here.)

The $4.42 average weekly income figure for 1989 is 46 percent greater than 1984 without adjustments for inflation. So we can conservatively say that children's income is not only keeping up with inflation (of around 5 percent) but exceeding it substantially.

Table 2–2 details children's income, spending, and saving by age. It reveals that at age 4 children have an average income of $1.78 per week, suggesting that many children probably receive income prior to age 4. By the time they are in primary school (age 7) their income has almost doubled to $3.12 per week. When children complete primary school at around age 12 their income has tripled from what it was in the first grade and reached $9.83 a week. The largest percentage increase (57 percent) in income is between ages 10 and 11; the next largest (37 percent) is between age 5 and 6. These increases closely coincide with children's entry into primary and middle school.

**TABLE 2–1**

*Average Income, Expenditures, and Savings
of Children: 1984 and 1989*

| | Weekly | | Annually | | National Estimates, Annually | |
|---|---|---|---|---|---|---|
| | 1984 | 1989 | 1984 | 1989 | 1984 | 1989 |
| Income | $3.03 | $4.42 | $157.56 | $229.84 | $4,729,793,640 | $8,641,984,000 |
| Expenditures | $2.72 | $3.07 | $141.44 | $159.64 | $4,245,887,360 | $6,002,464,000 |
| Savings | $0.31 | $1.35 | $ 16.12 | $ 70.20 | $ 483,906,280 | $2,639,520,000 |

**TABLE 2–2**
*Average Weekly Income, Expenditures, and Savings*
*of Children According to Age, 1984 and 1989*

| Age | Income | | Expenditures | | Savings | |
|-----|--------|--------|--------------|--------|---------|--------|
| | 1984 | 1989 | 1984 | 1989 | 1984 | 1989 |
| 4 | $1.08 | $1.78 | $0.49 | $0.83 | $0.59 | $0.95 |
| 5 | 1.12 | 1.98 | 0.90 | 1.31 | 0.22 | 0.67 |
| 6 | 1.28 | 2.71 | 1.25 | 1.98 | 0.03 | 0.73 |
| 7 | 1.85 | 3.12 | 1.80 | 2.59 | 0.05 | 0.53 |
| 8 | 2.50 | 3.41 | 2.31 | 2.66 | 0.19 | 0.75 |
| 9 | 3.52 | 4.83 | 3.19 | 3.20 | 0.33 | 1.63 |
| 10 | 4.05 | 4.88 | 3.39 | 3.28 | 0.66 | 1.60 |
| 11 | 4.79 | 7.69 | 4.33 | 5.05 | 0.46 | 2.64 |
| 12 | 5.49 | 9.83 | 5.26 | 6.90 | 0.23 | 2.93 |

A preliminary glance at children's income by age shows there are increases each year. Since most of their income is from parents (discussed in the following section), it appears that parents feel that children need more money as they get older. Probably, also, as children get older, they request more money.

## Sources and Purposes of Children's Income

Parents were asked to detail the sources and purposes of their children's income. The results are summarized in Figure 2–2. The largest single source of money for children is an allowance given by parents usually on a weekly basis. It constitutes around 53 percent of children's total income (up slightly from 49 percent in 1984) and is provided by around 55 percent of the households. Almost all parents said the main purpose of the allowance was to help children learn to handle money. An additional, frequently mentioned purpose was to permit the children to buy things for themselves. In around 60 percent of the families the allowance was linked to the children's performing household chores. However, this linkage was not formalized in most of these cases. For example, one mom who provided an allowance said that her son "is expected to help around the house."

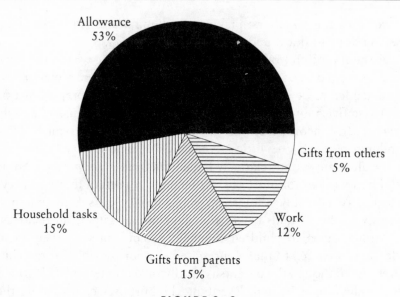

**FIGURE 2–2**

*Sources of Income for Children Ages 4–12.*

Parents who did not provide an allowance to their children tended to give children money "as needed" and often to tie these gifts of money (15 percent) to various occasions or to household tasks. Some gift occasions were family excursions, when the children go somewhere with other children, holidays, birthdays, high test scores, and last day of school.

Money received specifically for performing household tasks (15 percent) was often reported by the parents to be a way of teaching the children to earn money, or as one respondent said, to "teach them that money doesn't grow on trees." Household tasks were many and included washing dishes, vacuuming, feeding pets, emptying the trash, yard work, and tending to younger siblings. Typically the specific tasks were priced out, that is, completing a certain job earned a certain amount of income. Parents tended to treat this money as an addition to an allowance that could be earned by the child if he or she really wanted more income.

Around 12 percent of children's income is derived from part-time work outside the home. It is encouraged by some families more than others, mainly lower income households and single-parent households. The main types of part-time work were baby-sitting, yard work for neighbors, picking up aluminum cans for recycling, selling door to door, and delivering newspapers.

A small portion (5 percent) of children's income was in the form of gifts from others, usually grandparents and other relatives. These gifts tended to be related to special occasions or accomplishments.

These five sources of income are not mutually exclusive; a child may receive income from all of them. Within the extremes, a few children received very little income, while some received relatively large allowances and relatively large gifts from grandparents. Some children worked for most of their income. A pattern that was prevalent was a weekly allowance, some money gifts from parents, mainly for households tasks, and some money gifts from relatives.

Money given to children by their parents, in whatever form, clearly is intended to make purchase behavior possible for the children. Even though the parents typically talked in terms of "learning to handle money" when describing the purposes of providing the children with income, they obviously meant it from the standpoint of being a consumer. When the topic was pursued, there were always references to the children's spending—their high rate of spending, their careless spending, or their mistakes in spending.

## Children's Evaluations of Their Income

Throughout the 1989 household survey, children, when available, were involved. Their thoughts were elicited to confirm the amount and adequacy of money received. Except for most of the 4-year-olds and a few of the 5s, none of the children thought the amount of money received was enough. They said that there were a lot of things they wanted to buy and could not. They also often reported that their friends received more, particularly more in terms of an allowance. A small but significant number of the kids complained that there were not enough "things to do around the house" in order to earn money. Slightly related was the complaint by some of the children that they did not have enough opportunities to spend their money.

These evaluations by children of their income suggest a great concern for money, perhaps what *Fortune* magazine has termed "money enchantment."[2] Their desire to have more money and to buy more with it reflects a type of materialism that marketers are often accused of creating. A closer examination suggests that parents should share the responsibility for children's materialism, if that is what it can be called, for it is the parents who provide the money and some of the incentives to obtain it. Moreover, according to *Fortune,* parents are passing on to their children the value of using money to define who one is.

## Children's Savings

Contrary to the commonly held view that children spend all the money they can get their hands on, Tables 2–1 and 2–2 show that they do save some of their money. In fact, children are now saving nearly three times as much as they did in 1984. Of the $8.6 billion per year received by all children, they save around $2.6 billion of it, or approximately 30 percent. Table 2–2 shows that children of *all* ages saved relatively more in 1989 than in 1984. A study funded by *Sports Illustrated for Kids* in 1989 also showed that three-fourths of kids who receive an allowance save some of it.[3] So it appears that saving is popular among children. It is a popular idea among parents, also, who often talked about the value of teaching systematic savings to their children. They frequently mentioned articles in popular magazines such as *Money* and *Parents* that described how to get children to manage their money.

In both time periods the data indicate that children save a very substantial amount of the money they receive prior to age 6, then the savings rate declines dramatically. The rate climbs again at ages 9 and 10. In 1989 this higher rate continued, but in 1985 it sloped off again at ages 11 and 12.

Both parents and children confirm the relatively high rate of savings and describe savings programs in place within the home. The savings efforts appear not to be a problem for the 4- and 5-year-olds, but by the time the children reach primary school age, they become more reluctant to save. Said another way, when kids reach school age, they discover an increasing number of things to spend money on, including some of the money they have been saving.

The main purpose of the children's savings program is to learn money management, according to the parents, but that has different interpretations among households. Around half of the families believe that the practice of saving is inherently good, that it is a virtue that all children should practice. The intensity of this value among parents seems greater than it was in 1984, and may help explain the higher savings rate.

In the other half of the families there was a slightly different viewpoint. These families emphasize savings for their children also, but add that it provides money for future spending on relatively expensive items such as bicycles, computers, and vacations. In this case, saving money is viewed as necessary but it is a consumption-based practice.

As for the means of saving, roughly half of the children's money is saved in home depositories and half in commercial depositories. The *Sports Illustrated for Kids* study produced essentially the same findings. Preschoolers almost always save at home while nearly 60 percent of tweens (those 9–12) have commercial savings accounts. A few, in fact, had investment accounts with parents. All the children save at home in piggy banks and other containers (*Sports Illustrated for Kids* estimated the amount to be $31 at any one time), but the older children, beginning at age 8 or 9, also get involved in commercial savings of some sort with their parents' assistance.

In most cases, part of the savings at home is spent from time to time on high-ticket items, and to some extent this is true for the children's commercial savings as well. In a regional telephone survey of 190 households located within the sampling frame of the 1989 study, parents indicated that most children were using savings for Christmas shopping. In fact, with data from this survey it was estimated that children spent over $1.2 billion during the 1989 Christmas selling season, half of which may have come from savings. There is no way of knowing how much the promotional efforts expended at Christmas time by merchants were responsible for children spending this large amount of savings, but the amount seems significant to merchants whose sale volume is heavily dependent upon the Christmas season. And children did not spend this money with just any merchant. They have store preferences, as will be shown in the next chapter.

More banks are becoming aware of the relatively substantial amount of savings among children. At least two banks have been established to serve children—Young Americans bank of Denver and First Children's bank in New York City.[4] Some banks are beginning to do what banks did many years ago and commonly do in Britain, that is, visit schools for the purpose of getting children to establish savings accounts and then to deposit savings regularly through a representative such as a teacher or PTA volunteer. What this means is that an increasing number of banks are beginning to view children and their savings as an opportunity to develop a more loyal body of depositors as the children grow up. Banking to kids may not seem like an easy way to make money, and in the short run it isn't. But the fact that it is possible to develop a loyal group of customers (as banks apparently at one time had) is very appealing to this industry that is struggling to reestablish itself with a positive public image. Also, banking to children is an idea that if franchised may return some profits, and if publicized should attract some parents as depositors.[5]

## Children's Expenditures

Returning again to the two tables, we can see that of the $8.6 billion children receive as income, slightly over $6 billion is spent annually. While this is a somewhat lesser rate of spending than in 1984, the absolute amount is almost half again as much ($6 billion vs. $4.2 billion), or roughly a $350 million per year increase over the past five years.

Table 2–2 shows that some 4-year-olds do some spending; in fact, a few of them spend all their income during shopping trips with parents. But it is really when the kids get into school that they become spenders. It appears that they discover many more things to want as they interact with other school children, with teachers, and as they travel to and from school. For example, we found that children who walk to school make more store visits, usually to convenience stores, than those who ride. Incidentally, as described later in Chapter 11, this was also true for Chinese children in Hong Kong and Taiwan.

In Chapter 3 we will describe what children spend their money on and where they spend it, but it is important to emphasize at this point that the money they spend—the $6 billion—is all discretionary and can be spent on almost anything they wish. It is in this context that children are a significant primary market to many marketers. It should be noted, also, that while their $2.6 billion in savings makes them a primary market for the banking industry it also makes them a target market for sellers of high-ticket items.

During the past two decades personal expenditures of children have been estimated as follows.

| Year | Spending (in billions) | Change |
|------|------------------------|--------|
| 1968 | $2.2 | — |
| 1978 | $2.8 | 27+ |
| 1984 | $4.2 | 50+ |
| 1989 | $6.1 | 45+ |

These estimates suggest that children's spending, although sizable during the '70s, did not grow much—less than 3 percent per year between 1968 and 1978. But over the next ten years the rate of annual increase was around 11 percent. These figures tend to reflect increased giving by parents to their children, a greater emphasis by parents on children being self-reliant, and the increasing number of children.

These growing expenditures of children also explain, in part, marketers' increased interest in children as a market. For the concerned parent or consumer advocate who complains about the increasing advertising efforts aimed at children, these figures provide some of the explanation. As parents push children into the marketplace by giving them more money to spend, marketers pull on them in order to get a share of their growing expenditures.

## Overprivileged Children

While arraying the income data from the 1989 study of children's consumer behavior we were surprised to find that the highest incomes were not the domain of just the oldest children. In fact, a significant number of children at each age, 4–12, had relatively high incomes. Moreover, their spending and saving were significantly greater than those for all the children averaged together. Their economic status is shown in Figure 2–3, compared to children as a whole. These children were labeled overprivileged children (OPs) and studied separately. We discovered the following characteristics about them.

- OPs' average income is over twice the average for all children—$9.95 a week vs. $4.42. The additional income is derived mainly from larger allowances and gifts from parents. In total, OPs constitute only 18.5 percent of children but possess nearly half of children's total income.
- Parents of OPs both work in 77 percent of the cases and in 78 percent of those cases both are in professions (e.g. accounting, architecture, teaching). They therefore are usually in a position to provide their children with more.
- OPs' average saving is $3.58 per week compared to a figure for all children of $1.35—a rate of over two and a half times the average. OPs' savings patterns do not differ noticeably from children in general, although the OPs are inclined to use commercial banks slightly more as compared with saving at home. Also, the few 11- and 12-year-olds in the 1989 study who invest some of their money were identified as OPs.

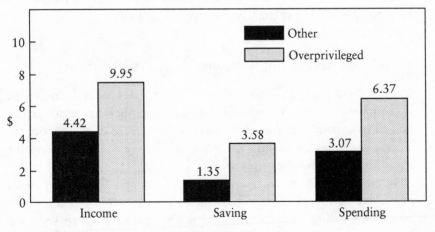

**FIGURE 2–3**

*Weekly Income, Saving, and Spending of Overprivileged Children Compared to All Children.*

- OPs spend twice as much as children on the average—$6.37 per week vs. $3.07. These extra dollars often go for items of higher unit cost.
- OPs purchase more designer-brand clothing, more consumer electronics and more sporting goods than the average spender of the same age.
- Younger OPs shop in specialty stores more than other younger children, and practically all OPs shop in department stores as compared to a small percentage of children in general.
- OPs participate in household responsibilities and decision making more than the other children. They feed the pets, vacuum, and clean more. They are involved more in decisions regarding weekend vacations and major purchases such as boats, and decisions about after-school activities.

Nationwide there are around 7 million children, ages 4–12, who could be classified as overprivileged because they average receiving, saving, and spending twice that of children overall. They constitute a niche of consumers that surely interests marketers of high-ticket items for children such as consumer electronics and signature clothing. Reaching OPs with marketing messages, however, may require specialized media such as direct mail. The kids' clubs that have become so popular probably have data on their members that will help to identify those that are overprivileged.

## Marketing Implications of Kids with Money

For the most part, children's money is parents' money being spent by children. It is all discretionary. In fact, no other consumer group has a larger proportion of their income earmarked as discretionary. This means they can spend it for whatever they want to, whenever they want to, wherever they want to.

What does this mean to marketers? It means some good news and some bad news. The somewhat bad news is that to get a share of that $6 billion that children spend marketers have to sell to a group of consumers that no one understands very well. Children are not like adults—they do not think like adults, and they do not act like adults. Since marketers are all adults, when marketing to children they are quite likely to make mistakes that translate into wasted dollars.

The good news is that selling to children as a primary market permits a marketer to earn additional revenues while establishing a relationship with children that could last a lifetime. The $6 billion that children spend may not be that big to many marketers, but a customer for a lifetime is. Thus, Coca-Cola or Hershey, for instance, may not be overwhelmed by the additional revenues that they obtain from children's current purchases, but if preferences are developed as result of those purchases, they have enormous value. Likewise, the $4 to $5 spent in stores each week by each child may not be viewed by many retailers as significant, but if those small expenditures are the beginning of a lifelong relationship between store and consumer, they are really worth thousands.

Thus, it may be difficult for many producers and retailers to spend advertising and merchandising dollars on children if the returns are viewed only on a current-year basis. But the potential of children's spending behavior becoming lifetime income for sellers means that children as a primary market are very important customers.

## Summary and Conclusions

In Chapter 1 we set out the steps children take in learning to be consumers and showed the final step to be that of making independent purchases. Of course, money is necessary for this step to take place; although the actual amount required for a youngster to make an occasional independent purchase is not great—perhaps a dollar a week. But this chapter has shown that children, on the average, spend over four times this much.

Children average spending $4.42 a week and on an annual basis for all children this amounts to over $6 billion. This spending obviously has more purpose to it than just learning to be a consumer, or just learning to handle money, as parents reported. The dramatic increase in children's income since 1984, most of which is derived from parents, suggests that parents want their children—expect their children—to be practicing consumers. The fact that money is given to children as early as age 4, and that the amount is increased every year, suggests that parents are encouraging their youngsters to assume the consumer role as quickly as they can.

Children are not shunning this responsibility as they might back away from the edge of the swimming pool when they first try swimming. Quite the contrary, they appear enthusiastic about it. Perhaps this is because being a consumer is an adult thing to do and children rush to be adults. Perhaps they understand the opportunities for satisfaction that await them in the marketplace. After all, from the time they were toddlers, they have been aware of the satisfaction-producing goods and services available in stores through their visits there with their parents and through television programming and advertising. Perhaps children want to be consumers simply because they sense that their parents want them to be consumers.

The income, spending, and saving data reported here testify to the fact that today the consumer life cycle begins in childhood, not in adolescence as it did before the baby boom. This is not the case just for the overprivileged child from the affluent family; it is also true for the lower-income and the lower-social-class families. The problems and opportunities that this relatively new development presents for marketers are numerous and complex and will be described throughout this book.

# References

1. The 1984 data is reported in James U. McNeal, *Children as Consumers: Insights and Implications* (Lexington, MA: Lexington Books, 1987), Chapter 3.
2. Myron Magnet, "The Money Society," *Fortune,* July 6, 1987, pp. 26–31.
3. *Sports Illustrated for Kids Omnibus Study,* Volume 1 (New York: Time Inc., 1989).
4. Michael Rozek, "Young People Get Lessons in Thrift and Banking: Learning about Business," *Update,* No. 4 (1989): 14–17.
5. Nancy Shepherdson, "No Child's Play, 'Kiddie Banks' Tap a Growing Market Segment," *Bank Marketing,* June 1988, pp. 28–32.

Nendy B.  TOYS "Я" US

FIGURE 3–1

# Children as a Primary Market:

## *Their Spending and Shopping*

The scene in Figure 3–1 shows Wendy, 9-year-old, shopping in a Toys "R" Us store in Houston, Texas. Wendy has no trouble at all envisioning herself loading up a shopping cart with toys as shown here. Moreover, her drawing shows she is quite familiar with the Toys "R" Us name, including the backward R, and familiar with merchandise other than toys, such as books, that can be found there. Wendy is part of the generation of new children consumers who was sitting in a shopping cart by age one, walked beside the cart at age 3, and started pushing one at age 5, perhaps a scaled-down model for children that is increasingly found in self-service stores. She is quite comfortable with "doing it herself" in a Kroger, K mart, or Kaybee store.

As this chapter will show, Wendy and a number of Kid Kustomers like her display an air of confidence about taking on a self-service store and coming out a winner. A major reason was demonstrated in the last chapter's discussion of kids as a primary market—kids at this age have a good deal of money to spend and a strong desire to spend it. In this chapter we will look at their actual spending—*what* kids buy and *where* they buy it.

## Products Purchased by Children

In a 1989 study of 1,018 households with children (described in more detail in Chapter 2) we asked parents and their children what the children buy with their own money. The answers are summarized in Table 3–1 alongside a similar report from 1984.[1]

**TABLE 3–1**

*Products Purchased by Children with Their Own Money*
*1984 and 1989*

| Product/Service | Expenditure and Share | | Expenditure and Share | |
|---|---|---|---|---|
| | 1984 | (%) | 1989 | (%) |
| Snacks/Sweets | $1,440,600,000 | (33.9) | $2,076,852,544 | (34.6) |
| Toys/Games/Crafts | 1,104,100,000 | (26.0) | 1,878,771,232 | (31.3) |
| Clothes | NA | | 690,283,360 | (11.5) |
| Movies/Sports | 771,200,000 | (18.2) | 606,248,864 | (10.1) |
| Video Arcades | 765,900,000 | (18.1) | 486,199,584 | ( 8.1) |
| Other | 162,300,000 | ( 3.8) | 264,108,416 | ( 4.4) |
| | $4,244,029,967 | (100.0) | $6,002,464,504 | (100.0) |

To some extent the findings are as expected. The majority of children's own money is spent on sweet things and playthings. But even this bears a closer look. The range of purchases in each of these two categories has been expanding. Consider sweets. This includes candy, gum, frozen desserts, fresh pastries, cookies, fresh fruit, and a wide range of beverages—carbonated, juice drinks, and flavored drinks. Fruits and fruit juice drinks were not reported in the 1984 study. It appears, based on a study of children's perceptions described later in this chapter, that children are thinking fitness more, and buying and consuming fruits probably reflect this value change. The $2-plus billion they spend on the snacks/sweets category has a great impact upon the total sales of several of these product lines. While the percentage of income spent on snacks and sweets remains essentially unchanged from 1984, the total amount spent has increased substantially and the makeup—what is actually bought—has changed somewhat also, although it is not reflected in the table. The term "snacks" here refers to nonsweet edibles—chips, nuts, popcorn, pretzels, and crackers—usually called salty snacks. Children's salty snack purchases have increased in volume, range, and frequency since 1984. This appears to be mainly a function of salty snack marketers who are providing a greater range of products backed up by increased advertising and promotion budgets of which more is targeted to kids. The 1991 advertising campaign to kids for Cheetos Paws from Frito Lay is a good example.

The toys/games/crafts category of children's purchases has grown since 1984, and now takes a larger share of children's spending—31 percent versus 26 percent. Probably the simplest explanation for this increase is the availability and purchase of a larger number of higher-cost-per-unit play items. Software for video games and radio-controlled vehicles are good examples of these higher-ticket items. Also, the supermarket-like environment that is increasingly found in play-item retailing is very inviting to children who grew up in a self-service environment.

The most dramatic change in children's purchases from 1984 to 1989 is in clothing. In 1984 there was no clothing category. The few purchases reported were tucked away in the gifts category. Now, children spend almost $700 million a year of their own money on apparel, including shoes. What has caused this explosion of clothing purchases? The answer is a complex intermingling of supply and demand factors. Kids have more money to spend—from income and saving—due to generous parents and children's ability to save more, and that permits purchase of higher-cost-per-unit items such as clothing. Also, children love conspicuous products that meet their needs for identification (with certain others) and separation (from certain others). Again, clothing items, including shoes, serve these needs well. Parents, who at one time made most of the purchases in this category for their kids, are now too busy working and increasingly are relinquishing the responsibility to their youngsters.[2]

On the supply side licensed brands, including designer brands, are more prominent in kids clothing, both in the department store price range and the discount store price range. Brands such as Esprit, Gap, Polo, Sasson, and Gitano, once only for teens and adults, are now available in kids' sizes and styles. Athletic shoes in particular that have significantly increased their targeting to children during the past five years. Expensive styles of these shoes, along with relatively high-priced designer brands of clothing are particularly desired and purchased by overprivileged children—the OPs described in the previous chapter who have twice the money to spend of most children.

The two categories of children's purchases that have *declined* significantly but together still constitute over a billion dollars in expenditures are movies/(spectator) sports and video arcades. In both cases part of the explanation can be found in changes in home life. Children (and their parents) are renting and buying videotapes and are playing video games much more, and therefore are spending more time at home with these items. (Working parents want their kids home more, either to take care of things while they are gone or to be with them when they are home.) In the meantime, on the supply side, movie theaters have increased their prices significantly and many video arcades have increased their appeal to older market segments. Both marketing actions probably have discouraged children as purchasers and have caused parents to discourage those purchases by their children.

The category "other" consists of over a quarter of a billion dollars spent on a very wide range of goods and services. Consumer electronics for gifts and personal use, music items, hobby items, fragrances, toiletries, flowers and plants are the main purchases in this category. Again, as with toys and clothing, relatively high-unit-cost items are noticeable in this category. Also, the role of marketers is important in stimulating some of these purchases. For example, the increased offering of plants and fresh flowers in a self-service environment is prompting children to give more consideration to the purchase of these items.

Throughout these spending categories, there are two significant changes going on among children as primary consumers. Children are spending more money than they did five years ago—$6.1 billion compared to $4.2 billion—and they are buying more high-ticket items. Both make marketing efforts directed to them more worthwhile. Moreover, these increases in purchases by children as a primary market indirectly reduce the costs of and encourage the practice of developing future customers from these children. More will be said about this possibility in Chapter 5.

## Children's Preferred Stores

Where children spend their money and where children *want* to spend their money often differ. Let us take a look at both of these dimensions of their spending.

Children begin visiting retail outlets with their parents at about the same time they learn to walk. By the time they are ready to enter school they have developed some "druthers" about stores. In general, children like and prefer stores that (1) are children-friendly, (2) their parents prefer, and (3) stock desired products in depth. The large number and range of stores that children visit early in life with their parents appear to be judged as good or bad according to these three attributes. There really is such a thing as a children-friendly store and children sense it. Like adults, children want to be wanted. A store that greets children (some greeters ignore them), provides gifts for children (cookies, balloons, e.g.), and has shopping facilitators for children (e.g., scaled-down shopping carts, eye-level displays) will attract children and make a good impression on them—an impression, incidentally, that may last a lifetime. Children tend to like what their parents like, in part to please their parents and in part because it's a sound criterion, and will often repeat negative and positive statements made by parents about stores, even including some of their voice inflections. It is logical that children would prefer stores that stock products for them, but we might not think immediately of the convenience store and super-market as much as, say, the toy store as preferred types. But convenience stores as well as supermarkets are "good stores" in general, according to kids, because both types have an abundance of snacks and sweets, often stock playthings, and often are children-friendly. More is said about these stores in the next chapter.

To the extent that children's store preferences are generalizable, they look like those shown in Table 3–2. There are no definitive lines between their preferences, but in general young children like the ease of convenience stores and the breadth of supermarkets. Older children prefer the breadth of discount stores (mass merchandisers) and the depth of specialty stores (toy, music, sporting goods,

**TABLE 3–2**

*Children's Preferences for Four Types of Stores*

|  | Age 5–7 | Age 8–9 | Age 10–12 |
|---|---|---|---|
| Convenience Stores | 1 | 1 | 3 |
| Supermarkets | 2 | 4 | 4 |
| Discount Stores | 3 | 2 | 2 |
| Specialty Stores | 4 | 3 | 1 |

e.g.). What perhaps is more significant in this ranking of children's store preferences is the types of stores that do not rank high with children even though they stock some products that children desire, for example, department stores and drug stores. There are many exceptions to this categorization of preferences caused by population area size, convenience, and special efforts of a particular store to attract or deny children. For example, department stores often are managed autonomously even though they are part of a group. And one or more of these stores may be favored by children because a store's management acknowledges children as potential customers and has policies and practices to serve them.

Thus, there are stores that children like and prefer to shop in if given the opportunity. However, children often must buy in stores that are most convenient. Children are limited by transportation and their parents' permission to visit stores. Therefore, children who walk by certain stores to and from school may spend money in those stores even though the stores rate low on their preference scale. Also, although they may not have chosen the mall or a particular store in the mall, children who are taken there by their parents may make purchases there. In interviews, we learned that one youngster made purchase-visits to a Kroger store almost daily. The reasons? It was located near her home and her parents sent her there frequently for household purchases. Consequently, she also made frequent purchases for herself at that store. Probably retailers ought to assume that some children are in their stores because of circumstances rather than choice and should take the opportunity to reduce the children's dislike or dissonance. They would be doing a favor for the kids, their parents, and indeed for their stores.

## Children's Independent Purchase-Visits

Tables 3–3 and 3–4 show the extent to which children made purchase-visits to stores in 1984 and 1989. Table 3–3 arrays the visits with parents during which the children make independent purchases. As mentioned in Chapter 1, this stage of consumer behavior may begin at age 4. The table shows that this is true for 30 percent of kids, by age 5, 54 percent, and by age 7, almost 90 percent. The average number of trips per week generally increases with age up to age 8, as does the average number of different kinds of stores

**TABLE 3–3**

*Children's Independent Purchase-Visits While Shopping with Parents*

| Age | Children (%) | | Average Number of Trips/Week | | Average Number of Different Stores | |
|---|---|---|---|---|---|---|
| | 1984 | 1989 | 1984 | 1989 | 1984 | 1989 |
| 4 | 16.3 | 30.1 | 1.8 | 2.0 | 1.5 | 2.0 |
| 5 | 58.2 | 54.0 | 2.0 | 2.0 | 1.6 | 2.0 |
| 6 | 60.4 | 65.2 | 2.0 | 2.2 | 2.5 | 2.3 |
| 7 | 100.0 | 88.8 | 2.7 | 2.8 | 2.5 | 2.5 |
| 8 | 100.0 | 99.2 | 2.6 | 2.7 | 2.8 | 2.8 |
| 9 | 100.0 | 99.2 | 2.8 | 2.8 | 2.8 | 2.9 |
| 10 | 100.0 | 100.0 | 3.1 | 2.9 | 2.9 | 2.9 |
| 11 | 100.0 | 100.0 | 2.8 | 2.9 | 2.7 | 2.9 |
| 12 | 100.0 | 100.0 | 2.4 | 2.4 | 2.3 | 2.5 |

visited, and then both figures level off. For example, by the time kids are in school, they make 2.8 trips a week to stores with parents to make independent purchases, and they make these purchases in 2.5 different stores. Both figures are substantially more than for preschool years, but not much different from the upper years. There are no noticeable differences in the measures between 1984 and 1989. Naturally the number of trips and the kinds of stores are primarily determined by the parents, but children do make store-visit requests, as described in the next chapter, and parents tend to honor them. So, the children do influence, to some extent, the number of visits and the types of stores visited with parents.

On their own, as shown in Table 3–4, children start making independent purchase-visits a bit later in life than with parents. They may walk or bicycle to stores or they may be taken by parents. Very few 4- and 5-year-olds go to the store alone, but by age 6 around half of children make a solo store visit. By age 7, about three-quarters are doing it, and upon reaching age 9 over 90 percent are performing as autonomous shoppers. The average number of store visits and number of different stores visited are fewer than with parents because of travel limitations and the like. But, by the time

**TABLE 3–4**

*Children's Independent Purchase-Visits to Stores*

| Age | Children (%) | | Average Number of Trips/Week | | Average Number of Different Stores | |
| --- | --- | --- | --- | --- | --- | --- |
| | 1984 | 1989 | 1984 | 1989 | 1984 | 1989 |
| 4 | 6.1 | 6.0 | 1.0 | 1.0 | 1.0 | 1.0 |
| 5 | 9.1 | 20.0 | 1.0 | 1.0 | 1.0 | 1.0 |
| 6 | 52.1 | 50.2 | 1.2 | 1.0 | 1.4 | 1.2 |
| 7 | 80.1 | 71.0 | 1.6 | 1.6 | 2.1 | 2.0 |
| 8 | 87.5 | 77.7 | 1.7 | 1.8 | 2.2 | 2.0 |
| 9 | 98.1 | 92.3 | 2.2 | 1.9 | 2.2 | 2.2 |
| 10 | 100.0 | 99.9 | 2.3 | 2.3 | 2.3 | 2.2 |
| 11 | 100.0 | 99.0 | 2.7 | 2.8 | 2.2 | 2.2 |
| 12 | 100.0 | 100.0 | 2.8 | 2.8 | 2.3 | 2.3 |

children have been in school a year or so, they make around two store visits a week on their own to at least two different types of stores. There are no significant differences in any of the data between 1984 and 1989, although there appears to be a slight tendency for a smaller percentage of children in the mid-years to shop independently.

These figures, overall, illustrate the development of children into consumers. By the time a kid reaches age 10, he or she is visiting and making purchases in an average of 5.2 stores a week or over 270 times a year. These figures are probably comparable to average purchase-visits made by many adults. (Actually, these figures and those above are probably understated since in many cases in the research a visit to a mall was counted as one store visit.) From this kind and amount of experience, children quickly form opinions about the marketplace, its stores, merchandise, and personnel. Also, they quickly gain knowledge about the marketplace, competence in how to operate there, and a sense of its purpose in a market-driven economy.

## What Shopping and Spending Mean to Children

Recognizing that children do get marketplace experience, that this experience produces perceptions about the marketplace, and these perceptions give direction to consumer behavior, an additional study was conducted in 1989 to determine what shopping means to children. That is, what kind of knowledge, feelings and views do children who have going-to-the-store experience possess about the marketplace.

To gather information a drawing technique was utilized since it is so difficult to elicit perceptions from children with standard inquiry methods. Drawing research has been used by psychologists for a century to study children's perceptions because children have trouble putting into words information that is stored as images.[3] After some trial-and-error iterations it was determined that the instruction that worked best for this study's purpose was, "Draw what comes to your mind when you think about going shopping." The only consumer-related cue word is "shopping," and the pilot studies showed that it elicited the widest range of response among children.

One group of children each was randomly selected from the second, third, and fourth grades of a middle-class school. Earlier, it was indicated that these children would have at least some minimum amount of marketplace experience. The experiment was carefully controlled by trained researchers. To make sure the perceptions revealed in the children's drawings were those of the children, rather than those of the experimenter, a systematic and objective application of categorization rules called content analysis was used. Some of the pictures that resulted from the study are displayed at the beginnings of the chapters in this book. The results were as follows.

## Types of Retail Environments on the Minds of Children

Table 3–5 ranks the retail settings portrayed in the children's drawings and shows that when children thought about going shopping they usually thought about the supermarket first. Supermarkets were drawn by children of all ages although they were the most popular choice of the youngest. This importance of the supermarket in the lives of these children may be explained by looking back at their early consumer socialization. Ever since they were able to sit erect they often were placed high atop a supermarket shopping cart from which they could observe the selections of all those wonderful treats that were provided by their parents. It was probably

**TABLE 3–5**

*Type of Retail Environments on the Minds of Children*

| Type | Frequency | Percent |
|------|-----------|---------|
| Supermarket | 45 | 40.2 |
| Specialty Store | 29 | 25.9 |
| Discount House | 15 | 13.4 |
| Department Store | 13 | 11.6 |
| Shopping Mall | 13 | 6.2 |
| Convenience Store | 3 | 2.7 |
| | 112 | 100.0 |

at the supermarket where the children first were taught to give money to the "storeman" or to actually purchase a sweet. Also, the supermarket is likely to be mentioned often by the children's parents whenever the topic of "going shopping" or "doing the shopping" arises. Finally, around 70 percent of the children in this study live in homes where both parents work. Consequently, many of the children are expected to do some shopping, or help with the shopping, and probably at a supermarket. One 10-year-old, for example, reported in the post-performance interview that when her mother let her out at school that morning she was given a five-dollar bill with instructions to pick up "burgers and buns" (hamburger meat and buns) after school and to buy something for herself. Children whose parents both worked tended to illustrate a supermarket more frequently than children of the same age from two-parent households where only one worked.

The second most frequently drawn type of store was the specialty store. In order of importance, the types of specialty stores illustrated were toy stores, music stores, sporting goods stores, ice cream stores, and computer stores. Specialty stores tended to be the choice of the older children, those 9 and 10, and to some extent of children of professional working parents. Older girls were more likely to draw a music store or a clothing store; older boys, a sporting goods store.

Discount houses such as K mart and Wal-Mart constituted the third choice of the children. While they were drawn by children of all ages, they were not drawn by older children from professional households. As children of parents in the professional class grow older, it would appear that discounters with their broad offerings lose some of their appeal and are replaced by specialty stores and department stores with their depth of assortment.

Department stores were the next most popular kind of store illustrated. The older girls tended to identify with the department store, mainly with the product area of clothing, particularly with designer-brand clothing. Only one boy illustrated a department store setting.

The convenience store was the least noted type of store. This appears contrary to previous reports that showed that convenience stores are very popular with children. A possible explanation for this difference is that children do not identify "going shopping" with the convenience store.

Six percent of the children illustrated a shopping mall rather than an individual type of store. Actually, more were expected since malls are such popular shopping environments. Also, for some children whose parents work, the shopping center is a good place to go after school. There, they meet with friends, examine an endless variety of merchandise and services, and feel comfortable and secure. Apparently, though, when children think about shopping, they think in more specific terms than about collections of stores.

In the content analysis of drawings by children it is often useful to speculate on what is *not* contained in the results but what might be expected. Drawing theorists explain that it is a sound assumption to expect children to draw objects they value.[4] Therefore, when expected objects do not appear in significant numbers of drawings, it is likely that they are not valued, or at least not valued as much as similar objects drawn by the group of children under study.

Already noted was the fact that convenience stores were included by less than 3 percent of the children. Fast food restaurants, shoe stores, drug stores, variety stores, arcades, and computer stores were not included at all, although one child illustrated the "Sears computer department." The omission of some of these retailing types was probably due mainly to the instructions given to the children. "Going shopping" logically might not evoke visions of fast food outlets, video game parlors or even convenience stores. However, the omission of drug stores and variety stores, for example, does appear to be a function of values since these outlets carry a large number of items of interest to children.

## Stage of Shopping Activity

To children, does "going shopping" mean going to the store, actually shopping, or coming home with the goods? Table 3–6 answers this question.

Essentially, "going shopping" means actually shopping. It means selecting, reaching for, and filling up a basket or cart to 82.2 percent of the children. Almost all of the children of working parents depicted themselves in the process of shopping.

Those drawings that portrayed children completing the shopping activity, around 10 percent in all, were usually by the oldest children. In 8 of 10 of the shopping completion cases the children had shopping carts overflowing with goods. The other two had their arms full of shopping bags and were exiting from department stores. Even at this very early age, some of their drawings seem to symbolize a "shop till you drop" mentality.

A small number of children attempted to depict the beginning of the shopping activity. The drawings showed them either leaving home (one was even entitled, "Go to store") or approaching a store or shopping center. These external views of the shopping setting, although small in number, probably were the most literal portrayals of "going shopping." Interestingly, all but one of these renderings were by younger children of single parents.

## Product Focus of Children "Going Shopping"

When children "think of going shopping" what products do they think of? Shopping for what? These questions were answered, in

**TABLE 3–6**

*Stage of Shopping Activity Implied by "Going Shopping"*

| Stage | Frequency | Percent |
|-------|-----------|---------|
| In Progress | 92 | 82.2 |
| Completion | 12 | 10.7 |
| Beginning | 8 | 7.1 |
| | 112 | 100.0 |

general, in Table 3–5, which ranks the types of retail environments that come to children's minds when they think about going shopping. But it is very important to the retail community to know specifically the children's product focus when shopping is on their minds. For example, do they mainly think of the snacks and sweets with which children are stereotypically associated?

The answer is much more complex, as Table 3–7 shows. In fact, the variety of products on the minds of children is so extensive— 271 in all—they were divided into foods and nonfoods to aid discussion. This large number of products evoked by the cue "shopping" is testimony to children's involvement in the consumer role as well as the extensive efforts of marketers that foster much of this involvement.

**FOODS.** The most frequently illustrated foods were not snacks and sweets in the traditional sense; they were vegetables (17.6 percent) and fruits (13.4 percent). Interestingly, the most noted products were not the ones advertised to children. One explanation for the popularity of fruits and vegetables among the children is that they are considered snacks and sweets in the relatively new fitness lifestyle that now pervades American households. Or perhaps in the children's minds fruits and vegetables require shopping, while the traditional snacks of candy, cookies, ice cream, and chips, all of which were pictured, are standardized and require less searching for and comparing. Including fruits and vegetables in the drawings was less of an age-related function than was drawing a supermarket.

Next in order of importance were soft drinks and cereal, each noted in 7 percent of the children's food drawings. Both are sweets from a child's standpoint, both are merchandised to children, particularly cereals, and both are traditionally associated with children. Meat, milk, and canned vegetables were each drawn eight times, or 5.6 percent. Other than milk, children might not be expected to emphasize these products. Equally unexpected were detergents (4.2 percent), eggs (3.5 percent), butter (2.8 percent), soup (1.7 percent), bottled water (0.7 percent), and fish (0.2 percent). The remaining items—bakery goods (4.2 percent), ice cream (4.9 percent), peanut butter (3.5 percent), cookies (2.8 percent), candy

**TABLE 3-7**

*Products Children Expect to Buy When Going Shopping*

| Product | Frequency | Percent |
|---|---|---|
| Foods | | |
| Vegetables | 25 | 17.6 |
| Fruits | 19 | 13.4 |
| Soft Drinks | 10 | 7.0 |
| Cereal | 10 | 7.0 |
| Canned Vegetables | 8 | 5.6 |
| Meat | 8 | 5.6 |
| Milk | 8 | 5.6 |
| Ice Cream | 7 | 4.9 |
| Bakery Foods | 6 | 4.2 |
| Detergent | 6 | 4.2 |
| Eggs | 5 | 3.5 |
| Peanut Butter | 5 | 3.5 |
| Butter | 4 | 2.8 |
| Cookies | 4 | 2.8 |
| Candy | 3 | 2.1 |
| Chips | 3 | 2.1 |
| Fruit Juice | 3 | 2.1 |
| Coffee | 2 | 1.4 |
| Popcorn | 2 | 1.4 |
| Soup | 2 | 1.4 |
| Bottled Water | 1 | .7 |
| Fish | 1 | .7 |
| | 142 | 100.0 |
| Nonfoods | | |
| Toys | 30 | 23.3 |
| Clothing | 18 | 13.6 |
| Video Games | 12 | 9.3 |
| Cosmetics/Toiletries | 10 | 7.8 |
| Skate Boards/Skates | 8 | 6.2 |
| Sporting Goods | 8 | 6.2 |
| Records/Cassettes | 6 | 4.7 |
| Stereos/Jam Boxes | 6 | 4.7 |
| Books | 5 | 3.9 |
| Shoes | 5 | 3.9 |
| Bicycles | 4 | 3.1 |
| Jewelry | 4 | 3.1 |
| Computer/Software | 4 | 3.1 |
| Stickers | 4 | 3.1 |
| Television Sets | 3 | 2.4 |
| Telephones | 2 | 1.6 |
| | 129 | 100.0 |

(2.1 percent), fruit juice (2.1 percent), chips (2.1 percent), and popcorn (1.4 percent)—are more expected choices of children.

**NONFOODS.** In addition to 142 food items, there were 129 instances of nonfoods contained in the children's drawings. Some of the children's drawings hinted at a one-stop shopping orientation by showing both foods and nonfoods as choices. For instance, Jonathan, a third-grader, sketched himself shopping in a supermarket, and above his head were aisle markers, one of which read, "Toys, Juice, Coffee."

Toys, which are responsible for around half of TV advertising to children, were at the top of the list of nonfood drawings as shown in Table 3–7. The classification of toys, which made up almost a quarter of the nonfoods, consisted principally of stuffed animals, dolls, games, miniature cars and trucks, and robots. Shown separately in Table 3–7 are the toystore-related items of bicycles, skate boards, skates, books, and video games. Most of the toys were depicted in self-service toy stores such as Toys "R" Us, but around 25 percent were shown in discount house settings (K mart and Wal-Mart) and in supermarkets. In half of the cases, toys were shown in shopping baskets or carts, usually heaped up, suggesting preferences for a self-service setting. Children of all ages included toys in their drawings and boys portrayed them slightly more than girls.

The second most popular category of nonfoods was clothing. To the children in this study, clothing is mainly a department store offering (Foleys, Dillards), and designer brands are essential (Esprit, Guess, Calvin Klein). Clothing also was shown in discount houses in a few drawings and even in a supermarket in one case. Older children, usually girls from professional working families, included clothing in their drawings. As noted in Table 3–7, shoes were also included in a few drawings but they were always shown in a department store or discount store setting rather than in shoe stores. Electronics were popular and included home video game sets, telephones, television sets, stereo sets, portable stereos, and personal computers. Cosmetics and toiletries (cologne, perfume, face cream, lipstick, shampoo) were shown in several of the girls' drawings and almost always by older girls. The girls also sketched jewelry (earrings, necklaces, and bracelets) in four instances.

*Price Consciousness of Children*

The 112 drawings were examined for the existence or absence of price consciousness indicators. Price consciousness indicators were defined as actual prices such as $1.98 and $10, words that would indicate price consciousness such as "sale" and "bargain," and depictions of money.

Eighteen (16 percent) of the drawings contained indicators of price consciousness. Ten drawings showed a variety of actual prices. Eight of these were in toy store settings while two were in department stores. Examples were a 25 cents sign hanging over a display of toys, a price tag with $30.00 written on it and attached to a doll, and a sign in a department store that said "Shorts $10.00."

The other eight indicators of price consciousness were words. In five of the drawings the word "sale" was used, all in clothing settings. In two discount house drawings the word, "special" was used, and in one the words "super buy" were displayed.

The relatively low percentage of children who demonstrated some price consciousness in their drawings is in keeping with other research findings that show that children are not very concerned with price. The somewhat high frequency of price consciousness shown among the toy store settings may be explained by the higher price of toys when compared to other products such as foods. Possibly, also, the pairing of toys with prices reflects the parents mentioning price often when the topic of toys arises. Children often report saving up for toys, which may cause toy prices to be more of a concern. The lack of price concern in the large number of supermarket drawings is probably a function of the relatively low prices of supermarket goods. Also, it could be a result of the low visibility of price markings that is more common in supermarkets than toy stores.

*Brand Consciousness of Children*

Prior research suggests that children are very conscious of brands and that they value certain brand names. A question of concern in this study was whether brand consciousness would show itself when children simply thought about going shopping. The children were only cued with the words, ". . . when you think about going shopping," not with such words as "product" or "brand."

Table 3–8 shows the 38 product categories that were present in the children's drawings and indicates which categories were represented by a specific brand and the frequency of representation. (It should be noted that several of these product categories, particularly fruits and vegetables, tend not to have well-known brands associated with them, so that the children would not be expected to assign brands to them.) Of the 38 product categories, children portrayed brands in 20 of them, or 52.6 percent. Nonfood items were somewhat more likely to be shown with brands than foods. Additionally, certain categories of nonfoods, namely toys, video games, records/cassettes, and clothing, showed a higher frequency of brand names than any category of food. In total there were 90 brands depicted in the drawings. The children also provided names of 22 different retail outlets such as Kroger and K mart, but these were not included in the measures of brand consciousness.

Almost 38 percent of the drawings depicted brands, even though they were not cued or requested; almost 53 percent of the product categories were represented by brands, and 32 percent of all the 271 products drawn possessed a brand name. All three age groups gave almost equal emphasis to brands in their drawings, as did both boys and girls. The inclusion of brand names (and store names) in the children's drawings without them being solicited attests to their value to the children and no doubt to the effectiveness of advertising.

## Children's Perceptions of Interior/Exterior Retail Environments

The drawings in this study provide an unique glimpse of the physical dimensions of the retail setting that children see when they think about going shopping. The shopping setting seems particularly difficult for children to describe verbally, but with pictures they are able to portray their perceptions of store-related colors, sizes, layouts, contents, even sounds, in one statement.

**EXTERIOR ENVIRONMENT.** Of the ten children who interpreted "going shopping" as going *to* the shopping setting, seven illustrated the exterior of shopping malls and two showed the exteriors of supermarkets. In all cases the exteriors were shown in dull colors and stereotypical designs as compared to bright colored and freewheeling interior designs. The exteriors of the shopping malls usually had signs on them either identifying a type of store, for example, "toy

**TABLE 3–8**

*Extent of Brand Consciousness Among Children*

| Product | Brand Indicated | Frequency |
|---|---|---|
| Foods | | |
|    Cereal | Yes | 5 |
|    Candy | Yes | 4 |
|    Cookies | Yes | 4 |
|    Soft Drinks | Yes | 4 |
|    Chips | Yes | 3 |
|    Ice Cream | Yes | 3 |
|    Fruit Juice | Yes | 2 |
|    Peanut Butter | Yes | 2 |
|    Bakery Foods | No | — |
|    Bottled Water | No | — |
|    Butter | No | — |
|    Canned Vegetables | No | — |
|    Coffee | No | — |
|    Detergent | No | — |
|    Eggs | No | — |
|    Fish | No | — |
|    Fruits | No | — |
|    Meat | No | — |
|    Milk | No | — |
|    Popcorn | No | — |
|    Vegetables | No | — |
| Nonfoods | | |
|    Toys | Yes | 16 |
|    Clothing | Yes | 8 |
|    Records/Cassettes | Yes | 7 |
|    Video Games | Yes | 7 |
|    Sporting Goods | Yes | 6 |
|    Cosmetics/Toiletries | Yes | 5 |
|    Shoes | Yes | 4 |
|    Stereos/Jam Boxes | Yes | 3 |
|    Bicycles | Yes | 2 |
|    Computer/Software | Yes | 2 |
|    Skate Boards/Skates | Yes | 2 |
|    Television Sets | Yes | 1 |
|    Books | No | — |
|    Jewelry | No | — |
|    Stickers | No | — |
|    Telephones | No | — |

store," or a store name such as Sears. Department stores were the most commonly named, which is probably explained by their emphasis as anchor stores in most malls.

**INTERIOR ENVIRONMENT.** Vitality and variety are the key descriptors for children's portrayals of the interior shopping setting. Seventy-four of the children's interior drawings were done in color—by choice—to demonstrate their perceptions of stores. Even most of those done in pencil possessed an apparent liveliness. Those in color frequently employed primary colors for walls, shelves, products, and floors. For example, floor tiles, which adults might not notice but children are very close to, were illustrated in ten drawings in checkerboard fashion of either red and white, blue and white, or black and white.

Every type of store was drawn by some children with an abundance of display fixtures. Fifty-two of the drawings, mainly supermarkets and toy stores, portrayed stores as consisting of shelf after shelf of products. True to scale, the shelves were usually shown as towering over the child shopper. In addition to shelving, checkout counters were shown in ten stores: six in supermarkets, two in toy stores, two in music stores. Besides the shelving and counters, there was an array of special, free-standing displays. They held the following products: clothes, video games, computer software, fruit and vegetables, guns, knives, and stickers. Also, two fourth-graders each carefully drew two clothing-draped mannequins in two department store settings.

One of the most striking features of the children's drawings was the predominance of shopping carts. Clearly, for there to be shopping there must be a means of gathering up the merchandise, according to 71 percent of these children. Of the 112 drawings, 63 contained shopping carts, 12 showed shopping baskets, and in four the shoppers had their arms full of shopping bags. With the exception of four drawings, the shopping carts were very large, often giant size. The strong, steel mesh of the cart was almost always apparent as was its handle, infant seat, bottom rack, and wheels. The wheels, particularly, often appeared overly exaggerated, but if we realize that most of these children spent at least two years next to those wheels—watching them turn, hearing them squeak, seeing them stalled by dried beans and other debris in the aisles—perhaps we can understand the emphasis given them.

There was also some use of signs in the drawings. Four drawings contained overhead aisle signs in supermarkets designating the location of such products as flour, coffee, and cereal. As noted earlier, there were several sales signs. Two drawings showed brand-specific banners hanging from the ceilings. Two checkout lanes were marked with numbers. And in one drawing there was a lighted sign that said, "Sale when red light is flashing." So children not only see and catalog what is at or below eye level, but they demonstrate keen awareness of even what is in the heights of the stores.

Finally, the value of the shopping setting to the children is demonstrated in the amount of detail provided in their drawings of store furnishings other than fixtures—items theoretically less noticeable because they are less directly related to the stores' primary function of selling. These included dressing rooms in two discount houses, restrooms in a shopping center, a Coke vending machine in a sporting goods store and a Pepsi-Cola vending machine in a music store, a public telephone outside a supermarket, fire extinguishers, trash cans, ceiling light fixtures, and even music (shown as musical notes) emanating from grills in the ceilings of two supermarkets. Such detail is unlikely unless there is much emotional involvement on the part of children, and this involvement is unlikely without a high value placed on the shopping environment.

## Emotional Tone

The emotional tone of a drawing is expected to reflect the feelings of the artist toward the object drawn and is manifested in the faces of characters in a drawings, use of colors, lines and shapes, and inclusion of various symbols. Since the children were allowed to draw whatever shopping-related picture they wished, as suggested earlier, a positive tone was expected.

There were 112 children figures and 31 adult figures presented in the drawings. Seventy-seven (69 percent) of the children and 13 (42 percent) of the adults were smiling, suggesting a generally happy, even fun, experience for the youngsters. Perhaps the smaller percent of smiling adult shoppers indicates that the shopping experience for adults is seen by children as more serious, or less fun, which may be a response to the negative remarks often made by parents about shopping.

Almost one-third of the children's faces appeared to have frightened expressions. Perhaps some children are intimidated by the towering fixtures, store personnel, and large numbers of people.

As reported earlier, bright colors were often used for store interiors, suggesting an air of excitement for the children. This excitement was punctuated by a variety of shapes (not all fixtures were angular), lines going in many directions (not just horizontal and vertical), and use of lines of varying thickness. Finally, rainbows were included in four drawings, the sun in two, and stars in two, hinting at an exciting tone.

In sum, there was a high degree of exhilaration portrayed in the children's drawings. Being permitted to shop is a very uplifting experience for most children, even though they may be initially intimidated by certain aspects of the shopping setting. Besides the anticipated satisfaction from the products available for purchase, there is the satisfaction derived from performing an adult activity. The mere fact that in their drawings children almost always put themselves into the shopping setting (in contrast, they depicted their parents only 27 percent of the time) attests to the positiveness of the experience.

## Independent/Dependent Shopping

When the children thought about shopping, not all of them thought about shopping independently. Of the 112 children shoppers, 31 were depicted as being with a parent, and specifically their moms. Thus, 72.3 percent definitely viewed themselves as independent shoppers. Of the 31 mother/child shopping situations, 12 of the children appeared to be *with* their mothers, that is, they were not shopping independently. All 12 of these children were eight-year-olds. The other 19 pairs appeared, however, to be co-shoppers in which both are making independent purchases. Therefore, when co-shopping is included, the degree of independent shopping displayed in the drawings increases to 88.8 percent.

The 112 drawings suggest that shopping tends not to be perceived as much of an interpersonal experience. As noted above, only 31 (27.7 percent) of the children shopped with others. In all cases the other shoppers were with parents, specifically mothers. There was no shopping shown with peers, nor with dads.

Only nine (8 percent) of the drawings included store personnel. All were clerks at checkout counters. Four of the drawings did show other shoppers—"other people buying things," as one child noted—

but no interaction with them. Perhaps the importance of store personnel to children has been overstated in past research or perhaps children hold enough negative attitudes toward them so as to exclude them in their drawings.

## Some Implications and Recommendations

Asking children to draw "what comes to your mind when you think about going shopping" naturally provides some of the same information as verbal inquiries, but it also produces additional and richer results. Children's minds seem to give somewhat different and more thorough directions to expressive behavior as compared to verbal behavior. Each resulting picture is a unit of thought, not a series of disjointed ideas linked together by an interviewer's questions. Retail managers wanting children's true store-related attitudes, perceptions, and evaluations may wish to consider picture drawing as a means for producing this information.

Several of the findings in this study of elementary school children's perceptions of the marketplace seem significant. The drawings show that even at this early age the shopping setting consists of much more to the children than just a place that stocks products to be exchanged for immediate gratification. It consists of specific kinds of stores identifiable by name that are perceived as the retailer intended—a multidimensional offering of colors, sounds, fixtures, doors, floors, displays, brands, products, prices, shopping carts, baskets, and bags, restrooms, dressing rooms, trash cans, potted plants, vending machines, telephones, and store personnel. It contains many products beyond those stereotypically associated with children and, very significant, many products not advertised to children. All of these things may come to the minds of children when they think about going shopping, now in the future, and may influence their choice of stores. Retail managers who are concerned about the development of their store images—and all should be—should take heed. The elements of those images begin in childhood as shown here, in fact, probably prior to age 8 (the youngest children in this study). The pictures in the children's minds that are reproduced in the their drawings are the foundational store images that will be modified and carried throughout life and evoked at purchase times. Consciously managing these images among children will help to build a customer base for the future when these children are at their peak as adult spenders.

The drawings demonstrate a strong childhood attachment to supermarkets, as compared to other store types. While this is explainable, it is nevertheless surprising in light of other research that shows supermarkets to be of somewhat less value to children. For supermarket firms that desire to build a lasting relation with children in order to have them as adult customers the study suggests a favorable opportunity. Related to supermarkets, the study results show a fascination of children with shopping carts. Apparently by serving as transportation for the child through aisles of want-satisfying products, and also as transportation for these items, as well as providing a means of holding parent and child in close proximity during shopping excursions, the shopping cart has endeared itself to children. It, more than any other item appearing in the children's drawings, seems to symbolize all the positives of shopping. Using these carts as an advertising medium, which is gaining increasing support, makes good business sense in view of these findings.

This study confirms findings of earlier investigations of children's consumer behavior that children are not very price conscious. However, it suggests that the price-consciousness that children do hold is product-specific to nonfoods, mainly toys. Retailers of nonfoods to children may want to address this price-consciousness if it is perceived as producing resistance to purchase.

This study shows that shopping is an emotional experience for children—fun for about 70 percent, frightening for about 30 percent. In both cases, however, the children's drawings show a zest for shopping that is coupled with a strong desire to own a variety of products. Retailers only need to insure that children are welcome in their stores in order to turn these positive shopping attitudes into profitable, long-term shopping behavior.

## References

1. James U. McNeal, *Children as Consumers: Insights and Implications* (Lexington, MA: Lexington Books, 1987).
2. Ellen Graham, "As Kids Gain Power of Purse, Marketing Takes Aim at Them," *Wall Street Journal,* January 19, 1988, pp. 1, 8.
3. Joseph H. Di Leo, *Children's Drawings as Diagnostic Aids* (New York: Brunner/Mazel, 1973).
4. Wayne Dennis, *Group Value through Children's Drawings* (New York: John Wiley, 1966).

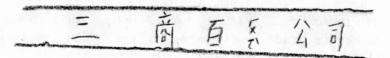

FIGURE 4–1

# 4

# Children as a Market of Influencers

**W**hen asked to "draw what comes to your mind when you think about going shopping," a fourth-grader in Taipei, Taiwan drew the picture in Figure 4–1. It shows her shopping with her mother in an appliance store and suggesting, "Buy me a TV set." A television set is a rather expensive request for a Taiwanese child, but not an unusual one. Taiwan is the second-wealthiest nation in Asia, and children there often influence the purchase behavior of their parents who are very children-centered.

It is also not unusual for U.S. children to make purchase requests while accompanying parents during shopping trips. One study, for example, shows that children average 15 purchase requests to parents during a store visit.[1] In addition to influencing parental purchases in the shopping environment, children make purchase requests in the home, in the car, at the movies, during television viewing, on vacation, at mealtimes, even in church. One mother told us that her 5-year-old invariably makes suggestions during church services about where to eat out after church.

The influence that children have on parental purchases is extensive and principally embraces the following areas:

1. Items for the children. This group of purchases includes snacks, toys, consumer electronics, clothing, and hobby equipment and supplies.
2. Items for the home. Children today influence some of the purchases by Mom and Dad of furnishings, furniture,

television sets, stereo systems, and foods and beverages for meals.

3. Nonhousehold items for the family members. These items often are major purchases and include vacations, automobiles, clothing, restaurant meals, and recreation things.

In addition to these three groups, there are others that are more difficult to classify. They include family gifts to the children's grandparents and to other relatives and neighbors, family donations to charities, license plates for the family car (custom plates), and vacation homes. Also, children often influence the parents' choice of stores, shopping centers, and shopping malls in which many household purchases are made. The influence on the choice of shopping settings can indirectly influence a large number of purchases and cause some offerings to be omitted from parental consideration.

## Reasons for Children's Influence

The influence that children assert on family purchases has been an area of concern among marketers ever since the advent of television programming in the 1950s, but it has become a much more substantive matter during the 1980s. The reasons for this were noted in Chapter 1 and can be summarized as follows:

1. Parents are having fewer children and therefore tend to give each child more things and more say-so in buying things.
2. There is an increasing number of one-parent households in which the child is expected to participate more in household decision making.
3. Having children is often postponed until later in life when parents' careers are established and nest eggs built. When children do arrive they are given much more attention. Part of this attention is in the form of letting the children join in with Mom and Dad when planning purchases.
4. In almost 70 percent of households both parents work (and are working longer hours) and they therefore expect more household participation from the kids. What parents used

to consider as influence is increasingly becoming children's responsibility.

These reasons for children's greater influence on household consumption are acknowledged by a wide spectrum of business experts:[2]

- "Mom and Dad, too busy making money to spend it, are surrendering the purse strings to their children." (Selina S. Guber, President of Children's Market Research, Inc.)
- "Kids have been empowered to make decisions that historically they would not have made." (Betsy Richardson, Marketing Director of Reebok International Ltd.)
- "With all the debate about whether the modern husband helps his working wife with housework, nobody thought to look at what kids are doing." (Horst Stipp, Director of Social Research for NBC)

There is an even more fundamental explanation for children's influence on such a wide range of household purchases. As shown in the steps of children's consumer development set out in Chapter 1, kids learn to obtain things by requesting them from parents. This is essentially the first stage in their consumer behavior. So, it is quite natural for them to ask Mom and Dad to buy a lot of things. While their initial requests are for personal needs such as sweets and playthings, eventually they are permitted, even encouraged, to request a wider range of items for themselves and for their households.

## Extent of Children's Consumer Influence

As noted, when children want commercial objects, it is a logical course of action for them to turn to their parents, who have been providing for them ever since they were born. Until age 2 or 3, parents completely determine what will satisfy their children's needs, but beginning at about this age, children are permitted some choice—for example, in flavors of ice cream and beverages and in types of toys. Because at this point children are unaware of many want-satisfying objects in the marketplace, their choice options and purchase requests are relatively few.

Starting at approximately age 2, children are exposed to an increasing number of advertisements targeted to them. The information in these messages, in combination with a great amount of information received during store visits with parents, provide the children with an increasing number of things to want. By age 5 or 6 this number has probably grown beyond the means of both child and parent to provide all the things wanted. Upon entering grade school the youngster finds it necessary to begin developing special persuasive techniques (often learned from peers) to be used on parents in order to obtain even a small share of a very long list of wants. At this point the parents often hear pleas like, "I wanna," "I gotta havva," "I'll die if I don't getta . . . ," and "Everyone's got one except me."

What things do children try to get their parents to buy? As indicated earlier, the number of different items is large and includes things for themselves as well as for the household. What is the cost of filling this want list? The total dollar amount has never been measured, although it has been estimated for a number of product categories where children's influence is thought to be extensive.

Because of the increasing importance of the influence of children on household expenditures, a study was undertaken by the author to develop some estimate—at least an educated guess—of the economic impact of this influence. The first step in this research was to review business magazines and journals to locate any estimates of children's influence on parental purchases of certain product lines. If two or more estimates for a category were found, the more conservative was used. Articles in which company officials were quoted provided names to contact by mail or phone for their opinions about children's influence on parental purchases of their industries' products.

This procedure produced estimates for around half of the product categories believed to be influenced by youngsters. In order to find measurements for the other product categories, we examined the research reported by others regarding what parents and children, rather than industry spokespersons, said about children's influence on household spending. That is, since we were unable to obtain enough judgments from marketers of the children's influence market, we turned to what we viewed as somewhat less credible estimates—those of the children themselves and/or their parents. We considered these estimates less credible not because of who conducted the research but because of the way the research was conducted. Usually parents and children of a household both are each asked the degree of influence of the children on parents' purchases, and their estimates usually disagree. Also, the results are often expressed in such terms as "a fair amount" or "a lot," and these are difficult to convert into dollars. But we tried by averaging the two estimates.

The final step in our research program was to reconcile figures—figures from industry officials, from parents, and from children. Further, we had to match these influence estimates with industry sales figures, for which there is variance, and remove sales not influenced by children. This produced still another estimated measure. For each product category we then estimated the amount of purchase by households with children. To do this we had to obtain data on number of families with children and judge their purchasing power in each product category. Information from the Bureau of Labor Statistics' Consumer Expenditure Survey provided some guidance for these measures. Articles from *American Demographics* provided some, also.

The net result of all this data juggling is the estimates of kids' influence on their parents' purchases found in Table 4–1. These estimates total more than $131 billion even though there are still some categories that could be added to the table. (One major category, for example, for which we were unable to determine the dollar influence of children was family vacations.) There are very substantial figures for some product categories—$8.8 billion for autos and $11 billion for children's clothing. Or consider foods. Children influence $22.75 billion in fast food purchases, but they influence even more than this in the home consumption of food. In the case of toys, for example, children's influence accounts for the lion's share of the industry's sales—$9.4 billion out of $13.4 billion. There are some relatively small figures such as $110 million for isotonic drinks like Gatorade, $860 million for pet foods, and $840 million for beauty aids for children. But none of these figures is insignificant for sellers in these industries because all want to influence the decision makers for their products.

Errors in this study of children's consumption influence are acknowledged. Inaccuracies result because the figures assume that the children's influence is of the same intensity in each category, that

**TABLE 4–1**

## Estimates of Children's Influence
### on Household Purchases

| Selected Products | Industry Sales $ (billions) | Influence Factor % | Sales Influence $ (billions) |
|---|---|---|---|
| Athletic Shoes | 5.60 | 20 | 1.12 |
| Autos | 221.70 | 04 | 8.87 |
| Bakery Goods | 26.10 | 10 | 2.61 |
| Bar Soap | 1.50 | 20 | 0.30 |
| Batteries | 3.00 | 25 | 0.75 |
| Beauty Aids (kids') | 1.20 | 70 | 0.84 |
| Bicycles | 1.00 | 40 | 0.40 |
| Blank Audio Cassettes | 0.39 | 15 | 0.06 |
| Bottled Water | 2.00 | 10 | 0.20 |
| Bread | 13.00 | 20 | 2.60 |
| Cameras (still) and Film | 4.55 | 12 | 0.55 |
| Candy & Gum | 10.43 | 33 | 3.44 |
| Canned Pasta | 0.57 | 60 | 0.34 |
| Casual Dining | 21.00 | 30 | 6.30 |
| Cereals (cold) | 6.90 | 20 | 1.38 |
| Cereals (hot) | 0.74 | 50 | 0.37 |
| Clothing (kids') | 18.40 | 60 | 11.04 |
| Consumer Electronics | 32.60 | 10 | 3.26 |
| Cookies (packaged) | 4.30 | 40 | 1.72 |
| Dairy Goods | 40.20 | 10 | 4.02 |
| Deli Goods | 11.10 | 8 | 0.89 |
| Fast Foods | 65.00 | 35 | 22.75 |
| Fragrances (kids') | 0.30 | 70 | 0.21 |
| Frozen Breakfasts | 0.55 | 10 | 0.06 |
| Frozen Novelties | 1.40 | 75 | 1.05 |
| Frozen Sandwiches | 0.27 | 30 | 0.08 |
| Fruit Snacks | 0.30 | 80 | 0.24 |
| Fruits & Vegetables, Canned | 3.00 | 20 | 0.60 |
| Fruits & Vegetables, Fresh | 43.40 | 6 | 2.60 |
| Furniture, Furnishings (kids) | 5.00 | 35 | 1.75 |
| Hair Care | 3.80 | 5 | 0.19 |

**TABLE 4–1 (continued)**

| Selected Products | Industry Sales $ (billions) | Influence Factor % | Sales Influence $ (billions) |
|---|---|---|---|
| Hobby Items | 1.00 | 40 | 0.40 |
| Home Computers | 3.10 | 10 | 0.31 |
| Hotels (mid-price) | 5.50 | 10 | 0.55 |
| Ice Cream | 7.60 | 23 | 1.75 |
| Isotonic Drinks | 0.70 | 15 | 0.11 |
| Jellies & Jams | 2.60 | 20 | 0.52 |
| Juices & Juice Drinks | 10.00 | 33 | 3.30 |
| Meats (packaged) | 17.10 | 13 | 2.20 |
| Meats (fresh) | 43.10 | 10 | 4.30 |
| Microwave Foods | 2.30 | 30 | 0.69 |
| Movies | 1.20 | 30 | 0.36 |
| OTC Drugs | 11.00 | 12 | 1.32 |
| Peanut Butter | 1.40 | 40 | 0.56 |
| Pet Foods | 7.20 | 12 | 0.86 |
| Pizza (frozen) | 0.92 | 40 | 0.37 |
| Pudding and Gelatin | 0.93 | 25 | 0.23 |
| Recorded Music | 3.40 | 20 | 0.68 |
| Refrigerated Puddings | 0.20 | 20 | 0.04 |
| Salty Snacks | 8.30 | 25 | 2.08 |
| School Supplies | 1.80 | 35 | 0.63 |
| Seafood | 7.30 | 10 | 0.73 |
| Shoes (kids') | 2.00 | 50 | 1.00 |
| Soda | 46.60 | 30 | 13.98 |
| Sporting Goods | 5.50 | 10 | 0.55 |
| Spreadable Cheese | 0.25 | 20 | 0.05 |
| Toaster Products | 0.25 | 45 | 0.11 |
| Toothpaste | 1.00 | 20 | 0.20 |
| Toys | 13.40 | 70 | 9.38 |
| Video Games | 3.50 | 60 | 2.10 |
| Video Rentals | 6.50 | 25 | 1.63 |
| Yogurt | 1.20 | 10 | 0.12 |
| Total | $766.15 | – | $131.77 |

there is parity among researchers of this topic, that combined estimates are better than single estimates, and that the extent of children's purchase influence is the same in all households. However, an attempt was made to be conservative throughout this exercise. Therefore, there should be more understating than overstating. Also, a few product categories should have been included but were not simply because estimates for them were too hazardous. Jewelry, for example. In sum, then, children are influencing at least $131 billion in household purchases. While it is only their influence—hints, requests, demands—that causes this money to be spent, it is almost as if the children spent it themselves. And that is how an increasing number of business firms look at it, and consequently target children as an influence market.

## Information Sources Underlying Children's Requests

When children make requests for certain toys and candy or suggest to parents a particular brand of stereo, where do they get these ideas? The typical answer would be advertising. At least a half-billion dollars in advertising is aimed at children, much of it intended to direct their influence on parental purchases. And it is not just television advertising—not in the '90s—but also radio, magazine, and newspaper advertising. And it is not only advertising of sweet items and playthings, as it was until the mid-1980s. Now there is advertising of clothing, shoes, fast foods, sporting goods, and toiletries targeted to children.

Research has shown that since the 1970s advertising has been the main source of children's product ideas, but just barely. A study in 1975, for example, showed that children's main information source for gift ideas was television advertising (27 percent of the time).[3] But an almost equally important information source was friends (26 percent), and this was followed closely by stores as an information source (22 percent), and then catalogs (15 percent). Today there are more sources and the percentages are probably different, at least for certain products. For example, in a proprietary study of children's attitudes towards styles and brands of athletic shoes, it was found that their major source of information about a new style of shoe was other children, usually older ones, 46 percent of the time. Other sources were stores (25 percent) and catalogs (15 percent), with advertising accounting for only 10 percent. These percentages were found to change, however, after the shoe style had become fashionable. Then, advertising became a somewhat more important source of information for the kid.

The fact that there are more information sources available in the '90s for young consumers than there were in the 1970s, is good for the children because they want more marketplace information. As indicated, while more advertising is targeted to children, and more of it is in media other than television, children appear to be placing more importance on other commercial sources relative to advertising than they once did. One Houston, Texas family with two children showed us an old issue of *What's Hot For Kids,* a magazine from General Foods. It had been used for its games (crosswords, connect the dots) by the children, but also had initiated some "Let's get some of this" from the children. In the case of media, then, television is still king, but magazines such as *Boys' Life,* newspapers such as *Class Acts,* club magazines such as Delta Airlines' *Fantastic Flyer,* and radio such as The Children's Radio Network are additional and increasingly important sources of product ideas for kids in the '90s.

In addition to advertising media, there is the almost equally important influence of stores. As noted above, the athletic shoe stores that are typically located in malls where kids hang out have become important sources of information for kids interested in running shoes. But this is true of many other store types. Given that a 10-year-old, for instance, may visit stores 250 times a year, and that each store visit may produce hundreds of units of information, many of which are physical as well as visual, little wonder that a growing number of retailers are merchandising to kids as consumers—present, influence, or future consumers. These merchants are lowering fixtures and display racks to kids' eye level, and some are even setting aside special areas for youngsters, such as is done in the Hastings (books, music, video) chain of stores, where merchandise can be examined from a kid's perspective. These stores know that the children may not be able to afford many of the items offered but that the youngsters are likely to request them from parents, both in the store and at home. The store is definitely a major information medium for the child.

A Portland, Oregon working mom told us that her 11-year-old often looks at her mail-order catalogs and makes requests from them. In fact, she jokingly related to us that he had even asked for a $3,500 bicycle from a Hammacher Schlemmer catalog. The convenience of catalogs in the home, their greatly increased numbers, and their specialization, along with the fun and excitement kids experience from receiving things in the mail have made catalogs an important source of product ideas for kids. In fact, catalogs have been sources of information and inspiration for decades, as many parents remind us, but for some time were overshadowed by television advertising. Now, due to social and economic changes, they are again important to households.

A great deal of information about stores, services, and products that influence children's purchase requests is now available to them in schools. It often comes in the form of education materials, such as the read-a-book-a-week program by Minute Maid which also contains information about Minute Maid juices, and educational tools such as Apple computers that in and of themselves are major units of information—a constant flow of information about the product to the children.[4] Personnel from retail stores and banks also visit schools to present information to the children about products and services, while other stores may host school field trips to their retail locations. Usually these retailers provide samples of products and/or coupons and discount programs during visits.

Finally, a large number of what are often called "nontraditional" commercial sources of information are targeted to children. These include advertisements on rental videos, product placements within movies, product samples distributed in school either in single or pack form, posters at school, television ads presented through classroom programming, and direct mail advertising.[5] All of these and other media are used to influence the influencer—to direct children's influence of parental purchases.

## Children's Requesting Styles and Appeals

To get parents to buy them things, children make verbal requests or requesting gestures. Their purpose, of course, is to obtain an object of interest to them, usually, although not always, something for immediate gratification. Their typical request is direct and usually begins with "Get me," "Buy me," or "I want." Sometimes it is more emotional and contains words such as "I just gotta have," "I must have" and "I'll die if I don't getta." Sometimes it is just a gesture, such as a toddler pointing to a product, or more intently, grabbing for the product.

In most cases, rather than just asking "May I have it," the child utilizes a *style*—a way of asking—and an *appeal*—the reason for asking—to increase the chances of obtaining the item(s) requested. Like marketers, the child appeals to the motives or needs of the parent (usually one parent at a time). Through learning from trial and error, from friends, and from marketers the child applies the most effective appeal through the most effective style. The appeals are large in number but fall into some general categories:

- Educational—"You want me to learn don't you?"
- Health—"Don't you want me to be healthy?"
- Time—"It'll save you time."
- Economy—"It'll save you lots of money."
- Happiness—"You want me to be happy don't you?"
- Security—"You don't want me to get hurt do you?"

Marketers may provide these appeals in their advertisements concurrently with appeals to the child. For example, one ad might say, "It's fun [for the child] and it's educational [for the child's parents]," or simply, "Have fun while you're learning," and the child seems to understand the focus of each appeal.

Like the variety in appeals, there are many styles the child employs in his or her request to parents for goods and services. And like the appeals, the style is learned mainly as a result of the parents' responses to each style. A positive response reinforces the style, a negative response extinguishes it. It is particularly in the style that acting ability pays off, and the child learns to switch from one style to another as a means of renewing a request. Some of the popular styles are these:

- *Pleading*—It is usually accompanied by words such as "puleeeze," "help me," and by repetition such as "mother, mother, mother."

- *Persistent*—This style involves repeating the request over and over at all opportune as well as inopportune times. Sometimes requests are accompanied by "I'm gonna ask you just one more time."
- *Forceful*—This is related to the demonstrative style that follows. It uses loudness and forceful words such as "I must have it," "Nothing will stop me from having it," and "I'll ask grandma if you don't buy it for me."
- *Demonstrative*—This is perhaps the height in acting. In younger children it means going stiff, holding the breath, or falling down on the floor screaming. In older kids it may entail refusing to leave the store or refusing to talk or look at the parent. Tears are often employed for effect.
- *Sugar-coated*—The words "love" and "wonderful" are usually invoked in this style: "I'll love you forever if you'll just get me one," and "Buying me one means you're the most wonderful father in the world."
- *Threatening*—This style usually focuses on the negative results that will occur if a purchase is not forthcoming: "I'll hate you forever if I don't get one," and "I'm gonna leave home if you don't buy me one."
- *Pity*—Finally, there is the negative result for the child rather than the parent if the purchase is not made: "I'll be the worst-looking kid in school if I don't have one," "Nobody will even talk to me if I don't have one," "Everyone has one except me," and "You never buy me anything."

All of these appeals and styles may be used in combination, but kids tend to stick to one or two of each that prove most effective for certain kinds of merchandise and for their own parents. While the examples given are mainly related to personal items for the children, these request styles and appeals are used also for obtaining items for the household such as a new television set, telephone, or living room furniture.

## Location of Children's Requests to Parents

There is a general rule that governs children's requests for goods and services to parents, a rule that is well known to marketers whose strategy is to influence these influencers: Children are most likely to make a purchase request for an object when in the presence of a stimulus related to that object. This rule sounds obvious, but it has numerous marketing, parenting, and public policy implications.

1. A marketer who wants to direct a child's influence on parental purchases of an object should target frequent communications to the child about that object in a variety of media including the retail setting.
2. Parents who do not want their child influenced by marketers, which in turn would produce requests from the child, should keep the child away from marketing messages.
3. If public policy makers believe it is wrong for marketers to attempt to influence children's purchase requests or to influence them at certain times, they must limit commercial messages aimed at the children at least at certain times.

From this general rule we can expect the child to make purchase requests during or soon after watching, hearing, or reading commercials, during visits to the shopping setting, while interacting with peers or soon afterward, and within the time zone of experiencing other marketing messages such as in the classroom, watching a movie, riding public transport, during auto travel with parents, or walking to school.

While it may seem to some parents or consumer advocates that children are bombarded with commercial messages—that is the essence of a report from Consumers Union,[6] for example—there actually are several additional, and perhaps more effective, opportunities for marketers to try to influence children's purchase requests. For example, research shows that children have a fascination with shopping carts and with the checkerboard designs of the flooring in many stores. Yet, neither is utilized as a message medium for children. Moreover, the retail setting is a most logical and most effective place for marketers to communicate with children. Children frequently accompany parents to stores, and the commercial influence there can produce purchase fulfillment since the products are present—within reach. Yet probably most retailers do little to take advantage of this opportunity, although many parents may feel that they do.

## Influence of Kids on Parents' Choice of Retail Outlets

The discussion to this point about children's influence on household purchases may be misleading in that it omits the significant influence that children also have on *where* their parents buy things. The fact that children have a lot of input regarding retail sources follows from the development of children's consumer behavior described in Chapter 1. As children are exposed to the interiors and offerings of stores by parents during the first few years of childhood, they develop likes and dislikes of kinds of stores and of specific stores. Their store preferences are enhanced and modified by preferences of parents and peers and by actual experiences with an increasing number of outlets. For example, research shows that by age 10 a child averages 250 store visits a year during which independent purchases are made.

Children make retail outlet recommendations to parents mainly on two occasions: When parents and children are going shopping together, and when parents shop alone and some of the purchases are expected to be for the children. In a 1989 study I found that when parents and children decided to shop together (often due to prompting of children), in almost 90 percent of the cases the children made recommendations regarding one or more shopping outlets. Further, in population centers of 100,000 and over, where there are a variety of shopping opportunities, children often suggested shopping centers and malls as well as specific stores.

When parents visit retail environments without their children but intend to buy items for them, the children offer store suggestions almost half of the time. One mom told us that she often called her son at home before she left work to get his opinion about food to bring home or movies to rent. He usually suggested Blockbuster's (video store) for the movies and Pizza Hut for the food. Another mom said that when the family ate out the children usually got to select the restaurant. If they chose McDonald's, she noted, it had to be a particular McDonald's because that one had more of a children's atmosphere (as perceived by the children).

According to one study, 14 percent of parents said that children have a say in catalog purchases made by the household.[7] Our 1989 study produced a similar finding (just under 20 percent), and in the case of clothing, a few households reported that kids suggested a catalog as an alternative source to going to stores.

By recommending to parents that they buy from a certain retail outlet, children are causing the parents to preselect an offering of goods and services. This has major implications for producers whose product lines could be omitted from parents' choice sets depending on the store recommendations of youngsters. Producers of items intended for children may wish to consider some cooperative advertising efforts with retailers. Producers of kids' products may also want to investigate the images of certain retailers among children even before they begin their selling efforts to that particular store.

Research indicates that a large number of retailers still do not take children seriously as either a current market or an influence market.[8] To the extent this is true these retailers are losing business and that loss will be compounded as time goes by. For all retailers, there is wisdom in giving special consideration to small children brought to their stores by their parents. These children should be made to feel comfortable and wanted as visitors and later as individual consumers. Retailers should keep in mind that children as well as adults are always seeking outlets in which needs and wants can be satisfied. The sooner that children sense that a particular store or store chain is a place for certain need-satisfiers, the sooner those youngsters will recommend the store to parents. Said another way, even kids are unlikely to recommend an object they dislike to a person they like.

## Parental Response to Children's Requests

There are about as many kinds of responses by parents as there are kinds of purchase requests by children. But research in this area permits some generalizations. There are essentially four parental responses: (1) make the purchase, (2) substitute another purchase, (3) postpone the purchase, (4) ignore or refuse the request. Let us briefly consider each of these.

**MAKE THE PURCHASE.** As a rule, parents honor children's requests around half the time. Most parents want to honor all of their children's requests, but because of economic limits and because of impact on the welfare of the child, they do not. Parents enjoy giving to their children, want the children to ask for things, and understand that requests are often logical. But parents often get angry at the frequency of requests, particularly in the shopping setting, and tend to direct part of their anger at the marketer. Children learn to sense this threshold and miraculously can closely calculate the number, type, and/or costs of items requested that are just below their parents' threshold of anger. Such skills are usually fully developed by age 10.

Parents are more likely to fulfill a purchase request made in the retail environment than one made at home. There is no simple explanation for this, but several reasons can be advanced. A purchase request at home may be viewed as less credible if it is described by the child as inspired by TV advertising, whereas a request in the store can be compared with the actual product. A request at home can be more easily delayed since it usually cannot be purchased then and the child is therefore somewhat less likely to persist. The child who makes a request at a store, however, usually recognizes that persistence is necessary because once they have exited the store the opportunity to obtain the product will be gone. Finally, the store is a public place, parents may honor the child's request rather than run the risk of a humiliating confrontation.

**SUBSTITUTE ANOTHER PURCHASE.** Parents may feel that a certain brand or type of product requested is too expensive, of poor quality, or inappropriate for their child, and offer a substitute. A confrontation may result, which the child may or may not win depending upon the parenting style. This may mean less satisfaction for the child and, of course, a lost sale for the marketer whose product initiated the purchase request. An average rate of substitution is not known but it may be a good reason for marketers to target both parent and child with promotional messages.

**POSTPONE THE PURCHASE.** As indicated above, postponing a child's purchase request is easier when the request is made at home than when it is made at the store, or even in the car heading toward a store. Parents often make postponements either for economic reasons—"You can have one when I get paid"—or because of the child's welfare—"You have had too much candy today." Sometimes the postponement is a ploy in hopes that the child will forget. In such a case, the parent can probably expect the request to arise again and therefore the sincerity of the parent to be tested depending on the viewpoint of the child about the parent's response style. Because parents generally like to buy for their children but postponements are often necessary, marketers must take this into consideration in their promotion programs.

**IGNORE OR REFUSE THE REQUEST.** For reasons already mentioned, the parent who receives a purchase request from a child may ignore it or refuse to honor it. Often, parents have an understanding with children about certain products—"Don't ever ask me to buy you chocolate"—or about certain times—"Don't ever ask me to look at something or buy you something when I am involved in buying something for your father." These caveats may not always work, but the parent may pretend not to hear in such cases. Refusals are just that. They may make sense to the parents although not necessarily to the children.

Ignoring or refusing a child's request happens often, but children may have trouble with these responses. Confrontations may result and arguments, spankings, or tantrums ensue, all of which can be embarrassing for both parties. There are ways that parents often can prevent these results and there are ways to deal with them, particularly if parents can depend on the help of concerned marketers. However, we will defer to the consumer educators and child psychologists who specialize in these matters. But let us comment about outcomes of not honoring purchase requests.

**OUTCOMES OF NOT HONORING PURCHASE REQUESTS OF CHILDREN.** Around half the time parents do not buy what their children request. As indicated above, parents make a substitute, postpone, ignore, or refuse the request. The results are the same for the child— no product. This outcome can produce conflicts between parent and child that takes several forms. In-store tantrums, going stiff, holding the breath, screaming, crying, threatening, and throwing things may occur, humiliating parents and causing them to "get old fast," as one mom said. The parents who cannot afford to honor most of their children's requests, or the parents who strongly believe that it is the parent and not the child or marketer who decides what the child receives, may pay a high price in embarrassment, frustration, and anger. While probably most children are playing the averages and do not get overly concerned about parental refusals, it is certainly possible for relationships between parent and child to be hurt.

In the heat of competition marketers may not think that damaged parent/child relationships can result, because they do not happen often, but it is in part the marketers' responsibility to be concerned about this. Naturally, the parent must bear much of the responsibility because it is normal for children to want things. Therefore, parents are expected to develop rules for dealing with requests.

### Parental Style and Children's Purchase Request

As indicated above, not all parents respond in the same way to children's purchase requests. While differences may be attributed to the economic conditions of the household, parenting style is often the explanation. By this I mean the patterns of thinking and behavior of parents in regard to rearing their children. Many books have been written on the subject of parenting style, and every mother has given advice to her married children about how to raise the grandchildren. This parenting style has a major impact on children's requests for goods and services just as it has on all interactions between parent and child.

While parents cannot be exclusively grouped into a specific type of parenting style, they do tend to follow or subscribe to certain defined patterns.[9] There are the *authoritarian* parents who discourage independence in their children and usually make all decisions for the children. At the other extreme are the *permissive* parents who avoid exercising any control over their children. Far from being disciplinarians, these parents are more like friends to their children. In the middle, so to speak, are the parents that can be described as *authoritative* who clearly are in charge but have flexible boundaries for their children that encourage autonomy for them. Finally, there are *neglecting* parents who for whatever reasons show little concern for their children's development.

All of these parents probably honor many of their children's purchase requests, but logically we might expect the authoritarian parent to discourage such requests, the permissive and the authoritative to encourage such requests, although for different reasons, and the neglecting parent not to respond to them. While there is no data to show us how such parenting types are distributed in our society, we might conclude that only the authoritarian will be unlikely to respond positively to their children's requests (assuming the children of these parents make requests). Also, marketers will not be very successful in trying to direct the children of authoritarian parents to influence their parents' purchases. Authoritative parents are likely to honor children's purchase requests to the extent that they fall within certain guidelines or the children have good reasons to avoid the guidelines. A dual marketing strategy will probably be more effective for this parenting type and perhaps slightly effective in the authoritarian family. Marketers are likely to be successful in influencing the children of permissive and neglecting parents, although neglecting parents' responses will be the lesser of the two. It may be difficult for nonpersonal marketing communications such as advertising and sales promotion techniques to take into consideration these parenting styles, but individual salespeople in retail settings can learn to identify them and work with them effectively.

## Marketers' Perceptions of Kids' Influence on Parental Purchases

In general, marketers are keenly aware of children's purchase requests to their parents, aware that these requests are honored probably half the time or more and that, in total, these requests are responsible for billions of dollars a year in spending by the parents. Expenditures of this magnitude cause many marketers to want a thorough understanding of the influence that children have on their parents' purchases so that they may participate effectively in its process. Others seem oblivious to it.

It appears that marketers hold at least four different viewpoints about children influencing their parents' purchases. Two of them acknowledge the importance of their influence while two do not.

1. *There is nothing that can or should be done about it.* Clearly, many retailers and producers believe either that there is little that can be done to affect children's influences on parental purchases or that children's influence is not major and therefore is not worthy of

concern. For example, one independently owned hardware / appliance store manager told us, "Maybe kids do pressure their parents to buy things, but not likely the things we sell." A vice president of a drugstore chain told us that he really did not want children in its stores because they are noisy and bothersome, implying that their influence on their parents' purchases was not a significant factor. In both of these cases, children's influence on parents' shopping and buying is practically ignored or even viewed negatively.

2. *Influence parents' thinking and they, in turn, will influence children's thinking.* The standard model of parent / child interaction assumes that parents determine essentially what their kids think and do. Therefore, the purchase requests that children make are presumed to be essentially echoes of what parents have taught them. For instance, children who want a toy that is advertised in their favorite magazine would request it from parents only if the parents previously had indicated that they considered that type of toy appropriate for the kids. Marketers who subscribe to this model direct most of their promotional efforts to parents, who are expected to pass on the information to their children. In this case, parents use the promotional information to instruct children about desirable products and stores and as rebuttals to inappropriate requests. Thus, the flow of influence would look like this:

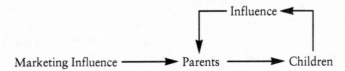

This model is commonly used, for example, in the children's clothing industry that primarily promotes to parents. Back-to-school advertising of children's clothing to parents by retailers such as Sears and K mart and by brands such as Gitano and Levi are suggestive of this strategy. When Sony entered children's consumer electronics with its My First Sony line in 1987, it chose to target mainly parents. It continued this practice with its first entry into children's toys—Sony's Electronic Sketch Pad that retails for around $100.

The parent-to-child-to-parent model of consumer influence particularly accommodates children's indirect influence, that is, it permits parents to take into consideration their children's product and brand preferences when making purchases for the children. In this case it is assumed that the parents at some point have discussed what products and brands suit the children's wants and have these plugged into a special evoked set (those few items that come to mind when one decides to make a purchase) that is triggered when the parents think about making purchases for their kids.

This model is probably not as common as it once was because it does not function as effectively as it did prior to the 1980s. It is harder for marketers to reach parents with a promotion message related to children than it used to be because Mom and Dad are both working and both working longer hours. Also, parents of the '80s are encouraging their children to be more self-reliant and to make more consumer decisions for themselves as soon as practicable. The dual strategy model described next is probably more effective for marketing to these families.

3. *Influence parents and children simultaneously.* This model of parent-child interactions assumes that children have substantial influence on the purchase behavior of parents but that parents must be persuaded, also, of the merits of a particular product in order to get them to make the final purchase decision. The model also recognizes that the amount of yielding of parents to children's requests varies, depending perhaps on the product sought by the children and according to parenting style. Finally, this model recognizes that parents and children make joint purchase decisions for many products. Therefore, in all these cases both parties should be the focus of the marketer who seeks to satisfy the wants of children. The flow of influence would look like this:

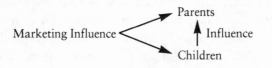

Kool-Aid, Nike, and Nintendo are examples of brands that appear to target both parent and child. There are many others. All three of these brands target some separate advertisements to the two parties. Kool-Aid also develops a lot of its advertising campaigns so that both parent and child are targeted simultaneously.

This dual marketing strategy may appear more costly than just targeting either the parent or the child, but the objective is to make sure to reach the decision maker(s) as effectively as possible.

4. *Influence the child who influences the parents.* This is the model that was advanced in the 1950s when television programming to children first came about. In essence it said that advertising can influence the wants of kids, who in turn make advertising-influenced purchase requests to parents, who make purchases to satisfy the kids. The flow of influence looks like this:

Marketing Influence ⟶ Children ⟶ Parents

The thinking underlying this model differs only slightly from that in the previous model where parents and child are both targeted. In this latter case it is believed that even though children influence parents, parents hold the purse strings and must also be influenced.

This model is commonly practiced by the producers of the two largest categories of goods that children want and often buy for themselves—sweets and play things. Most of television advertising to children consists of messages about sweets—sweetened cereal, beverages, confections, frozen novelties—and about playthings—toys, bikes, skateboards, video games—and these messages are usually very persuasive in terms of how their products satisfy the needs and wants of children. The result is that the children either seek and buy the advertised items with their own money or—because there are so many things to want—usually they request the items from their parents. It is significant that many of these advertisements are cast in such a way that they appeal to the child as both a primary market and an influence market. As we will see in a later chapter, this often-used model of marketing influence on children's influence of parents does not utilize advertising alone but is the focus of an array of marketing efforts.

## Marketing to Children as Influencers

Marketers direct marketing strategies to children as influencers for 100 billion reasons—because children influence at least $100 billion in household purchases. It is actually a complicated way to sell something and marketers would not do it if it were not worthwhile. But the plain fact is that parents give this indirect purchasing power to their children, and in order to compete most effectively, marketers must influence it.

The marketer's basic rule is simple: Sell to the decision maker. If the youngster decides what brand of running shoes he will wear and Mom buys them, then the marketer will most likely direct primary selling effort to the child. To the extent a purchase is the result of joint decision making, as it often is for children's goods, then persuasive efforts must be directed to both decision makers. Because there is a very real possibility that the marketer's message may not be relayed correctly to the parents from the child, and because parenting styles and consequently parent-child relationships differ among families, it is logical to direct the message to both child and parents. Also, if there is some controversy regarding the particular product or service, messages directed to both will reduce it.

There is really little need for a marketer to suggest the influence act to children—to tell children to "Ask mom to buy some for you," or "Tell your parents about this wonderful new product." Requesting items is a natural act of children. All that is necessary is to inform children of an offering and create desire for it, in the case of a child-related product, or create a favorable attitude in the case of a household-related item. Once the desire is present for a child-related item, children will either try to buy the product with their own money or ask parents for it. The marketer need only make sure of the availability of the product to the child and/or parent.

Appeals to children as an influence market may differ somewhat from appeals to children as a primary market. In addition to appeals to motives for wanting the product the marketer may provide additional appeals so that the youngster will be encouraged to request the product, particularly in the case of high-ticket items. The appeals directed to parents often will differ, too, from those directed to children because parents may have different reasons for wanting the product. For example, both the child and parents may want certain jeans because they are fashionable and of good quality, but the parents may also want them to launder well.

Finally, marketers must realize that most appeals to children as an influence market reach some children who should not receive the message. That is the nature of most advertising and selling media. Thus, it is possible to create desires among children whose families cannot afford particular products or do not want their children to have them. While this is practically unpreventable because of the nature of marketing to large numbers, it nevertheless should be a concern of all marketers.

# References

1. Joann Paley Galst and Mary Alice White, "The Unhealthy Persuader: The Reinforcing Value of Television and Children's Purchase-Influencing Attempts at the Supermarket," *Child Development,* December 1986, pp. 1089–1096.
2. Ellen Graham, "As Kids Gain Power of Purse, Marketing Takes Aim at Them," *Wall Street Journal,* January 1988, pp. 1, 14.
3. Andre Caron and Scott Ward, "Gift Decisions by Kids and Parents," *Journal of Advertising Research,* August 1975, pp. 15–20.
4. Cyndee Miller, "Marketing in the Classroom Raises a Furor: Scholastic Inc. Says a Sound Education Must Be a Primary Goal," *Marketing News,* September 11, 1990, p. 2.
5. Joseph Pereira, "Kids' Advertisers Play Hide-and-Seek, Concealing Commercials in Every Cranny," *Wall Street Journal,* April 30, 1990, pp. B1, B6.
6. *Selling America's Kids: Commercial Pressures on Kids of the 90's* (Mount Vernon, NY: Consumers Union Education Services, 1990).
7. *Between Parents and Children: A USA Weekend-Roper Report on Consumer Decision Making in American Families* (New York: USA Weekend, 1989).
8. James U. McNeal, *Children as Consumers: Insights and Implications* (Lexington, MA: Lexington Books, 1987).
9. Les Carleson and Sanford Grossbart, "Parental Style and Consumer Socialization of Children," *Journal of Consumer Research,* June 1988, pp. 77–92.

**FIGURE 5–1**

# Kids as a Future Market:

*Reaching Them Through a Multidimensional Segmentation Strategy*

**C**hildren often think about their consumer behavior as it might be when they are adults. They can be overheard beginning their sentences with, "When I get big I'm gonna buy a———" and "When I grow up I'm gonna get a———." "I'm shopping for all my clothes," is how a future-oriented fourth-grader who drew the picture in Figure 5–1 imagined it. In a post-drawing interview, she said that she does buy some clothes for herself now, and she hopes to buy all of her clothes soon. She really can envision herself as a future consumer shopping for and purchasing her wardrobe. So can clothing marketers—retailers and manufacturers—and some of them believe that as their future customers, children's patronage should be cultivated now so that they will favor the firms' offerings when they reach market age. Competition dictates it, they would say.

An increasing number of marketers are targeting children as a future market and often as part of a marketing program that targets them as a current and/or influence market. For example, the South Hills Mall in Poughkeepsie, New York found itself in competition with a new upscale mall. One of its competitive responses was to develop a club for kids through which it promotes the mall to children (who, in turn, will most likely suggest it to their parents). Such an effort not only provides additional customers for the mall now, but assuming the children are treated well, it will help provide a steady stream of peak-buying future customers as these kids grow up.

Whether it is the Poughkeepsie mall, a store in that mall, two million or so other retailers, or the 365,000 manufacturers, they all have to be concerned about the nature and source of their *future* customers. Children begin developing brand preferences and store preferences in early childhood, even before they enter school. And not just for child-oriented products but also for such adult-oriented things as gasoline, radios, and soaps.[1] If a marketer's offering is not included in these preferences at some point, the offering may be skipped over or rejected when the subject comes up for consideration in the future—at market age.[2] In harsher terms, just as children learn to like certain stores or products and their brands, they also learn to dislike some. Those that are disliked will not be given much consideration as the children grow into bona fide consumers. Rarely do children go to the store and buy canned spinach, for example, when they start spending their own money.

At a retailing symposium a representative of a specialty department store described the 18-to-35-year-old women who are the store's primary target customers and how the store went about marketing to them. In an informal discussion afterward the store executive was asked at what age the store begins appealing to this customer body. "We start with the 18-year-olds," he answered. "What if you competitor appeals to her at 17? Or even 7?" he was asked. "I guess that is a possibility," he responded. Indeed it is. More and more, retailers and producers are reaching out to consumers early, often in childhood, to build awareness and liking among them so that when they reach market age, they can be more easily converted into customers. What is being suggested here is that as people move through the life cycle, roughly defined by their age, they become potential customers for certain products and certain stores. The basic question for marketers is: In what stores will they first purchase certain products and what brands will they first buy? Before reaching the market age for a particular product or store, the potential customer probably has already formed some product, brand, and store preferences, often in childhood. If specific marketers have participated in the development of these preferences, there is a good chance the children will patronize their offerings.

That is what we want to talk about here—children as a future market and how marketers respond to them. Specifically we will show that appealing to youngsters as future markets is often done, and probably most effectively done, through an integrated marketing strategy in which children are courted as two or three markets simultaneously. Thus, children who are primary customers (as described in Chapters 2 and 3) and influence customers (as described in Chapter 4) are also *all* the future consumers for potentially *all* firms for *all* offerings. As future consumers, then, they are even more significant than the other two children's markets—the current and influence markets.

## Children as a Source of Future Customers

There are only two sources of new customers for a retailer or producer: competitors who already have them or new customers who have not yet entered the market. Customers of competitors have to be switched over—switched from K mart to Wal-Mart, from Kellogg's cereals to General Mills' cereals. By definition, then, they can be switched back. In fact, that is the typical scenario. Customers are switched back and forth among stores and brands through the use of coupons (in free-standing newspaper inserts), prices ("everyday low prices"), premiums ("free baseball with five proofs of purchase"), or some unique attribute such as location (of a new Circle-K store) or credit plan (Sears' Discover Card). Sometimes such practices result in profitless competition, and at the very least, in thinner margins.

Children who have not yet entered the marketplace are the other source of new customers. When nurtured, they tend to become more loyal customers for marketers than those obtained through switching strategies. However, a relatively long period of nurturing is needed before they become bona fide customers for a particular product or store. For example, 7-Up, who counts children as its future consumers, has to nurture them until they reach their teen years when they become the major consumers for soft drinks. AT&T, who targets children in grade school as future customers has to wait for perhaps twenty years before the children reach its market age. During the waiting period, whatever length it may be, a marketer has to spend money to grow customers from childhood even though there is little if any return. But the ultimate results— the most basic return—are theoretically more faithful customers than those switched from competitors. That should mean more satisfaction for both consumer and marketer.

## The Importance of Loyalty in Cultivating Kids as Future Customers

Every marketer wants loyal customers—customers who definitely prefer the marketer's offering and buy it most of the time—but today there seems to be very few of them. There was a time, however, when people commonly had favorites—a favorite department store, favorite bank, favorite doctor. Now, as likely as not, they go to the department store in the nearest mall, the bank that is on the way to work, and to the nearest "doc-in-a-box" for medical help. The notion of loyalty hasn't disappeared, but the long-term practice of developing it is less favored than short-term strategies of brand-switching and store-switching. Instead of businesses trying to grow their own customers, they more often try to get them already grown from competitors. But as observed, it is difficult to make a loyal customer out of one who has been switched from competitors. The customer who has proven to be switchable, can therefore be switched back, or switched to a third competitor. Metaphorically speaking, as a result of current marketing practices, many consumers have become butterflies, flitting from one sweet deal to another.

Appealing to children as future consumers, when done right, can produce a very loyal customer. That explains why McDonald's, as a good example, cultivates children as a primary source of new customers. It has found that they tend to become loyal, often for a lifetime. It follows rather naturally. If year by year children are shown the outstanding attributes of a company, along with its products, services, and brands, then the awareness, understanding, and belief that result are bound to translate into children growing up and turning to that company's offerings whenever they reach that company's market age and their wants cause them to consider products like those that a company offers. The legions of loyal McDonald's customers, ages 2 to 92, are well known, well documented in writings, and attest to this premise. One *Fortune* magazine article, for example, referred to this situation as the "McDonald's Mystique."[3] But the term "mystique" suggests that there is no logical explanation for the loyalty of McDonald's customers. There is. It is plain and simple "cradle-to-grave marketing" at its best.

There is a consumer-side explanation for consumer loyalty.

Loyalty-proneness inherently exists in people, at least to some degree. All of us, particularly at a young age, are looking for dependable relationships (even while trying to achieve a degree of autonomy).[4] The belonging (affiliation) need, which causes us to seek cooperative relationships, is very strong among children. Also, children are looking for order in their lives. There are so many new things to encounter that some order is necessary to cope with them all. A trusting relationship in which satisfying acquisitions can always be expected helps give order to an increasingly complex life. And children also need to avoid the frequent embarrassment and humiliation that come from doing the wrong things. A good relationship with marketers can provide assurance that items purchased are the correct ones. Thus a steady, dependable relationship with certain sellers can provide for all three needs—affiliation, order, infavoidance (avoidance of humiliation)—as well as others. So, when the opportunity for a loyal relationship exists, children, as well as many adults, are likely to take it.

The trouble is, much of the time a long-term relationship with a merchant or even a brand may not be readily available. As indicated, marketers want them. However, they too often do too few of those things necessary to develop such relationships and instead rely on switchable customers whose brand and store preferences are not strong. This does appear to be changing as some businesses take a longer-run approach to developing a customer body. (It may be a lesson learned from the Japanese, but is more likely intuitive).

What does it take to transform a youngster into a loyal future customer? It requires *commitment* on the part of both customer and marketer.[5] But a consumer is not likely to commit himself or herself without first perceiving a commitment on the part of the marketer. That is what is still too uncommon—marketers demonstrating commitment to consumers, particularly young consumers.

Let us carry this reasoning one step further before we return to the basic premise. Commitment on the part of the marketer means consistent evidence that the firm is trying to satisfy the needs and wants of specific customers. After all, why does a customer come to the marketplace or select a particular brand? To satisfy needs. And it doesn't take a brain surgeon or a rocket scientist to know how to satisfy customers. Most customers, including children, can tell us.

Consider just one practice of retailers that is sure to demonstrate *lack* of commitment: out-of-stocks. Looking for the advertised product on sale and not finding it on the shelf. Looking for one's size among a rack of shirts or shoes and not finding it. Looking for the small box of cereal and finding only the large one there. All these are out-of-stocks and sure to displease. "If they advertise it for sale, it ought to be for sale," is the sort of remark that children who accompany their parents to the store may hear. The children assimilate these complaints and feelings and based on them develop nonloyal feelings toward some sellers. So, whether it be frequent out-of-stocks, long checkout lines, difficult return policies, poor parking, or a host of other unsatisfying activities, we can be sure that children who are looking for loyal relationships will not develop them with firms who specialize in such recurring practices.

There are actually many significant impediments to the development and maintenance of loyalty among young consumers as they advance to market age, but they can be summarized in three words: (1) consumers, (2) competitors, (3) company.

- *Consumers.* Other consumers, mainly parents and peers, can cause children to lose faith, or not develop confidence in a retailer or producer. Children take cues from parents, and if they hear their parents bad-mouthing a marketer, for example, for the out-of-stocks mentioned above, the youngsters are likely to follow. As children reach their teen years, they also become susceptible to the influence of peers who may express negative feelings about a marketing source. Peers, for example, often define what products and stores are "cool." It is important to keep in mind that most customers complain about bad experiences with merchants, but only 5 percent complain to the merchant. The other 95 percent complain to anyone who will listen, including their children.
- *Competitors.* Very logically competitors will try to attract customers or potential customers from other competitors. As noted, customer-switching is standard fare and consumers come to expect such activities as price-cutting, couponing and give-aways. Very low prices, for example, at one store may test the commitment of loyal customers at another

store, particularly during periods of recession. Comparison advertising that disparages a loyal customer's favorite store or brand can eventually change the allegiance of that customer.

- *Company.* Even a company that is practicing a marketing strategy of growing customers from childhood can be its own enemy. For example, during uncertain economic times operating costs often are cut and the costs most often cut are those least directly related to profits. Since a customer-growing program is difficult to relate to the bottom line, it is likely to get cut—in the name of belt-tightening. At the time of this writing, one convenience store chain is reducing promotion programs targeted to children. There is no way to know, regrettably, the long-term costs, if any, of this effort to reduce short-term costs. Put more positively, one loyal customer for life might be worth $50,000 to a convenience store, $100,000 to a supermarket, and $150,000 to an auto dealer.

## Building a Loyal Relationship with Children as Future Customers

If there is to be some assurance that children will become future customers of a firm, an enduring relationship must be established with them. Otherwise, they are anybody's customers. Assuming they will not be actual customers until their teen or adult years, how does a firm build a relationship with children that will last for that time span? The answer can be found in the following model.

This model suggests that in order for there to be patronage *action* in the future, children must be made *aware* of a firm, its products, and mission; their *interest* in the firm must be generated and maintained; and their *belief* in the company as a provider of satisfactions must result. Let us look at these stages separately, although they are actually indistinguishable parts of a process.

**AWARENESS.** While it is obvious that there must be awareness of a firm among children before they can develop a relationship with it, how to create that awareness is not so obvious. Fortunately, the child is an eager learner with enormous amounts of not-yet-suppressed curiosity. Therefore, frequent presentations of the firm's logo, slogans, and brand names within the child's environment will produce awareness of a firm. This is relatively easy for those sellers whose products are a normal part of children's daily life—books, crayons, clothing, food, for example. Probably there is not an adult who doesn't remember as a kid being aware of Crayola crayons—their colors, their package and wrappers, and above all, their aroma. And these adults relive that experience with fond memories when they become purchasers of Crayola crayons and other Crayola products for their kids. Such future action as this began with childhood awareness. However, for such awareness to be possible, the firm must make its name and brand names prominent. Many producers fail to create this awareness and therefore forego the opportunity to build a relationship with children as future consumers. This appears to be true, for example, for some clothing items such as pajamas, socks and gloves, and for some food items such as flour, sugar, and spices.

Creating awareness of a firm among children who do not consume the firm's products is more difficult and requires a different strategy. In this case, the firm's name or its products' names should be *paired* with objects of children's frequent involvement. For example, a life insurance company or a bank can give its name prominence by providing kids with book covers bearing its name and logo.

Whether a firm's products are a normal part of the children's life, such as school supplies, or a part of adult life such as autos, creating awareness for them should utilize all communications means in order to be as effective as possible. Producing awareness among children does not happen automatically for any firm, although for a firm like Coca-Cola it is relatively easy. The combination of Coke's advertising, signage, logo-laden trucks, and pervading packaging creates a major presence in practically everyone's environment. In fact, what Coke does is recommended to any company that wishes to create awareness among children. Most companies, however, do not have Coke's communications budget and must necessarily be more selective in their efforts. What is suggested is a combination of advertising, publicity, sales promotion, and packaging for creating awareness so that together a presence will result that is somewhat comparable to that of Coke.

**INTEREST.** Even though a firm makes its company symbols apparent to children, the children probably will not take much interest in them unless they are perceived as positive symbols—as potential need satisfiers. Crayons, for example, are usually viewed by children as having the potential to meet some of their important needs. What needs? The need for play, particularly, but also others such as belonging and sentience (the need for sensory experiences). Crayons give children a stimulating way to express themselves, hours of fun, and they produce conspicuous results that are often displayed by happy moms or pleased teachers. Pajamas are potential need satisfiers, too. So are jeans. They both produce warmth and comfort and play. But jeans are more frequently presented as need-satisfiers by pairing them with a number of producers' and retailers' names, and they are associated with many other positive products such as toys, trucks, and cowboys. Pajamas for whatever reason are not.

What about baking soda or sugar? Such products are probably perceived as having much less need-satisfying potential than crayons to a 6-year-old. This is true of hundreds of other products that also should be developing future customers. So, how do they do it? The answer is in the pairing—pairing with objects of significance. For example, when I was a kid, Arm & Hammer baking soda provided an order form on its package and in its magazine ads that permitted mom or a child to order a set of "bird cards." Each card had a beautifully illustrated picture of a bird with a good description on the back. Birds have significance to children! Like crayons, pajamas, and jeans. They had significance to me, and as a result of that collection of cards so did Arm & Hammer baking soda. Arm & Hammer did a good job of creating awareness and interest in a product and its brand that had little significance to a kid by pairing it with something that did have significance. The use of the premium for children in tandem with an adult product created interest in the baking soda that was rekindled each time the pictures of the birds were examined. As time went by, an awareness of the baking soda itself grew as its baking possibilities were introduced, and over time a very favorable image of that product was developed.

Kraft's answer to creating awareness and maintaining interest in products not usually targeted to kids has been the Kraft Cheese & Macaroni Club. Through the means of a club the firm is able to respond to children's need for play while informing them of Kraft products. The club concept has recently blossomed as a means of communicating to children about child-oriented, as well as adult-oriented, products and services.

**BELIEF.** Getting children to believe in a business firm and its products and missions is not difficult if there is awareness of them and if there is interest in them. The key is getting children to see a firm and/or its products as *actual* providers of satisfaction—in much the same way as mom or dad, grandma or grandpa can provide satisfaction. Interest can be maintained as long as there is perceived need satisfaction, but for belief to occur and continue, actual satisfaction of needs must be experienced. Being seen as a provider of satisfactions is relatively easy for a producer or seller of crayons, cereal, clothing, even automobiles, but it is more difficult for many other firms, for example, for a communications company (such as AT&T), a producer of bathroom tissue (such as Scott) or a hotel chain (such as Hyatt). Yet, all three companies have programs with this purpose. At AT&T, in an effort to develop future consumers from childhood, an education program has been developed for first-graders that teaches the benefits and use of communications devices such as the telephone. Although it is still too early to assess its results, the program is liked by many school teachers (which will please the children and their parents), and the children are learning how to use the telephone which provides them actual satisfaction. Thus, children's need for affiliation (with parents and teachers) and the need for security are met.

Today many companies are aligning themselves with programs and movements intended to protect and enhance our environment. Such efforts, when communicated to children, have the potential to produce belief in a firm. Likewise, if a company can ally itself with universal values such as patriotism, national defense, and good health, it is likely to nurture belief in it among children. It should be noted, however, that most value systems are difficult for children to conceptualize until they reach age 7 or 8.

Through the use of premiums a firm can create actual and substantial need satisfaction among children regardless of its degree of involvement with them. For example, if a firm sets up a reward system whereby children identify it as the provider of rewards, the satisfaction derived from the rewards can maintain belief in that firm. Consider this personal example. As a third-grader, I was called to the auditorium stage at a year-end ceremony to receive a prize for being neither absent nor tardy for the school year. What an exciting event for a kid. And, even more exciting was the fact that the prize was presented by the principal, a man who was revered by both teachers and students. The prize was the highlight of the experience. It consisted of a double-drawer case of pencils, crayons, and other school items, and I perceived it as a very expensive gift. The case was covered in a beautiful red leather-like material and embossed in gold with the words *Coca-Cola.* From that time on I loved Coke and honestly believed it was a notch above any other soft drink in quality. Indeed, my very positive attitude toward that brand came not through the medium of soft drinks but through school supplies. It is interesting that I did not buy Coke then. It seemed expensive—it was available only in six-ounce bottles that sold for the same price as colas in twelve-ounce bottles— and it seemed, also, to be more of an adult beverage. But for all my adult life it has been my preferred soft drink.

There are other examples like this. Pizza Hut established a program in schools to encourage frequent reading by children. Called, "Book It," the program rewards children with "One Free Personal Pan Pizza" for meeting monthly reading quotas. The main feature of programs such as this is to provide actual satisfaction of some of the children's needs so that they begin to see the firm in this role.

It is important for business firms that do not produce products of obvious significance to children to utilize *high involvement* and *credible* media for communicating information about themselves to children in order to help obtain and maintain interest. The print media—newspapers, magazines, books—are particularly useful. They trigger left-brain involvement that deals with reading. Also, as compared to television, print media, particularly children's magazines, tend to have a lot of inherent credibility. Thus, whether attempting to create awareness, interest, or belief, getting high-involvement learning among an audience provides the most effective way. Besides the printed message, spoken messages from credible sources such as parents and teachers work well. This is why parents and teachers and other role models are so effective in instilling values, and this is why we see these significant persons portrayed in television advertisements targeted to children.

**ACTION.** The action of concern here is future action—purchase or patronage on a regular basis. This is expected to occur in young adult years or at some other appropriate time in the life cycle if the customer-growing strategy of a firm is effective. However, action of some sort along the way to market age is desirable because it produces the high-involvement learning mentioned above. For example, getting children to cook with Arm & Hammer baking soda or Imperial sugar and to see the role of these ingredients in the results is an excellent way to generate future action—purchases and use—when the cooking role becomes more important. This might mean targeting cookbooks to children or to parents and children, perhaps as follow-ups to premiums such as the "bird pictures" noted earlier. It also suggests the participation of companies and their products in various activities for school children—science projects, spelling contests, raising farm animals, for instance.

Marketing programs that encourage hands-on participation for children are recommended whenever possible in order to get high-involvement learning and to provide them actual satisfaction. Therefore, a firm should strive for children's participation with its products even if its products tend to be adult-oriented. Banks can set up savings accounts for children as well as special in-bank services for children. Auto producers can set up safe-driving schooling through simulators. Ditto for producers and sellers of bikes and motorcyles. And all firms can provide for some kind of hands-on experience for children during specially designed field trips to their facilities.

As nurtured consumers reach market age and shop in a given store or buy a particular product for the first time, some of the appeals that they were introduced to as children should be used. These link the pleasant and secure childhood relations with those of the future. The playgrounds attached to most McDonald's restaurants are a signal to teenagers to come in and feel at home just as they did when they were kids. Interestingly, we might expect playgrounds to turn away teenagers who are striving to be grown up. But the playgrounds at McDonald's are like a beacon to many teens who remember the fun, food, and family from childhood.

## Marketing to Kids Using a Multidimensional Segmentation Strategy

It may be difficult for some companies to justify a separate marketing effort targeted to children as a primary, influence, or future market when the returns from it appear small, or are in the distant future and are hard to measure. An investment firm, auto manufacturer, or beef producer, for instance, may view such an undertaking as unworthy and even ludicrous. Yet, members of these three industries, and others, have begun reaching out to children using a multidimensional market segmentation strategy that targets them as not one but as two or three markets. Children may be targeted as primary and influence markets, primary and future markets, influence and future markets, or as primary, influence, and future markets. All four combinations are in use. For example, a soft drink that is purchased primarily by adults and only in small amounts by children may be marketed to kids as a primary market but additionally as a future market. The future market possibilities can make efforts aimed at the small primary market more justifiable to top management. This is the thinking of 7-Up that targets children, teens, and adults. This combination strategy also is used by Nike, for example, for its athletic shoes. It allocates a portion of its $50 million advertising budget to children and the rest to teens and adults.

On the other end of the children's market spectrum are those products not purchased or used at all by youngsters, such as autos and investments—and baking soda. Firms in these adult-only industries are increasingly recognizing children as a future market and also as a market of influencers. While they may occasionally feature their products in various promotion efforts to children, mainly they emphasize their company names, brands, and missions. Fidelity Investments, for example, put together a learning package for grade-school youngsters that teaches them about money management. Fidelity, in turn, hopes to develop awareness of its name among children and their parents, and that the children will grow up with a positive attitude towards Fidelity's services. The Kansas Beef Council, in a regional promotion of beef, aimed a sweepstake at children by mailing posters and entry forms to 2,800 Kansas primary schools. Winners had the chance to appear on a poster with George Brett, the Kansas City Royals' star. Again, the purpose was to obtain a positive acceptance from children to a product line, in this case beef, believing that the favorable attitude eventually will influence their parents' purchases as well as the children's future purchases.

All producers and all retailers of consumer goods will find it beneficial to target children as future customers. Additionally, in most cases children can be wooed concurrently as an influence market. Those producers who make products desired by both children and adults, such as soft drinks, clothing, and sporting goods, and those retailers that sell products for both children and adults such as department stores and mass merchandisers, are in an unique position to target children as members of all three markets.

Such multidimensional market segmentation efforts aimed at children are expected to produce a life-long relationship between children and a firm and consequently a steadily increasing flow of new customers at different decision ages for the firm's offering. Because this segmentation strategy nurtures and develops future customers rather than winning them over from competitors through brand-switching strategies, it theoretically produces more faithful customers.

## Managerial Suggestions

Children's annual expenditure of $6.1 billion alone makes them a worthy market target for thousands of retailers and producers of items that please the palates and play of kids. The fact that children also influence up to $132 billion of family purchases, and that they are a future market for all goods and services, makes them premium market material for most businesses. Moreover, if treated right today, they can contribute substantially to the future success of a business when they reach their peak buying period as adults. In fact, if won over now, they are likely to be more loyal than customers obtained through brand-switching or store-switching strategies.

If a business firm is not now targeting children as one or more of the three markets, and plans to, the following four pointers should help.

**GET TOP MANAGEMENT INVOLVEMENT.** Marketing to children is very different from marketing to adults. It is not just selling scaled-down adult items. Fisher-Price found this out when it introduced a $250 camcorder for kids in 1987 that ended up being perceived more as a toy. Depending on the company, there will be different requirements for many of its departments—selling, advertising, research. Thus, targeting kids is a decision that should be made at the top. Also, it takes an investment-for-the-future kind of attitude. Selling to children as a current market usually does pay off immediately, but it takes much longer to get payoffs from them as a future market. Charging such costs to current marketing budgets could create some real conflicts unless top management supports it. Also, because of the time required—perhaps twenty years in the case of AT&T's Adventurers program targeted to first-graders—there is bound to be executive turnover. Formal top management commitment will keep the effort on an even keel through these changes.

**PUT SOMEONE IN CHARGE WHO KNOWS CHILDREN.** There is lots of room for error when marketing to children—improperly age-graded advertising that misses the target, the opening / closure of a package that forgets about the limited dexterity of kids, or selling merchandise for kids through a channel of distribution that children avoid because it is not considered children-friendly. The plain fact of the matter is that children are wired differently from adults and the most astute marketer may err if he or she does not possess a sixth sense about kids. Someone who does possess such a skill should be in charge or at least provide advice and/or approval for kid-targeted marketing efforts. At AT&T it is the Youth Market Manager, at Binney & Smith it is the Director of Child Development. The title may not be so important but the responsibility is.

**UTILIZE THE ENTIRE COMMUNICATIONS MIX.** There is a tendency to think of television advertising when we think of communicating with children as consumers. Television is a great medium for creating awareness and interest in products of immediate importance to children. But it is easy to become a "Johnny-one-note" and not take advantage of the array of communications tools at the disposal of the business firm.

To get children aware, interested, and believing in a firm and its products and missions requires more active involvement than that provided by television advertising. Contests, sweepstakes, and premiums get children involved. Advertising in print and on radio creates great believability. Advertising in all media—broadcast, print, outdoor—creates a presence that any one medium just cannot achieve. Publicity in the school and home environments and in all media lend credibility to a firm and its missions.

So, utilizing the entire communications mix is necessary in order to produce a lasting relationship with children. Advertising can't do it alone. Just as there is a tendency automatically to think of TV advertising when informing children, it is just as automatic to forget the important role of store salespeople, store displays, and product packaging in long-run communications efforts.

**WHEN MARKETING TO KIDS, WEAR KID GLOVES.** Children are consumers-in-training. Anyone can fool them, deceive them, cheat them. It takes a mighty good marketer to satisfy children's wants and needs and not do any of these things, intentionally or unintentionally. If someone in the firm fails to check against such occurrences, one can be sure that someone on the outside will. Therefore, all elements of a marketing strategy targeted to children should be parent tested, as described in the later chapter on research.

# References

1. Lester P. Guest, "Brand Loyalty—Twelve Years Later," *The Journal of Applied Psychology* 39, No. 6 (1955): 405–408.
2. Here we are referring to the concept of the evoked set. See James U. McNeal, S. W. McDaniel, and Denise Smart, "The Brand Repertoire: Its Contents and Organization," in Patrick Murphy et al., eds., *1983 AMA Educators Conference Proceedings* (Chicago: American Marketing Association, 1983), pp. 92–96.
3. Penny Moser, "The McDonald's Mystique," *Fortune,* July 4, 1988, pp. 112–116.
4. This discussion of loyalty and its underlying needs is based on Henry A. Murray, *Explorations in Personality* (New York: John Wiley & Sons, 1938).
5. Jacob Jacoby and David B. Kyner, "Brand Loyalty vs. Repeat Purchasing Behavior," *Journal of Marketing Research* (February 1973), 1–9.

# PART THREE

# Marketing to Kids as Customers

The Children's Jewelry Category is Swiftly
Creating A New Generation of Shoppers

Bank
for kids

Children Are Spending More at Retail

Delta's "Fantastic
Flyer Program"
for kids

Toys 'R' Us returns
to pitch aimed at kids

Hotels and Resorts
Are Catering to Kids

K mart
focuses
on kids

Bowlers try to lure
kids into alley

Fast-food firms find
fortune in children

Shopping carts for kids

Burger King courts kids

Talbots is ready to kid around

FIGURE 6-1

# 6

# Retailing to Children

**S**ince retailers and parents are about the only sources of products and services for satisfying children's needs, children hold them both very dear. It has only been during the last decade that many retailers have acknowledged this relationship with children and have turned it into a two-way affair. The newspaper and magazine headlines in Figure 6–1 attest to this new retailing effort. And it's not just a few fast food restaurants and toy stores. It is across the board—bowling alleys, banks, airlines, hotels, clothiers, and mass merchandisers. Perhaps the one headline, "Children Are Spending More at Retail" explains it best. Kids have so much more spending power today than they did a decade ago that retailers have to take notice.

There are still major segments of the retail industry that refuse to recognize children as bona fide customers. These will be described in this chapter along with those retailers that are courting children. In general, though, the relationship between kids and retailers is much improved and is likely to get even better as merchants realize that there are only two sources of new customers: competitors and children.

## Reasons for Retailers to Target Children as Consumers

Reflecting on the preceding chapters, we may conclude that retailers know the following facts about children as customers:

1. *Children are three markets in one.* Children spend over $6 billion annually of their own money at retail outlets,

directly influence almost $132 billion in household purchases from retailers, and will ultimately buy all the products that retailers sell.

2. *Children save over $2.5 billion annually of their income.* This money may be saved at home or in commercial depositories, and may be spent later. For example, during the 1990 Christmas selling season children pulled over $700 million out of savings and spent it in retail outlets in addition to their regular spending of around $500 million a month. Also, $2.5 billion saved is potentially $2.5 billion spent at a bank.

3. *Children buy a relatively wide range of products and services.* Children are major buyers of sweet things and playthings, but they also spend a lot of their income on clothing, consumer electronics, entertainment, and hobbies. Their spending is all discretionary; it can be spent on about anything they choose. Thus, the relatively wide range of items they want and buy also may cause them to choose a wide range of retail outlets.

4. *They make purchases in a wide range of retail outlets.* Children begin to make independent purchases as early as age 4 or 5, and by age 10 they are making over 250 purchase visits a year to stores. They buy playthings at toy stores, mass merchandisers, supermarkets, and convenience stores, and they buy sweets from an even broader range of stores.

5. *Children co-shop with parents.* Children go shopping with parents as both independent consumers and as decision makers for potential household purchases. Thus, anytime a child is in the store with parents, he or she is a potential customer just as the parents are—and a potential future customer as well.

6. *Children form opinions, perceptions, and preferences about retail outlets.* Children enter the marketplace with very positive feelings toward stores because they perceive the stores as warehouses of satisfactions. The large number of interactions that children eventually have with retailers permit, encourage, and compel children to form many more cognitions and feelings about those retailers. These cerebral

results, in turn, provide directions and suggestions for
future store visits and purchases.

Given these six basic facts about children and their relationships
with purchase outlets, how are retailers responding to them? How
*should* retailers be responding to them? To the extent that research
results permit, we want to provide answers to both questions. Before we do, however, let's consider some implications of the above
six statements about the children's market in the context of today's
retailing environment.

Around the time of this writing, *Discount Store News* announced
that Wal-Mart had been declared the largest retailer in sales among
mass merchandisers, taking over the number one position from
Sears and blowing by the number two, K mart.[1] Sears tried to fight
off this challenge, ironically, by copying Wal-Mart's everyday low
price policy which only resulted in more lost revenues and profits
for the giant. K mart, the king of discounters for a couple of decades, responded to Wal-Mart's dash for the pennant by also copying some of Wal-Mart's merchandising methods while matching it
stride for stride. Sears in the meantime struggles for its very survival
and is rumored to be considering the disposal of its huge catalog
division just at a time when catalog sales are booming.

Also, around the time of this writing, headlines in a special report
in *Advertising Age* magazine announced, "Department Stores in
Fight of Their Lives."[2] This declaration referred specifically to department stores' substantial loss of sales in cosmetics and fragrances. The article noted that women have changed their shopping
patterns during the past few years and are buying fewer cosmetics
and fragrances in department stores and more in cosmetic specialty
stores, drugstores, supermarkets, and by mail order. Elsewhere we
read about department stores having to reorganize to survive, some
are on austerity plans, and some, such as the renowned Sakowitz
department store of Houston, are closing their doors.

Some major convenience store chains, including 7-Eleven and
Circle-K, have had financial difficulties and are finding it necessary
to pull back, sell off, and cut costs in hopes of becoming profitable
again. And we hear similar messages from some supermarkets (e.g.,
Safeway), drugstores (Revco), mass merchandisers (Ames), specialty children's stores (Child World), showroom stores (Best), and
electronics stores (Circuit City), to name only a few.

Thus, struggle and declining profits seem to characterize retailing at this time although there are a few shining stars such as Toys "R" Us, Nordstrom's, The Limited, and of course, Wal-Mart. Why such sounds of doom and gloom in the environment where people *must* go to meet most of their needs? Most retailers would blame the Middle East war and the recession for this 1991 situation. But how, then, would they justify the successes noted? We will not get in line to explain this struggle, or its successes and failures, but only spotlight it in order to provide a current context for discussing the children's market and retailers' responses to it. However, to repeat a point made in Chapter 5 that hints at a long-term solution to these retailers' problems, *there are only two strategies that will provide new customers for a store—switching customers from competitors or developing them from the pool of potential customers getting ready to enter the marketplace.* It appears that most retailers try to obtain customers from other retailers because these people are ready to purchase. But drawing them away from competitors is expensive, requiring heavy advertising, premiums, couponing, and price concessions. The result too often is profitless competition that has positioned some of the retailers mentioned above in the negative column. If, on the other hand, customers are developed before and during their entry period to the marketplace—mainly in childhood—they tend to grow into loyal customers who cost less to keep.

The six highlighted facts mentioned earlier about children as a market indicate that growing customers from childhood is indeed a viable and logical strategy for retailers. Children begin coming to stores as infants, and by the time they enter the first grade they are beginning to make purchases on their own—beginning a lifetime journey through marketland. The opportunity for retailers to develop regular customers from these children is not something that has to be fought for—it is foisted on them by the children and their parents. Retailers need only follow already delineated strategic paths within the context of their particular store types to win a legion of loyalists among these young consumers.

The concept of growing loyal consumers from childhood is not something that was invented in this book. It has always been around. Every retailer wants loyal, repeat customers, but knows that it is often hard to see them through the dog-eat-dog, day-to-day kaleidoscope of competition, particularly when they are only three or four feet tall. In one of our exploratory studies of children as consumers we observed children shopping for fragrances during the Christmas selling season in a department store. One 9-year-old who wanted to surprise her mother with an expensive fragrance for Christmas eased up to the fragrance counter and began smelling the samples. The salesperson behind the counter ignored her until the child took a sample bottle of cologne from its display and sprayed some on her wrist. The saleslady leaned over the product-laden counter and said "Oh no, you better not do that. Where is your mommy?" Interpretation: "You're some mother's kid. Why aren't you attached to her?" Not, "You're a potential customer for life if I treat you right." This incident occurred in a department store that is reporting financial difficulties.

Thus, we can see that a number of retailers are not doing great, many are struggling, some are dying. At the same time we can see new, first-time customers—children—coming to stores with enthusiasm, excitement, money, and motives. Ironic, indeed. We will examine retailer responses to children as consumers to see if we can explain this irony, and to see if we can suggest a more successful relationship between these two—one that will produce the most satisfaction for both.

## Retailers' Responses to Kids as Customers

In the fall of 1984, we surveyed major U.S. retailers by mail to determine if they acknowledge children as consumers, if they actively seek children as consumers, and if they have policies and practices aimed at children. The results were first reported in *Children as Consumers* in 1987 and essentially showed that just over a third of retailers were children-oriented.[3] We replicated that study in the fall of 1990 and the spring of 1991. The results of the two studies will be compared here so that we may see any changes that have taken place during this brief but very significant period of time. It was significant because during the last half of the 1980s children's status as consumers increased dramatically.[4]

### Research Procedure

The 1991 study of retailers' responses to children was modeled after the 1984 study in order that we might make legitimate comparisons between the two time periods. The last half of the 1980s was a time of intense marketing efforts to children according to a literature report; yet not much of that literature specifically described children-oriented retailing practices.[5] Therefore, we wanted to know if the growing intensity in marketing to children was as much a phenomenon among retailers as it was among manufacturers.

In both studies we contacted the retailers we believed to be the major players in each of ten retail categories. These ten categories were chosen because we believed they represented retailers having a legitimate interest in children as consumers. We intentionally omitted one category—toy stores—because we felt it unnecessary to demonstrate the extent to which they were involved with young consumers. We used an open-ended letter, rather than a questionnaire, addressed to the chief executive officer of each of the major retail chains, and in the case of some department stores, to the chief operating officer of each store. The department stores that were treated separately were known to have a great deal of autonomy within their groups. The letter asked the same questions as it did in 1984 and all respondents were promised anonymity.

The letters went out to 176 executives (157 in 1984), and after one follow-up 62 responded, or 35 percent (92 responded in 1984 with a 59 percent rate of return). We received six refusals and these combined with those who did not reply at all produced a 65 percent nonresponse rate. This nonresponse rate is apparently normal for today but it is regrettably high and probably is due in part to our sending the letter directly to the CEOs, and in part to not using a simple check-off questionnaire. We acknowledge our bias in selecting only major retail chains. We know that smaller, independent retailers often target children, but we thought that reports from the largest retailers in each category would best reflect what is actually happening out there. The study was also biased because our sampling lists did not include service retailers such as banks, video rental and sales stores, and arcades. Neither were mail retailers included. We will say something about these omitted categories and their relationships with kids after we present the results of the 1991 study and compare them with those from 1984.

### Findings

The categories, the number of retailers contacted in each, and the response rate of each are shown in the first three columns of Table 6–1. Four of the categories—department stores, variety stores, convenience stores, and discounters—had response rates of 24, 25, 25, and 27 per-

**TABLE 6–1**

*Types of Retailing Firms Classified as Children-Oriented,*
*1984 vs. 1991*

| Type | # Contacted | Responded No. | Responded % | Children-Oriented % '84 | Children-Oriented % '91 |
|------|-------------|---------------|-------------|-------------------------|-------------------------|
| Department Stores | 67 | 16 | 24 | 45 | 75 |
| Variety Stores | 4 | 1 | 25 | 25 | 100 |
| Discounters | 15 | 4 | 27 | 80 | 75 |
| Supermarkets | 20 | 9 | 45 | 32 | 78 |
| Convenience Stores | 8 | 2 | 25 | 100 | 50 |
| Restaurants | 21 | 8 | 38 | 39 | 75 |
| Drugstores | 3 | 1 | 33 | 0 | 0 |
| Apparel Stores | 15 | 8 | 53 | 22 | 50 |
| Hotels/Motels | 13 | 7 | 54 | 25 | 43 |
| Other (Specialty) | 10 | 6 | 60 | 22 | 50 |
| 1991 | 176 | 62 | 35 | | 68 |
| 1984 | 157 | 92 | 59 | 37 | |

cent, respectively. Except for department stores, where the actual number of responses was relatively large, these categories are suspect in terms of their measures. The overall return of 62 stores, however, appears to provide a broad picture of major retailing.

The last column shows the extent to which the reporting retailers are children-oriented, and in this case, the results are presented side by side with the 1984 measures. A firm was judged to be children-oriented if it stated that it had one or more policies or practices targeted to children as potential customers. According to these data almost twice as many retailers were children-oriented in 1991 as compared to 1984—68 percent versus 37 percent. Clearly, retailers significantly upped their interest level in children as consumers during the last half of the 1980s.

Looking more closely at the last column in Table 6–1, we can see that nine of the ten categories of stores have a higher rate of child orientation. The degree of orientation by discounters (mass merchandisers) did not increase, but it was already relatively high in 1984. Thus, the 75 percent in 1991 is not statistically significant compared to the 80 percent of 1984. In four cases the extent of children orientation at least doubled, in three more cases it almost doubled. The already high rate for discounters did not change as noted; the percent for hotels/motels increased over 50 percent; and only drugstores remained exactly the same. However, the rates for several of these categories are based on such a small number that we cannot place much confidence in them. Overall, though it is apparent that a children orientation is growing rapidly among retailers.

Table 6–2 describes those activities that caused the 42 retail chains to be classified as children-oriented. The first group of figures shows the number of retailers practicing each activity. The second group shows the percentages for children-oriented retailers, while the third group shows the percentages for the total sample. There are significant changes in these indicators of children orientation between 1984 and 1991. There was a slight increase in shopping/buying facilitators. The increase is not statistically significant but the fact that 90 percent of the stores provide some of them is notable. These activities acknowledge children as special customers who require special assistance. Included are eye-level displays and fixtures, downsized shopping carts, children's menus, and bicycle racks. The percentage of children-oriented retailers targeting some kind of promotion to kids significantly increased from 52.9 percent to 80.1 percent. This category includes any marketing communication effort such as in-store promotion and television advertising. The amount of store personnel training for the purposes of assisting children increased slightly. Here, we are referring to store employees being trained, for example,

**TABLE 6–2**
*Retailers' Children-Oriented Activities:*
*1984 and 1991*

| Activity | Number of Retailers | | Children-Oriented Retailers (%) | | Total Sample (%) | |
|---|---|---|---|---|---|---|
| | '84 | '91 | '84 | '91 | '84 | '91 |
| Shopping/Buying Facilitators | 29 | 38 | 85.3 | 90.1 | 38.5 | 55.7 |
| Consumer Education | 28 | 12 | 82.4 | 28.6 | 30.4 | 13.1 |
| Promotion | 18 | 34 | 52.9 | 80.1 | 19.6 | 50.1 |
| Store Personnel Training | 17 | 26 | 50.0 | 61.9 | 18.5 | 37.7 |
| Ethical Practices | 14 | 10 | 41.2 | 23.8 | 15.2 | 13.1 |

to assist children with change-making at the checkout counter or with making exchanges and obtaining refunds. Ethical practices did drop significantly which may suggest either that stores are devoting less attention to them or that there is little else to do in this area of serving children. Keeping dangerous products and sexually oriented magazines out of children's reach are typical examples of ethical practices. Two stores also reported liberal responses to children shoplifters in order not to burden them with it for a lifetime. Consumer education activities dropped very significantly. Some stores still offer field trips and printed materials for classroom use, but their number has declined dramatically. Perhaps the negative press that has been given to commercializing the classroom has caused this change, or perhaps retailers feel that such efforts are needed less by children.

## Some Retailers Target Children, Some Don't

In 1984, slightly over one-third of retailers were reported as children-oriented; in 1991, just over two-thirds. Even with all the shortcomings of this study, the signal is pretty clear. Kids are rapidly being acknowledged by the retailing community as potential customers. Perhaps the large number of purchase-visits that children make in the marketplace is awakening retail managers to the fact that kids represent market opportunity. In any case, merchandising to children is becoming part of the overall competitive strategy of a significant portion of retailers.

Now that this new information about retailing to children has been displayed in Tables 6–1 and 6–2, let us try to glean the meaning and implications from them. We will take small lumps of them for analysis. First, let us look at the retailers who are *not* child-oriented according to the data.

### Retailers Not Oriented to Children

One-third of retailers are not children-oriented according to our study. Actually, the figure is probably higher because (1) we don't know enough about the chains that did not respond to our study, but we believe there was a tendency for nonrespondents not to be children-oriented, and (2) some of those that responded are just now entering the children-oriented mode and still need to learn to do it better. Respondents who did not view children in a special light ranged from adamant to apologetic. One CEO wrote, "[Our store] is strictly an adult store. In fact, children accompanied by their parents are not very comfortable in our stores." In the other direction, another said, "We don't have any policies or procedures related to young people but it is a thought-provoking idea."

Respondents offered two reasons for not being oriented to children: (1) They believed that all customers should be treated in the same manner, or (2) they felt that theirs were exclusively adult-oriented stores. In some ways, stores that treat all customers equally might be viewed as children-oriented. For example, one store executive stated that, "We do not have any different policy for handling younger customers than other customers. We treat them all well." Most likely children would be treated well in those stores. But would they be treated as potential customers or as children? For instance, one store told us, "Children who shop in our stores are always with a parent who is the customer." In this store, the youngster is unlikely to be treated as a potential customer but as the kid of a potential customer. There is a difference, a marketing difference. If the child is not viewed and treated as a potential customer, he or she may not feel like one in that store, perhaps ever.

Not acknowledging children as potential customers because a store is oriented to adults only—the second reason for not being children-oriented—may be shortsighted. There are no offerings for today's adults that will not eventually be purchased by today's children. The store that does not acknowledge this, and does not let children know that they are appreciated as future customers, may indirectly be reducing its number of future customers, particularly future loyal customers.

These responses suggest that in 1991, as in 1984, there are still a number of store executives who, for what they believe are good reasons, do not view children as either a current, influence, or future market. These executives who are found in all the retail categories studied here, simply cannot envision the market potential of kids for their particular line of retailing.

## Children-Oriented Retailers: Extent and Nature

To the extent that the percentages given in Table 6–1 are representative of major retail categories that are children-oriented, we can see that some categories are more focused on children than others. We might expect some variance since the offerings of some of these retailers vary in attractiveness to children as a primary market. For example, the offerings of mass merchandisers such as K mart are of more interest to children as potential customers than apparel stores or hotels. Therefore, we might expect more children-centeredness among discounters, and this is the case.

The least child-oriented, or those retailers with the lowest percentages, are apparel stores, drugstores, hotels/motels, and specialty stores. These lower percentages might be expected to some extent since these stores usually offer less to children as a primary market. However, in this day and time we might not expect low percentages from any categories. Let's look more closely at each type of retailer.

**APPAREL STORES.** We received reports from women's apparel, men's apparel, and family apparel stores. As might be expected the family stores were more oriented to children—providing credit cards (through parents), video areas for entertaining and selling, visual displays targeted to kids (signs, posters, lights, fixtures), and kids' fashion shows. When there was a focus on kids among the apparel stores for men or women, it often had the purpose of making shopping easier for parents—video centers, kids' reading centers, and kids' sitting areas. Thus, there was more baby-sitting than customer growing.

Most of apparel stores did not seem to see kids as future consumers who ought to be made welcome now. Yet, as long ago as 1986 *Stores* magazine reported that there was a heightened interest about children in fashion wear and that manufacturers such as Esprit and Liz Claiborne were extending their junior and misses looks into children's clothing.[6] And by 1988 this same magazine was asking, "What's hot in [clothing] retail?" and answering, "Anything having to do with kids."[7] Thus, changing attitudes and dressing patterns among kids would suggest a great opportunity for clothiers to grow customers from childhood.

**CONVENIENCE STORES.** The two convenience store chains that responded showed lots of concern for kids as current and future customers. Young children, particularly, have a strong preference for these stores because of their convenience (to home and/or school) and their relatively wide assortment of kid-pleasing items. The two chains responding in this study acknowledged this "love affair." In return, sweets, toys, and reading materials are displayed at eye level, along with kid-oriented promotions, and some are attended to by vendors who understand and help the stores cater to children as current consumers. For example, one executive wrote that ". . . vendors pay special attention to the stand-alone shippers that they provide to our stores in order to appeal to children."

In addition to the typical sweet things and playthings, these stores rent and sell videos for children. One has bicycle racks, both have clubs. In one club the orientation is on food and beverages, and it is well organized with special mailings and rewards for cumulative purchases. The other is not yet organized but will focus on rewards for accomplishments such as high grades. Both are intended to develop positive attitudes and allegiance among children.

**DEPARTMENT STORES.** This retail category showed a substantial increase in its orientation to children. In most cases the reporting stores acknowledged kids as current, influence, and future markets. There is a more intense and sustained focus on children as current consumers (as compared to 1984) as store managers recognize that kids, particularly kids from high-income families, have more money to spend and are spending more of it on high-ticket items such as designer-brand clothing. There is an increase in displays at kids' eye level, more visual dazzle, somewhat more willingness on the part of salespeople to demonstrate to children, and more tie-ins with school life. Along with teen boards, there are now kids' boards (or combinations), there are fashion shows, and there are many more in-store and media promotions than in 1984. Special shopping times are being set aside for kids at peak selling seasons—no longer are kids limited to just the kids' department. And events is the operative word—events during peak selling times, events during slow times, events tied in with school, events tied in with parents—all geared to making kids feel special. It sounds like having a favorite department store might come around again as some of them try very hard to develop loyalty among youngsters.

**DISCOUNTERS (MASS MERCHANDISERS).** Discount department stores, or discount stores, or mass merchandisers—all three terms are used by the industry's literature—have acknowledged the spending and spending-influence of children at least since the 1984 study. Some of the activities they target to children resemble those of the department stores discussed above, only perhaps more solidified. Discount stores utilize advertising more, and in general aim more external promotion to kids. They use clubs, tie-ins with schools, and in general maintain frequent contact with kids. Within the stores there is more merchandise for children than there was in 1984, although there does not appear to be much more merchandis*ing*. None of the discounters appear to be long on merchandising, or on special services for kids, or on personnel training, focusing instead on cost maintenance and reduction. Overall, though, discounters definitely see kids as part of their customer mix and give them lots of consideration when buying and stocking goods, particularly in terms of bringing in new lines of merchandise such as health and beauty aids.

**DRUGSTORES.** This category offers a number of items that appeal to children. In fact, it probably stocks as high a percentage of total items with appeal for kids as do discount stores. Yet, as in 1984, these stores report little in the way of an orientation toward children. Also, the wide range of items stocked by drugstores produces an appeal to families overall, but the stores seem not to acknowledge children as influential. Finally, if they see children as their future consumers, they do not acknowledge it.

It is difficult to tell (from our studies) if drugstores see themselves as an adults-only retail type, and therefore don't feel kids belong there, or if they don't see themselves as stocking goods that are of interest to kids. And it is difficult to tell if they perceive that kids are their future and should be part of their current merchandising strategies.

**RESTAURANTS.** The restaurants that were contacted in this study were chain restaurants. Most of them that responded could be classified as either fast-food restaurants, cafeterias, or family sit-down restaurants. Most of them don't see kids as current consumers— as coming to the restaurant on their own and making their own purchases—but as members of a family. Therefore, most of the restaurants treat the children as either future customers, or as influencers. All have children's menus, although most selections are only small portions of adult items. One exception was a restaurant that used "extensive marketing research to develop new menu items for children" employing test marketing and taste tests. The result was intended to be a highly desirable set of food items uniquely designed for kids and acceptable to their parents. Most of the restaurants offer premiums for children and see the premium area as a basic means of competing for the favor of children—often even more than foods. Around half of the restaurants advertise to children, and others have plans to do so. Also, about half have some kind of personnel training that targets kids and their satisfaction.

A few of the restaurants are involved in some type of consumer education in which a combination of field trips and educational materials for schools are in use. Some of this consumer education also is made part of in-store promotions. With nutrition and fitness becoming even more important to adults and children, restaurants are in a position to offer some vital consumer education.

Most of the restaurants appear to be performing a balancing act between targeting adults and children. The adults targeted may or may not have children with them, thus producing two market subsegments. A few restaurant chains have decided to focus strictly on the adults, even to the point of ignoring children as their future customers.

**HOTELS/MOTELS.** Reports from hotels and motels have about the same tone as those from restaurants. Most are trying to satisfy both children and adults, including families. They recognize the opportunities to serve these two or three segments (depending on how they are perceived), but find it to be a tightwire act. Satisfaction of children ranges from special programs and room amenities just for them to simply introducing a children's menu in their restaurants. And like some restaurants, some of the hotels seem to feel that they can't serve two masters, so they choose adults who have the spending power. One hotel, for example, said that "the hotel does not direct marketing efforts toward younger consumers" because "the activities of the hotel are geared toward an older clientele." Further, its restaurants had children's menus but it "does not market the fact that children's menus are available."

Like many of the restaurants, motels and hotels recognize that kids are not usually independent consumers, and most seem to feel that children do not make independent decisions at a hotel or motel. One hotel said its shops were leased and it did not have control over their merchandising, implying that the shops were unimportant to children who stay at the hotel. On the other hand, another hotel stated that its shops were focusing on kids much more by adding new lines of merchandise at eye level, and by introducing an entertainment/food unit just for its young consumers.

It appears that hotels and motels, as well as eating and drinking establishments, are choosing sides. They either will appeal to the adult segment without children or the adult segment with children. Each will experience a burden of sorts. The adult-with-children hotels/motels will need the budget and staff to provide a truly child-satisfying environment, not just children's menus and a game room. The adult-only hotels and motels will need to develop plans to attract future, loyal customers in some way other than targeting young consumers.

**OTHERS (SPECIALTY STORES).** The product lines of the six store chains classified as specialty stores in this study were sporting goods, giftware, books, consumer electronics, and music. Somewhat like hotels and restaurants, these stores are deciding to focus on either adults with children or just on adults. They generally feel that their products are not for kids except for the book stores. In the latter case, there is a tendency to emphasize products for kids (books, videos, accessories), eye-level displays, and a club through which frequent promotions are done. The music store stocked a line of items for kids but seemed not to want to emphasize it. The sporting goods store and one of the gift stores focused on the family more with a separate space for children set aside with play/entertainment items. Like hotels and eating places, the family-oriented specialty stores seem uncertain about the extent to which to give children separate attention while the adult-only stores seem not to be concerned at all with children as future customers.

**SUPERMARKETS.** Supermarkets have done an about-face since 1984, with over twice the percentage reporting to be children-oriented, and the efforts of practically all of them extend well beyond the "cookie credit card" stage. The child is now a focus in personnel training classes, in display strategies, in consumer education and community affairs programs, in promotion programs, and in ethical practices. Most supermarkets run the gamut of trying to please the young consumer and build loyalty among them. One supermarketer echoed the sentiments of most of the others: with "We recognize that young children are the shoppers of the future and developing customer loyalty and trust with young consumers is very important to us."

Ethical practices, consumer education, and community affairs programs often flow together under the banner of "nutrition." Teaching nutrition and encouraging good nutrition are blended with community membership and community responsibility, and all are focused on kids. Promotions are often the vehicles for these activities.

Probably no retailing type has a better opportunity to build long-term relations with children than supers. Children learn their early consumership there, more than in any other store. And it starts at age one or two. So, whatever is learned at the supermarket is put in place early. This relationship is a two-edged sword, however. Children become early critics of dirty floors (they are perceived as antithetical to food) and of malfunctioning carts (a cart with bad wheels is like a bicycle with a flat), and they quickly pick up on the complaints of parents about out-of-stocks and deceptive pricing. Thus, supermarkets have the earliest opportunity to create a love or hate relationship with kids—with all their future consumers. Since 1984 they have focused increasingly on love.

**VARIETY STORES.** With only one variety store reporting a child orientation in 1984 and in 1991, it is difficult to profile their views about kids as consumers. That one store does some eye-level displaying and some community affairs work with children. The broad offering of variety stores should have an appeal to kids, and their open displays should encourage store visits by children. Together, these two features provide opportunities for variety stores to build relationships with youngsters. However, the study results do not permit an assessment of variety stores' efforts at bonding with children.

## Nonstore Retailing

Nonstore retailing was not a part of the study reported here and is not currently a major factor in marketing to children. It has the potential, however, and it is showing signs of becoming a more important force. *Vending* machines have always had an appeal to young consumers because of their convenience and their visible offerings of sweets and beverages. Probably some of children's earliest purchases are made from vending machines in spite of what seems like a concerted effort to place the coin slots out of reach of children. Probably, also, a significant number of children's impulse purchases are from vending machines. However, the $19 billion vending industry does not appear to be interested specifically in children as current consumers and gives no hint of future interest.

The *telephone* industry offers another possible nonstore channel of distribution for marketing to children although it seems the 900 segment has chosen instead to shoot itself in the foot by attempting to dupe kids with purchase-of-air opportunities such as Dial-a-Santa and Dial-a-Muppet.[8] There are some hints now that the industry is trying to get its act together through some self-regulation. If it does, it has a chance to participate in something that children like to do almost as much as buying things—namely, talking on the telephone.

Perhaps a simple solution to the problems the telephone industry faces in becoming a viable channel of distribution to children is to change the 9 to an 8. The 800 numbers would not offend parents or deceive children into paying for the privilege of buying from a merchant, and they would permit a variety of marketing opportunities, particularly relationship building.

*Catalog* sellers are on the verge of delineating children as a major potential market. There are already a number of children catalogers out there that discovered in the 1980s that children like to receive mail, like to look through Mom and Dad's catalogs, and are doing some catalog shopping with parents. Now, there are catalogs that specialize in toys (e.g., Green Mountain Express) and clothing (e.g., 7th Heaven), as well as more general ones from retailers such as Bloomingdale's and J. C. Penney.[9] With data bases being created that identify homes with children—often through clubs for kids—it is only a matter of time before clubs start some mail sales through their own specialized catalogs. And as magazines and newspapers especially for kids grow in circulation, they will increasingly offer some type of mail sales, perhaps in conjunction with a catalog seller. As children spend more time at home, alone and with parents who are opting more for the sofa over restaurants and shopping and socials, catalogs, which are increasingly popular with adults, will grow in popularity among children.

*Clubs* constitute another nonstore channel of distribution. Clubs may be part of retailing operation—for example, K mart's Gym Kids Club and J. C. Penney's Sesame Street Kids' Club—but more often they belong to a manufacturer such as Nintendo, Lego, Keebler, and Kool-Aid, or an advertising medium such as Nickelodeon or Family Circle. Clubs for children have been around at least since the advent of kids' radio in the 1930s and 1940s, but they experienced a rebirth, actually an explosion, in the 1980s.[10]

While kids' clubs can be classified as belonging to either retailers, producers, or media, they all appear to be nonstore retailers in varying degrees. Thus, their merchandise offering (as part of their reading and playing features) generally can be classified as either goods related to one brand, one retailer, or one licensed character or group of characters, or goods of a general nature.

It is difficult to say how many kids' clubs there are, but at a national level there currently appear to be around two dozen; at a local level, probably ten times that many. The force behind their sudden development again is data base marketing (DBM), the ability to do mass marketing at a one-on-one level. Since the technology of data base marketing is in its infancy, we certainly can anticipate more kids' clubs as DBM matures.

## Service Retailers

The research findings that were discussed earlier were related almost exclusively to product retailers. The particular exception was hotels and motels, a number of which are targeting children. But there are other retail service units that focus on children as a potential market. *Video rental-sales* stores are targeting children with product lines, in-store promotions and displays, kids' play and entertainment sections (corners), and clubs. Additionally, as already noted, retailers such as convenience stores, supermarkets, and bookstores are promoting videos to kids. This is an industry that has an automatic appeal to our TV generation of youngsters and their parents. Building loyalty with kids might automatically be expected of this segment of retailing.

Of course, the terms "automatic appeal" and "automatic loyalty building" could as aptly be applied to the *video arcade* retailers. Here children spend a half-billion dollars a year of their own money and an additional large amount of Mom and Dad's money. Game arcades, like video rentals/sales, have an inherent appeal for children, and children carry this habit into their teen and young adult years. The Nintendo company, for example, appeals to all three age groups with its advertising campaign. The arcade industry, however, is made of many small though often chain-owned units, as is often the case in the video rental industry, and thus there are fewer media advertising and promotion programs. The lack of such promotional activity appears to lessen loyalty building by this $6–7 billion industry even though children often grow up to be adult video arcade patrons.[11]

*Movie theaters* are another service retailer that often targets kids as customers. Along with spectator sports—mainly professional football, baseball, and basketball—the two attract around a half-billion dollars of children's own money plus a good deal of parents' money spent on behalf of the children. Because these entertainment retailers' primary markets are adults, they have to develop strategies that appeal to both segments without alienating one. But generally it's the kids who end up being alienated; therefore, they are finding similar entertainment at home. United Artists theaters, for instance, is attempting to build loyalty with movie-goers through more frequent advertising and by permitting easier purchase of tickets with automated teller cards, but it does not appear to be targeting such efforts among its youngest audience with the most potential.[12]

Another class of entertainment retailers that tend to see children as current, influence, and future consumers is what might be classified as entertainment parks. The most visible of these are Disney Land and Disney World and their complementary units. There are other large entertainment centers that compete with Disney and there are many relatively small ones. Finally, within this category of smaller parks we might include private zoos, miniature golf courses, carnivals, and circuses. While Disney and its competitors devote some national advertising to kids and/or families, the smaller units rely on local advertising media, promotions, and publicity. All of them must compete with other entertainment retailers for a share of children's money and minds. Because virtually all of these entertainment retailers specialize in play, they are natural attractions for kids.

As observed in an earlier chapter, *banks* are increasingly targeting children for services, mainly savings accounts. Again, this is primarily an adult industry, and trying to attract children without offending adults—who banks have conditioned to feel stiff and mature when using banking resources—is particularly difficult. Probably the most success has been accomplished with off-premises banking conducted at elementary schools such as that done by the Twiglet bank in Miami. The club concept is also being used successfully by banks to separate kids and grown-ups. The First National Bank Kids' Klub of Pulaski, Tennessee won a "Best Sales of a Retailer" award from the Tennessee Press Association for its efforts in banking to children.[13]

Finally, some nonprofit service retailers (some of them are for profit, too) target kids. These include zoos, museums, and hospitals. In all cases they are trying to appeal to children as one or more markets. Zoos and museums seek children as current and influence consumers, particularly, while some hospitals are trying to build relationships for the future.

## Conclusions and Recommendations

It is clear that during the last half of the 1980s the nature of retailing to children changed dramatically, and not for the worse but for the better—for retailers and for children. Retailers could have let up or given up, saying that marketing to kids is too difficult, controversial, and not noticeably beneficial to the bottom line. But they didn't. The studies cited in this chapter have shown that retailers increased by almost twofold the extent to which they include children in their marketing strategies and tactics. Some acknowledge children as a current market for goods and services, some treat them as a market of influencers, and some see children as a future market that should be developed now. Many of the retailers acknowledge children as two or all three of these markets with a multisegment segmentation strategy.

There is a negative side to all of this change. Not all retailers are making the change; not all acknowledge children as one or more potential markets. For example, drugstores appear not to see children as a market of purchasers, nor as influencers of parents' purchases or as the next generation of customers. Drugstores are not alone in this view; one third of retailers share it. This third sees its business as an adult business or at least as one in which children do not deserve to receive separate marketing treatment.

To some extent, the retailing strategies that are targeted to children also have a negative side. While there is a substantial increase in promotion to children and a sustained high level of use of shopping/buying facilitators, retailers have not increased much the training of store personnel in assisting children, and they have reduced substantially the amount of consumer education and ethical practices targeted to kids. All three of these activities—training personnel, consumer education, and ethical practices—are interrelated. Store personnel that are sensitive to the needs of children can be the vehicles of consumer education and ethical practices. But given the attitudes of many store personnel towards serving customers in general, much less the youngest consumers, the likelihood of advancing the level of consumer education and ethical practices seems small.

Some suggestions and recommendations are offered, first to those stores that do not acknowledge the market potential of children, and second to those stores that do. Stores that are not children-oriented should institute a public relations program targeted to children in order to produce a long-term favorable store image among them. These stores must assure themselves of a steady stream of new customers who want to come to those stores for overall satisfaction, not just for the lower price that is often offered to customers to switch from another store. Such a program, if managed by someone who understands the language and thinking of children, prepares the children with a good image of the store so that when they reach market age they can more easily be converted into lifelong, satisfied customers of the store.

For stores that wish to become children-oriented there are four major recommendations:

1. *Train store personnel so that they are better prepared to assist children who are new consumers and often need help.* Child-oriented stores report that they are doing more to bring children and their parents into their stores through promotion and in-store shopping/buying facilitators. But it is inconsistent to encourage youngsters to patronize a store without preparing its personnel to make sure things go right for these new consumers. In effect, the store personnel need preparation to make up for the preparation that children do not yet have. In the case of self-service, self-selection stores, the checkout people, stockers, and counter people should be given training to assist children in locating goods, paying for them correctly, and getting the correct items so that returns (and dissatisfaction) are reduced. Personnel in self-service stores are notoriously underpaid and notoriously uncaring about customers. Training will help, particularly if top management supports it.

Full-service stores should focus more on salespeople and prepare them to deal with children. It appears that for many professional salespeople (especially those who work for commission) serving children can be humiliating. For these people, particularly, some training is needed that will help them understand the value of the child consumer and convince them that children deserve *at least* the assistance and courtesies given to the adults.

One type of training might be effective for all store personnel in all stores. Each week they should write 100 times, "Kids are my future."

2. *Provide more consumer education.* Retailers are cutting back

on consumer education when they should be increasing it in order to help children develop consumer skills and knowledge. Children will be more effective shoppers and buyers in stores that provide such education. This means the children will be better satisfied consumers. Consumer relations (or public relations) personnel should visit with kindergarten and elementary school officials and teachers to jointly develop consumer education programs that will meet the goals of both parties. What is being recommended here is not a selling program; it is a consumer education program. It helps the school, the store chain, but most of all, the children.

3. *Institute more ethical practices.* Serving children is not the same as serving adults. Adults have developed a set of values; children are developing theirs. Children will do the wrong things. They need help to do the right things. For instance, the 1984 and 1991 studies discussed earlier showed that many stores keep sexually oriented materials out of the reach of children. There are many other products and practices that children should not be subjected to until they have a value system in place. For example, they should not be able to examine firearms or buy glues that may be harmful without their parents. Consider this example: A supermarket chain has just opened a video rental and sales store. It is roomy, flashy, exciting, and inviting to children. It has a very large children's section next to a bank of video games. Above the games is a sign that says that children are not allowed to play the video games during school hours. That's an ethical practice. But the very first object encountered when one walks into the video store is a large display of bubble gum sold in pouches to look like chewing tobacco and in round tins to look like snuff. That's an *un*ethical practice!

4. *Do research to support marketing strategies targeted to children.* Even as parents we don't understand children very well, and our understanding doesn't necessarily improve when we become retail decision makers. As noted earlier, some restaurants do taste tests and market tests to determine potential new products for children because these restaurants recognize that children's tastes are not like those of adults (even though most restaurants apparently don't see a difference). Some simple research designs will help properly locate products in a store, test the product mix offered to children, check the appropriateness of the fixtures for children, check the special services for children, and measure the satisfaction of children. Would a retailing firm make a decision to

go after a new market segment, promote to it, lay in new products for it, develop new services for it, and then not check to see if the new market segment is satisfied? That too often is done.

Finally, about the worst thing that could happen is to decide to target children as a market, to do a good job of satisfying them, but to alienate their parents. That can be a disaster. The new video store described above with its tobacco look-alike bubble gum display will probably alienate some parents—the very people who pay the bills. The key to making sure this kind of thing does not happen is to *parent-test* all strategies and tactics aimed at children. Just as stores have teen advisory boards and children's advisory boards, they should have parent advisory boards through which all children-related activities can be tested.

## References

1. "Wal-Mart, K mart Battle for No. 1 Spot." *Discount Store News,* February 18, 1991, p. 2.
2. Laurie Freeman, "Department Stores in Fight of Their Lives." *Advertising Age,* March 4, 1991, p. 29.
3. James U. McNeal. *Children as Consumers: Insights and Implications,* Lexington, MA: Lexington Books (1987), Chapter 4.
4. An analysis of writings on the topic showed a steep upward incline in number of publications on the topic during this period. See James U. McNeal, *A Bibliography of the Research and Writings on Marketing and Advertising to Children* (Lexington, MA: Lexington Books, 1991), Chapter 1.
5. Ibid.
6. Janet Wallach. "Some Strategies for Selling Sophisticated Updated Fashions for Trendy Little Girls," *Stores,* August 1986, pp. 44–48.
7. Muriel J. Adams, "Hot New Retail Formats: Retail Concepts That Are Finding a Special Niche in the Market," *Stores,* February 1988, pp. 34–44.
8. "ACT Calls on FTC to Restrict TV Ads for Phone Services Aimed at Children," *Broadcasting,* August 12, 1985, p. 36.
9. Merri Rosenberg, "Baby Boom Gives Birth to Boom in Direct Marketing," *Adweek,* November 30, 1987, p. 50.
10. Al Urbanski, "Focus on Clubs," *Food and Beverage Marketing,* July 1990, p. 35.
11. Donald Porter, "Game Players Escape Reality with a Short Flight to Fantasy." *Ogden (Utah) Standard-Examiner,* December 22, 1989, p. E2.
12. Marcy Magiera, "Movie Chains Test Brand-Building," *Advertising Age,* March 4, 1991, p. 43.
13. "'Kiddie Banking' 101: The Art of Marketing to Kids on a Shoestring," *Marketing Update (Bank Marketing Association),* February 1990, pp. 1–4.

# Kids upfront sizzles to $200M

**Radio tunes into children**

### At last, a great paper for kids

#### Book club will target toddlers, teens

## Gen'l Foods aims magazine at kids

## Cable kid sales are bullish

### Children's Advertisers Master Art Of Slipping In Their Commercials

## Kids targeted by new networks

## Publishers' efforts book parents, kids

# Kids' game shows

### Comics Publishers Woo Kids

**Nickelodeon takes pitch direct to kids**

# A NEW WORLD OF KIDS' MAGAZINES

FIGURE 7-1

# 7

# Advertising to Children

The headlines shown in Figure 7–1 are taken from various business magazines and newspapers and summarize rather well what is going on in the area of advertising to children. Television advertising is still the favorite medium for reaching out to kids, but other standard advertising media—magazines, newspapers, radio—have been gaining presence in the children's market. Also, relatively new forms of advertising have appeared that have the ability to target children with greater accuracy than the standard media. They include mail, home videos, video games, movies, and schools. Moreover, marketing strategies targeted to children are increasingly being found to be more effective when advertising is integrated with other marketing communications efforts.

## Advertising as Part of the Marketing Communications Mix

### The Second Generation

Marketing communications to children, including advertising, are now entering their second generation in which noncompeting firms may produce *joint communications efforts,* in which *one source* may coordinate all communication efforts under an umbrella called integrated marketing, and in which *one channel* may be used to carry all the communications. For example, a joint effort has begun between Pizza Hut and Nickelodeon that is an attempt to link the two in the minds of kids. "The pizza chain and the cable network will join together on promotion, in ads, and in a new Nickelodeon magazine," according to the *Wall Street Journal.*[1] The initial joint effort is set for three years and is valued at over $60 million.

A good example of using one source for all communications was Tyson's entry into the kids' dinners market in 1990 with its Tyson's Looney Tunes Meals.[2] It turned the entire job over to the Stern Walters advertising agency. Through its parent company, Kathleen Harrington Communications, Walters handled all advertising, sales promotion, public relations, and licensing.

Just as there may be one source of marketing communications to children, there also may be one primary channel for carrying the various communications. More companies are relying on the *club* concept through which to advertise, publicize, and promote to kids. Clubs are unmistakably a kids' channel which may be used for both communications and distribution. Burger King recently sent a "Fun Stuff Book" through the mail to the 2.7 million members of its Kids Club in which it included games, contests, and coupons, not only for Burger King but for noncompeting marketers.[3]

While television advertising has always received the major attention among marketing communications efforts directed to children, during the last half of the 1980s sales promotion (the topic of the next chapter) quietly moved into the lead, at least in terms of dollars spent. New children's advertisers, such as apparel, athletic shoes, fast foods, beauty aids, and toiletries, as well as the old standbys—sweet things and playthings—are finding greater use for coupons, contests, and premiums than ever before. Vastly increased sales promotion expenditures are occurring particularly in firms and in media with kids' clubs such as Burger King in fast foods and Fox Kids' Club in television. Also, entire industries that are modifying their marketing strategies to include children, such as restaurants, tend to be heavy users of sales promotion.

The 1980s also witnessed more public relations efforts aimed at kids, including the publicity that can be found in all children's media and the in-person publicity of celebrities and licensed characters who visit stores, malls, and schools on behalf of firms. It appears that publicity's high credibility is causing it to be in demand in marketing programs directed to children. For example, the typical newspaper targeted to kids now appears to be as much of a vehicle for publicity as it is for advertising.

Packaging in its role as "silent salesman," is more important in the children's market as children are shopping more, both on their own and with parents. Packaging is being designed to give better visual "sales talks" to children in self-service settings as well as at home while they are in use. Kids' cereal packages, for instance, have experimented with additional panels in order to provide more print space that can be used to target kids at the breakfast table with sales messages and premiums.

## Marketing Communications Expenditures

The increasing importance of all marketing communications to kids within the overall marketing picture can be put in better perspective is we look at its costs. Spending on marketing communications, including advertising, has become much more robust in recognition of the growth in the economic power of children. Kid Kustomer now commands higher fees, so to speak, from the marketing arena because of the power of her economic punch. It is difficult, however, to know the actual amounts spent on the various marketing communications targeted to children since no person or organization tracks and publishes them. Some periodic estimates are made about children's television advertising expenditures but they are rare for the other media. Even though overall sales promotion spending has increased enormously during the 1980s and now surpasses advertising spending, that portion devoted to the children's market can only be estimated.

To attempt to arrive at even a ballpark figure of the total expenditures on marketing communications directed to children is hazardous. But Table 7–1 represents a summary effort based on various literature and personal interviews. The television advertising dollar estimates are fairly accurate and probably conservative, but those for the other media and for other related costs are strictly "guesstimates," although intended to be conservative, too. In total, advertising expenditures to children amount to $1,003,500,000 of which $709,500,000 is for standard media costs, $24,000,000 for other media, $200,000,000 for point-of-purchase advertising, and $70,000,000 for production costs. The largest expenditure, $690,000,000 is for TV advertising. Yet, even this figure does not include prime time ads that target both kids and parents. Also not

**TABLE 7–1**

*Estimated Expenditures on Marketing Communications to Children*

| Advertising | | |
| --- | --- | --- |
| Television | | |
| Network | $210,000,000 | |
| Spot | 200,000,000 | |
| Syndication | 200,000,000 | |
| Cable | 80,000,000 | |
| Total | | $690,000,000 |
| Radio | | |
| Includes radio stations that mainly target kids and those that do some programming to kids | | $2,000,000 |
| Magazines | | |
| Includes old standards, new titles, those based on licensed characters, those that are part of clubs, those going into schools, and comic books. | | $15,000,000 |
| Newspapers | | |
| Includes ads in newspaper comic sections, newspapers going into schools, and local and regional newspapers | | $2,500,000 |
| Other Media | | |
| Direct mail (includes catalogs) | $10,000,000 | |
| Ads on videos | 1,000,000 | |
| Product placement in movies and game shows | 11,000,000 | |
| In-school ads and posters | 2,000,000 | |
| Total Other Media | | $24,000,000 |
| Total for Media Advertising | | $733,500,000 |
| Point of Purchase | | |
| Includes any materials inside and outside stores that mention brand names | | $200,000,000 |

**TABLE 7–1 (continued)**

| Advertising | |
| --- | --- |
| Advertising Production Costs | $70,000,000 |
| Total for All Advertising Spending | $1,003,500,000 |

| Sales Promotion | |
| --- | --- |
| Includes premiums, contests, coupons, sampling, 800 number provisions | $1,362,214,000 |

| Public Relations | |
| --- | --- |
| Includes publicity and in-person relations | $2,000,000,000 |

| Packaging (consumer) | |
| --- | --- |
| Design and materials for all containers including labelling and tags | $2,500,000,000 |
| TOTAL FOR ALL MARKETING COMMUNICATIONS | $6,865,714,000 |

included in any of the advertising spending figures are fees paid to celebrities to appear in advertisements (e.g., Michael Jordan, Michael Jackson), and fees paid for licensed characters to appear in ads (e.g., The Flintstones, Bugs Bunny).

Estimates for children's radio were most difficult because of the floundering nature of that medium. The figure of $2,000,000 was derived from conversations with members of the industry. The figures for magazines and newspapers are based on looking at rate cards, pages, and number of these media that accept ads. The estimates for "other media" are based mainly on a variety of figures given in business magazines. For instance, the $11,000,000 for product placement is 10 percent of an overall figure found in an article on the topic. Point-of-purchase advertising, which is growing rapidly according to the recent study on retailing to children reported in Chapter 6, is set at 5 percent of overall estimated spending of $4 billion.

The expenditures for sales promotion were obtained by using a ratio that is implied or mentioned in business magazines and suggested by data gathered by Donnelley Marketing Inc.[4] These sources indicate that, of the total monies spent on advertising and promotion by consumer packaged goods companies, between 30 and 40 percent goes for media advertising, and 60 to 70 percent for promotion. For example, in 1988, Hershey Foods spent $97 million on advertising and $245 million on promotion, or a ratio of around 28 to 72.[5] This kind of expenditure ratio apparently is characteristic of the food industry, which also is the main industry that targets kids. Since it is reasonably certain that around $733.5 million was spent on children's advertising (not including point-of-purchase advertising or production costs), and assuming an advertising/sales-promotion ratio of 35/65, we can estimate spending on promotion at around $1,362,214,000 ($733.5 million ÷ .35 × .65). Like the advertising expenditures, this figure for sales promotion does not include celebrity and licensing fees. Neither does it include costs for maintenance of kids' clubs.

The figures for public relations and packaging also were developed by using overall total spending data. In the case of packaging, there was the additional problem of how to separate the marketing communications costs of the package. It was finally concluded that 10 percent of the gross amount spent on consumer packaging would be assigned to the children's market and half of that figure would be allocated to communications. Therefore, the estimated spending on packaging for communicating to children amounts to around $2.5 billion. The public relations figure of $2 billion was determined by simply taking 5 percent of the total gross expenditure of $40 billion and allocating it to the children's market. Both figures seem conservative in view of the extensive use of these two communications tools in marketing to children.

In total, then, the estimated expenditure for all marketing communications come to $6,865,714,000. Of this, $1,003,500,000, or around 15 percent is for advertising. If we compare this figure to the combined purchases of children ($6.1 billion) and the purchases influenced by children ($132 billion), or $138.1 billion in total, we can see that spending on advertising to children is much less than one percent of potential sales to them.

## Changes in Advertising Media Targeted to Children

The estimated expenditures among the various advertising media targeted to children shown in Table 7–1 are all notable changes from a decade ago when only spending for television was significant, and even that was relatively small. For example, one estimate of spending on kids' TV in 1983 was $100 million, or less than one-sixth of today's spending.[6] In the early '80s there was no measurable radio being targeted to children, there were no significant newspapers except some comic-strip type ads in the Sunday comics, and not much in the way of magazines either, the most notable being some comic books and the durable *Boys' Life*.

Today, as shown in Table 7–1, much more television advertising is being targeted to kids and much more advertising in what sometimes is termed the "alternative" media—all the other media that might be used to reach kids. Let us take a closer look at each of these media in order to point out some of the changes that have taken place that account for some of the changes in spending.

## Television

The total dollars spent on television advertising to kids have increased during the past decade mainly because of an increase in available advertising opportunities during this time period. The number of independent television stations practically tripled during the 1980s, cable became legitimate, reaching over half of TV-viewing homes, and syndicated programming grew from a minor factor to a powerhouse. Kids even got their own television channels or a major share of a channel. For example, Nickelodeon, which came on line in 1983, now claims to have more kids watching childrens' programming than the three broadcast networks combined. Not only has commercial inventory increased, it has been divided into more parts as a result of the advent of fifteen-second commercials. Finally, in addition to standard kids' fare, there has been an increase in prime-time programming that appeals to youngsters and which adds to the potential inventory of commercial time available for reaching kids.

The wide range of children's programming now available on television has made it possible to segment the audiences into more homogeneous viewers. No longer are all programs geared to the entire group of youngsters aged 2–11. Instead, a particular program's major audience may be preschoolers, tweens, or any age in between, and a correct buy made among networks, independents, and cable by an advertiser can deliver most kids of all appropriate ages.

The greater availability of advertising time, the wider range of programming, and the segmentation possibilities have attracted a larger and much more complex mix of advertisers to children's TV. During the past couple of years, we have witnessed the appearance of new product lines never before advertised on television. These "nontraditional advertisers," as some members of the television industry call them, include apparel, athletic shoes, frozen and shelf-stable kids' meals, fast foods, and toiletries. More new advertisers can be expected during kids' time as the economic power that kids wield becomes more apparent. For instance, at the time of this writing two major hotel chains are considering national advertising to children. With the inventory of television commercial time on kid-vid now limited by law, any newcomers buying national time are likely to drive up the price of a unit of advertising time. This, in turn, could lead some television advertisers to give more consideration to some of the alternative media described below.

## Radio

The change in radio advertising to children is its reemergence. Radio for kids essentially disappeared in the 1950s with the advent of television programming for kids, but it has been trying to make a comeback. The comeback is a struggle, however, since most kids want pictures with their sounds. After all, kids are generally picture-people—they file away visual codes at least as commonly as they do verbal codes. So, one of the problems radio is experiencing is trying to attract kids to what probably appears to them to be half a loaf. Another problem, of course, is attracting advertisers, most of whom probably didn't listen to radio much when they were kids.

A *Wall Street Journal* report states that one major effort in kids' radio in 1990 was the Children's Radio Network that opened shop at WWTC-AM in Minneapolis.[7] A satellite-based programming service, it hopes to attract the under-12 set with special music not heard much on radio—some through requests—mixed with some educational fare and some reruns from old radio. It already has attracted advertisers such as McDonald's and Domino's Pizza plus a number of local advertisers. In Orlando, Florida the Kids Choice

Broadcast Network's Imagination Station was to begin a similar operation but apparently put it on hold. There are also radio stations that target a part of their programming to kids. This approach to the children's market may be the most logical for the radio industry in view of the startup costs and the problems that have been reported so far.

The concept of kids' radio could not be described as "on a roll" given the near-failures in the '80s, but it appears now to be "breaking out all over"—in the United States as well as Canada and the United Kingdom, although it is on a small scale. The fact that children's programming does not have a rating system that is understood and accepted by potential advertisers probably keeps some advertisers from considering it. Once radio finds a way to position itself—as entertainment and/or education, as different from TV, as beneficial to parents, as a member of alliances with other media, with school systems, with churches, with computers, whatever—so that advertisers can better see its potential benefits, it will most likely do well. After all, it is a portable, go-anywhere medium. Neither a TV nor a comic book travels quite as conveniently. Maybe, in addition to traditional media, its main competition is the portable cassette player and the two-way radio.

## Newspapers

There has always been some newspaper advertising directed at kids, usually placed in the comic section, and usually in the Sunday edition. It is still around, but just barely, having been severely reduced in stature by television advertising. Typical newspapers are no longer considered a viable medium for reaching children as a potential market.

But *newspapers for kids*. That's another story. Newspapers for kids didn't disappear, and now they are making a comeback—even more than radio for kids. Kids are introduced early in school to the concept of their own newspaper through *The Weekly Reader* or other similar publications. Therefore, they, their parents, and their teachers are at least somewhat responsive to the idea of kids' papers. Several newspapers specifically targeted to kids appeared in the mid to late '80s. *Young American,* started in 1983, billed itself as "America's Newspaper for Kids." Its distribution system (out of

Portland, Oregon) included both metropolitan and community newspapers as well as classrooms. *Bear Essential News for Kids* is another West Coast newspaper for kids that looks a lot like *Young American,* and like *Young American,* this Phoenix-based newspaper is not directly affiliated with a regular newspaper. *Class Acts,* on the other hand, is a newspaper for kids that is a product of the *Fort Worth Star-Telegram* and is a weekly insert in that newspaper. It is also available as an insert for other newspapers, and was adopted by the *New York Times* in the fall of 1990.[8] These three kids' newspapers have in common a desire to provide a business-supported newspaper that will inform children, participate in their education, and help them develop their reading skills as well as change their negative attitudes about reading.

There could be an image problem for kids' newspapers that stems from traditional newspapers. From a child's point of view, the typical newspapers in the home probably are not fun or very interesting. Most newspapers do little to welcome children or to satisfy any of their predominant needs. Like banks, they cast themselves as very adult. One possible exception is the *Milwaukee Journal.* It developed a program targeted to kids with the goal of getting them to read the *Sunday Journal.*[9] A contest was developed in which children were quizzed about certain items that appeared in the paper. Over 10,000 kids entered the contest in a month. So, there may be a model here that could be used by other major newspapers.

The apparent strength of the kids' newspapers from an advertiser's point of view is their ability to reach a specific geographical area. Unlike independent television stations, however, there is not yet an independent newspaper for kids in every major geographical region that will provide the comprehensive coverage needed by many national advertisers. As the newspaper industry recognizes the need to grow newspaper readers, it will most likely embrace the concept of kids' newspapers—somewhat like what the *Fort Worth Star-Telegram* is attempting to accomplish with *Class Acts*—and there will become a national network of them. In the meantime, they do provide local businesses with a good opportunity to reach kids.

## Magazines

Probably no specific advertising medium targeted to children is any more trusted by them than *Boys' Life* magazine, due to its long life and long association with scouting. This kind of credibility exists overall, to a greater or lesser degree, in the children's magazine industry with perhaps one major exception—comic books. Comic books are still too often associated with the "grow six inches in six weeks" type of advertising in the minds of many children and parents, although they have been trying to change that image.

The general credibility of children's magazines apparently continues to be an attraction for publishers and advertisers since around 75 new ones were introduced during the brief period of 1983–1990 (although not all accept advertising). Even though most children are not avid readers, publishers recognize that parents view magazine reading by children as developmental and educational. In fact, it is this learning/teaching aspect of children's magazines that probably most helps their image (but not that of comic books, ironically). Magazines, consequently, are bought as gifts for kids by parents and also by grandparents.

While advertisers may not be flocking to magazines, many now are treating them as a normal part of their media mix for the children's market. Advertisements for most of the typical children's products—for sweet things and playthings—can now be found in children's magazines. And increasingly, and logically, in view of children's magazines' good image, advertisements of products for children as *future* consumers are showing up in them, such as airlines, communications, and computer ads. Because children's magazines have appeal among parents, advertisers of high-ticket items that may require the parents' financing often can be found in kids' magazines—for example, bicycles, video game sets, running shoes, clothing, and consumer electronics.

Children's magazines are on the verge of becoming a major player in children's media, second only to television, but there are still some problems to resolve. One is how to remain fun and still focus on reading; or, perhaps, how to be a magazine but not a comic book. The danger of a focus on reading is it will not attract most children, only their parents. If the focus is too much on fun—for example, lots of comic-strip format—the magazine may not please the parent.

Attracting national advertisers on a regular basis is still a problem for kids' magazines. The size of the audience that is delivered is often not perceived as attractive enough by a national advertiser. Perhaps strategic alliances among several kids' magazines or among magazines and other media, as is increasingly being done among adult magazines, would overcome this problem. For example, *Sports Illustrated for Kids,* a new star among children's magazines, is part of the Time, Inc. publishing group that recently merged with Warner to form Time Warner. It might be packaged with other Time Warner properties (magazines, videos) to make the magazine a more viable advertising medium to kids.

There is also a view among some advertisers that ads in kids' magazines will not get kids' attention the way TV ads can. Probably there are no studies that support this belief, but it is commonly held. Ironically, such a notion may result from the many not-so-fun advertisements in children's magazines, but it doesn't have to be this way. For instance, the relatively new technology of pop-up art, such as that by Intervisual Communications Inc., and the three-dimensional photography that is being applied to advertising by such firms as 3DMARK, Inc., would be fun for children, and even permit them to have a free toy by removing the pop-up or 3-D item from the magazine. Not a bad idea—a magazine ad that keeps on selling to the same consumer.

### Other Media

Writing in the *Wall Street Journal,* Joseph Pereira observed that advertisers to children are "concealing commercials in every cranny."[10] What appears to be concealment to the writer is probably the number of relatively new media that are being used to reach the kids' market. These include direct mail, home videos, in-store videos, in-school means, and product placement in movies and game shows. Some video game machines in arcades, for example, flash "winners don't use drugs" messages when they are not in play.

Advertisements on videos that children rent and buy are relatively new, so new in fact that there are no accepted ways to measure their results. Such ads supposedly permit accurate targeting of children with specific interests, for example, in certain types of movies and/or certain actors, and in specific activities such as car racing.

Experiments with new in-store advertising media have been going on for several years and involve advertising on shopping carts, in shopping aisles and shopping areas, and at checkout counters.

These are in addition to the standard point-of-purchase advertising through displays, shelf-talkers, banners, and signs. For instance, for its in-store system, Sight & Sound Entertainment advertises, "If you have something to sell to kids and their moms, we know where you can find 3 million of them. It's Kids 'R' Us, the 180-store clothing division of Toys 'R' Us."[11] Advertising inside the store, where children are increasingly found, provides the advertiser with an opportunity to influence sales at the time children are in a buying mood.

Mail advertising to children is on the increase because data bases make it feasible. Also, the fact that children like to get mail—like to be counted as a member of the household—makes mail advertising even more likely to be read than similar mail to adults. The mail ads may be from clubs the child joined, product-based clubs such as book clubs or model-building clubs, or from catalog companies. Some of the letters, booklets, and catalogs that children receive in the mail may require as much reading as some of the magazines they buy, but because these items came by mail, children don't seem to mind the reading. To the extent that this is the case, publishers of children's items may want to emphasize home delivery more.

In-school advertising is being talked about more, and in a more critical manner, because of the increasing amounts of it and because of the advent of television advertising in schools. (Criticisms of TV advertising in schools seem to be directed mainly at the Whittle Communications' Channel One system, because of its intrusive nature and because the firm flaunts its ability to buy its way into schools.) The increase in advertising in schools is due, of course, to the increasing market potential of kids and the fact that schools are places where kids can be found in large numbers. In-school advertising takes an endless number of forms—scoreboards and billboards in athletic areas, posters, pamphlets, book covers, lesson plans, films, and vending machines.

There is a backlash, of sorts, going on against school advertising.[12] Some parent groups, teacher organizations, and school systems are seeking a more commercial-free environment. A major portion of schools acknowledge, however, that business is an important partner to schools, particularly to those that are underfunded. But advertising must be more subtle and should always have an important educational goal if it is to be acceptable to the school community.

Finally, the hottest new advertising medium in the children's market is the movies—not *at* the movie house but *in* the movies. Interestingly, this is usually not called advertising, but instead, product placement. The term is accurate in the sense that its purpose is to get a product displayed and/or used in a movie. The notion has been around in small ways for a long time, but the movie *E.T.* vaulted it into prominence when it made Hershey's Reese's Pieces an overnight success. The fees usually range from $20,000 to $50,000, although some fees supposedly have been six figures. Product placement agencies work with the movie industry as well as the television game show industry to find appropriate outlets for clients. Sometimes firms form a strategic alliance to get products displayed in a movie. That was the case when Burger King appeared in the movie *Teenage Mutant Ninja Turtles* which in turn was promoted by Burger King.[13]

The movie industry alone is taking in around $1 million a week from product placements, with kids' movies getting their share. Some movie producers are even announcing their fees well in advance of the production schedule in order to attract advertisers, as Disney reportedly did with its movie *Mr. Destiny*.[14] The forty or so game shows a week on TV may be returning an amount similar to that for product placement in movies, although there are still few children's game shows to use as a medium. Substantial growth is expected in product placement even though it is difficult to measure its effects.

## Effects of Advertising to Children

What happens when an advertising campaign is targeted to kids? Assuming the ads speak the kids' language and appeal to their needs, a chain of events similar to the model shown in Figure 7–2 may result.

The model suggests that an ad campaign (rarely one ad) produces attitudes and behaviors among an audience of children. The attitudes are toward the product, the brand, its producer, seller, even the advertisement and advertising in general. The behavior may be

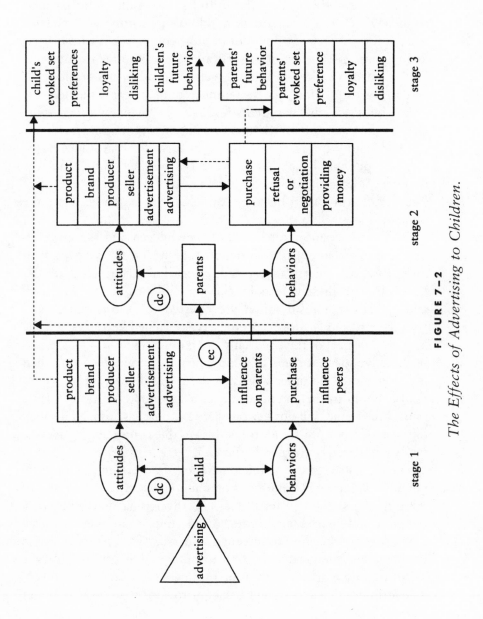

**FIGURE 7–2**

*The Effects of Advertising to Children.*

even more extensive and result from the complex of attitudes. We call this an A–B (attitude–behavior) relationship. (Later on we will refer to a B–A relationship—the attitudes that result from a particular behavior.) The behavior may take three forms: (1) behavior toward the product—looking for it, at it, comparing it with others, and buying it; (2) behavior toward the parents—influence attempts on parents by children in order to get them to buy the product advertised or to provide necessary funds; and (3) peer influence.

The influence on the parents results in behavior by them—purchases, provision of funds to the children, negotiations with the children, and refusals. The parents, in turn, form attitudes based on these possible behaviors—toward the product, the brand, the producer, the seller, the advertisement, and advertising in general (the same attitudinal objects as the child but not necessarily the same attitudes).

Finally, the resulting attitudes of the children and the attitudes of the parents interact to produce a liking or disliking of products, brands, sellers, advertising, which will determine later behavior toward these objects by children and/or parents. The likes and dislikes that result often are referred to as preferences and loyalty (for brands, stores, product types). The likes, importantly, also become part of the children's and parents' *evoked set*—the two or three brands that come to mind when the purchase of a product is contemplated. In other words, if children and/or parents do not hold a brand in their minds, and in a favorable position in their minds, the brand will not be considered at purchase time. This may likewise be true of specific stores. It is in this context that advertising is a powerful influence on purchasing.

The model suggests possible outcomes of advertising that are favorable to marketers who focus on children as any one or more of three markets. As a primary market, advertising may produce a purchase and favorable attitudes. As an influence market, advertising may cause the child to inform and persuade the parent, who in turn may buy the product and/or form favorable attitudes toward it. As a future market, advertising produces liking and other favorable attitudes that can trigger behavior toward a product at a later time.

The model of advertising to children has been roughly divided into three stages. In the first stage advertising influences children to buy products and/or to get parents to make purchases. In the second stage, parents consider the product at the recommendation of the child. In stage three, the attitudes of the child and parents that have been induced by advertising and purchase behavior determine their future behavior toward advertised products.

There are limitations to the model in Figure 7–2. It shows advertising effects in isolation—without the use of other communication efforts and without the influence of other producers and retailers. Because there are, in fact, so many marketers advertising to children in order to get them to purchase, to influence their parents, and to form favorable attitudes toward the marketers, children can not and will not process all the messages. Other communications tools are obviously necessary. Sales promotion efforts such as coupons, contests, and premiums can often stimulate action faster and more effectively than advertising or than advertising alone. Public relations programs sometimes can create favorable images in the minds of children better and faster than advertising or advertising alone. Properly designed packaging can have enormous impact on children and their parents once they enter the purchase environment. In sum, the model in Figure 7–2 is limited because it does not show the environment of advertising and the use of the other elements of the communications mix. It does, however, demonstrate the possible effects of advertising if properly executed.

## Encoding/Decoding Problems in Advertising to Children

Regardless of the type of advertising or the advertising media employed, the goal of the marketer is to inform and persuade an audience of children, and almost always to compete with other marketers for their favor. But there are problems, lots of problems, in communicating with children, some of which have no standard solutions. These problems can be classified, for sake of discussion, as encoding (ec) and decoding (dc) problems. The model in Figure 7–2 shows the locations of these ec/dc problems with ec and dc symbols.

Directing advertising communication to children entails attempting to inform and persuade them as members of three markets. As a primary market the marketer desires some *action*—purchases, store visits, phone calls, letters—from children who are just learning how to do these things. As an influence market the marketer wants the children to *communicate* to their parents the *same message* and the same enthusiasm as that received from the marketer, with the purpose of persuading the parents to purchase. As a future market the marketer wants the children to *remember, like,* and *favor* the marketer's company, products, brands, and ideas. All this communication is supposed to be coordinated and to take place in an environment that contains thousands of other competitive communications directed to the children, that contains the children's parents under time, social, and financial pressures, that contains the children's schools, churches, and family relationships (including broken ones), and contains public policies that are as variable as the winds. All in all, the chances of communication problems between marketers and children are very great.

Let us sort out some of these problems and shed some light on them. In order to do this we will look at them as either encoding (ec) or decoding (dc) problems although they usually are not separable (ec/dc).

## Encoding Problems

All the problems of designing advertising messages for children are related to one underlying problem—understanding children. They are a special case. When talking to marketers about the problems of communicating to children, we may head, "I understand that. I have kids of my own." What that statement means is, "I understand my kids; therefore, I understand other kids." One actually does not follow the other in many cases. We understand our own children *reasonably well* because we are around them a lot and are able to read their *nonverbal* as well as their *verbal* transmissions. Still, how many times do we preface our remarks to our kids with, "I don't understand you. . . ." For example, "I don't understand you; all you ever do is want, want, want!" We do this because we don't understand them. How much less may we understand children in other environments, in other families, with other values?

What we don't understand about children very well is how they think—how they process and retrieve information. Children, particularly those below the age of around 100 months, think differently from adults—they reason, evaluate, estimate differently. Because we don't adequately understand how they think, we often misunderstand their language, or probably more accurately, we assume their language is about the same as ours, only more limited. Yet, when we listen closely to them as toddlers, or first-graders, or tweens, we often hear them use different words than adults. Then, to make matters worse, when we adults develop marketing communications using those words in order to communicate with them more effectively, we often use them incorrectly because we don't know their exact meanings. Karen Forcade, president of Youth Research, has devoted a good deal of her professional life to trying to understand the jargon of childhood that she hears in interviews with children so that she can explain it to her advertising clients. She does a good job of it but only because she works at it, over and over and over. So, marketers do not understand children's language very well and therefore make mistakes in encoding messages for them.

Let's take it a step further. Since we don't understand kids' thinking very well, we often misinterpret what they think about the adult world—about our language, our possessions, our likes and dislikes. These misinterpretations usually stem from one or two errors in our thinking—from believing children like what *our* children like, or from believing that children like what *we* like. Jon Berry, writing in *Adweek,* tells about Tim Price, a creative director for Foote, Cone & Belding, who used to start his ads to children with, "Hey, kids," because his client believed that it was necessary for cuing the kids.[15] Today, his new clients, such as Levi Strauss and Nintendo, believe that ads should begin, and continue, with lots of action. In both cases, however, the ads could be wrong since they are based on what the clients *believe* about children's thinking. For example, in the case of the high-action ads, the presentation of words and symbols may be too fast, and therefore too complex, for young children who are just beginning to process language. Consequently, they may mentally skim over the messages and not comprehend them, much in the same way they do when asked to read orally and do not understand a word. They just sort of hum it and go on.

Would encoding errors be reduced if we let children handle the advertising communications task on the assumption that children understand children better? In pursuit of appropriateness in encoding messages to children, some firms have done just this. For example, Polaroid, when it introduced its new Cool Cam camera for kids, used ads that had been designed by children in a contest. Whether the idea worked well for Polaroid is not known, but probably it was not any more effective than if it were done by adults. Children may understand children better than adults but it is unlikely that they possess better marketing communications skills than adults.

Thus, we seem to be stuck in the middle, not understanding youngsters very well but communicating to them the best we can in order to meet business goals. In that middle ground, we may not make the extra effort to understand children well because we are too consumed with financial objectives, but we may not achieve those financial objectives very well either, because of all the encoding mistakes we make in our marketing communications to children. Then, because of the resulting mistakes, public policy makers, consumer advocates, and parents all may be offended, begetting additional problems for marketers.

Does this mean that every word and symbol of marketing communications targeted to children should be tested? For the most part, yes, at least until there is substantial evidence that there is a history of effective dialogue between child and marketer. Does all this cost more (as compared to marketing to adults)? Maybe not in extra money, but it requires an investment. Marketing to the littlest consumers doesn't necessarily result in the littlest expenses. The encoding errors in advertising communications are still too many and too frequent to make one believe that marketers are very high on the learning curve of understanding children. For example, the consistent use of wording that children do not understand in television advertising disclaimers, as demonstrated in research, is a good example of this misunderstanding. An investment in pure communications research should minimize this problem.

## Decoding Problems

The encoding problems in advertising communications to children discussed above boil down to marketers not understanding children. Decoding problems come about because children often do not understand the communications of marketers (which may be due in part to marketers not understanding children). To exemplify this circular problem, consider a statement often found in cereal advertisements and on cereal packages. It says, "Part of a nutritious breakfast," or words to that effect. What does this statement mean to children? One 6-year-old said it meant, "It's good for you." Is this the meaning that was intended to be communicated by the encoder? The fact that some kids may interpret it as "good for you" may result in their believing that a particular cereal is an adequate breakfast. This is almost the opposite of the intended meaning of that statement. Is this interpretation the result of an encoding or decoding error? Or is it a combination ec/dc error? How could the statement be improved? Tests would tell us. For instance, "Some assembly required," when tested, showed that preschoolers didn't understand it. Further tests showed that what they could understand was, "It must be put together before you can play with it."[16] Perhaps the statement with the cereals should read, "For a healthy breakfast, you have to eat other things with this cereal."

Decoding problems result when advertising communications are not understood or are misunderstood. Since marketers know too little about the information-processing ability of children, it is difficult to predict the extent to which these decoding problems will occur in a given communications situation. For instance, it is known that children's ability to understand varies with age. In general, the older the children the more likely they are to understand messages from adults. But the degree of comprehension can vary a great deal. Some children may understand better than others of the same age because of their enriched environment or their greater experience with the subject of the communications. In fact, chronological age itself may not matter as much as mental age in explaining the variance in children's understanding of communications.

In addition to age, children may bring to a communication a different mindset—the regulative and directive conditions of the mind at a given time—than the one anticipated by the communicator. For example, a child almost always has play on his or her mind. When targeted by a public service announcement to avoid drugs, particular youngsters may not take the message very seriously, and may even ignore it. There are certain mindsets common to kids which direct or regulate the responses made to communications. These include wanting to play, wanting to be free of authority, wanting variety, wanting to hurry day-to-day events, wanting to be grown up, wanting to overcome a great force. Any one of these mental sets may produce nonresponse, hurried response, and incorrect response to communicated messages. For example, some first-grade students were shown a print advertisement in which a spokesperson with his hand extended said to the reader, "Put it there, partner." The encoder meant for it to be a friendly gesture—the symbolic offer of a handshake in order to get interaction from the reader. One of the children thought the spokesperson was "trying to play a trick" on someone while another thought he was offering to play golf. Both of these very different interpretations may have been influenced by a play mindset.

Children decode with the words and symbols that are stored in their mind at a given moment. A typical 3-year-old, for instance, probably has no more than a thousand words stored. Probably not any of those is the word "assembly," as in, "Some assembly required," or even the simple word, "tab," as in "Lift tab to open." What happens when these two words are encountered by the 3-year-old while viewing a television ad? We do not know except on a case by case basis. But the responses would most likely distribute themselves randomly rather than around the intent of the encoder.

We will list four of the major ec/dc problems that are likely to occur as a result of advertisers communicating with children. However, the list is not complete and solutions to the problems do not exist in formula form.

1. *Adult language encoding/child language decoding.* This is the most obvious problem in advertising communications to children, but it does not have an obvious solution. It is more likely to occur in mass communications targeted to a wide range of ages than with communications to narrow age groups. Only testing will tell if the problem exists.

2. *Adult symbol encoding/child symbol decoding.* This problem is difficult to separate from the language

problem, but here I am referring to nonverbal language—color, sound, dress, body language. Decoding most of these symbols comes through socialization over time. For example, the white smock that symbolizes the medical profession may not yet be a part of a child's repertoire. Or the color red may be associated with Christmas and Valentines in the child's mind but not also with danger as it is in the adult's mind.

3. *Adult motives encoding/child motives decoding.* This problem is more related to mindset. For example, one is supposed to be sad about death, frightened by unknown creatures from other planets, and excited by the concept of springtime. In all three cases the child may respond differently—curious about death, curious about creatures from other planets, unconcerned about springtime. While all humans apparently possess the same needs or motives, those that are predominant vary according to age, culture, and individual personality. Adults therefore cannot be sure what motives kids bring to a specific communications situation or what additional motives are triggered by the communications.

4. *Adult values encoding/child values decoding.* Children often value frogs; adults often don't. Adults value the environment; children may not. The point is that values come with socialization, and at various rates, and therefore what a child likes at a particular time, what is important at a particular time, simply may not be the same as the marketer expects. Probably the most that can be expected is that children's values will mirror those of their parents. This suggests that in some cases communications to children ought to be segmented on the basis of their parents' characteristics.

## Observations and Recommendations

The year 1990 will probably go down in advertising history as the point at which advertising to kids became big business. During that year, total advertising expenditures related to the kids' market reached an estimated $1 billion.

The plain fact is that the kids' market has taken on great importance to large numbers of consumer goods companies. Advertising to kids has become an important way to *communicate* with that market as well as an important way to *compete* for it. The net results are an increase in advertising opportunities to kids—new media, more inventory of existing media—and an increase in advertisers.

As companies spend more money on advertising to kids, and as that advertising gets more competitive, there is legitimate concern about its effectiveness. Some of this concern arises out of recognition that it is difficult to know how kids think. In effect, marketers spend large sums of money on advertising to kids, but they do not know how effective the effort is or how much more effective it could be, simply because they do not have good knowledge of children's information processing.

Marketers may not know how effective their advertising to kids is, but they can do things to make it as effective as possible. Specifically, they can give it the three P-tests—*pro test, parent test,* and *pilot test.* The *pro test,* is an examination of the ads by a person who is professionally trained and experienced in understanding children. As indicated earlier in this chapter, most advertising problems boil down to not understanding how kids think. A person with academic training in child psychology, educational psychology, or elementary education, and who is experienced in communications (preferably marketing communications), can more easily discern problems and potential successes in advertising to be targeted to children. This is not to suggest that advertising to children is a science that can be taught, but only to indicate that a combination of certain experiences can make a person better than average at judging the potential effectiveness of such advertisements. Such a person also would be useful in evaluating other marketing communications to children such as promotion, publicity, and packaging. In theory, such experts could earn their pay through the elimination of costly errors in advertising programs to children.

A *parent test* is an examination of advertising efforts by a group, perhaps a panel, of parents in order to bring an objective, parental opinion to bear on an advertising strategy or tactic. These are not people whose children are grown, and they are not people who design the company's advertisements and happen, also, to have children. The parents referred to here are moms and dads who have kids age 2–12, and who are not directly associated with the firm doing the advertising. These parents, if properly selected, can provide opinions about how other parents might perceive an ad as well as how their children might perceive an ad. Their evaluations should complement those that result from the pro test. With the opportunity for error so great in children's advertising, producing ads that are understood, liked, and accepted by a panel of parents is a big accomplishment. It should be assumed that the ads that emanate from a firm will always be under scrutiny by consumer advocate groups. So the parent test can assure that the ads are more likely to be acceptable to such groups. Overall, the parent test, when conducted correctly, provides information about the possible responses of three groups to a firm's advertising program—kids as a primary target, parents as a secondary target, and consumer advocates as people concerned about fairness to children as consumers.

A *pilot test* is a small-scale study of the effectiveness of an advertisement among an appropriate group of children. It is the sort of thing that is usually done with any advertising program. With children's advertising it is even more critical. Knowing what responses kids will make to an ad before millions of media dollars are spent on it can be an important, but relatively inexpensive piece of information. Who does the pilot test? It could be done internally or externally, although an external effort is usually more objective. A handful of research shops specialize in kids marketing. They could do the pilot testing on a contractual basis, and they could be expected to improve, work faster, and charge less as they gain experience with a particular advertising group. Of course, most agencies are set up to do this kind of work also, but often it is difficult to be objective when one is judging his own work.

The three tests—they are not really tests as much as they are assistance in planning—do not have to cost a lot, do not have to take a lot of time, and can be easily controlled for security purposes. In fact, to save time and money and maintain security, all three activities can be handled by one office within the company or one external shop. The purpose of the three P-tests, in combination, is to make advertising efforts targeted to children as effective and as publicly acceptable as possible. While such tests might ordinarily be used for any and all advertising, they definitely should be used when advertising to kids because of the greater risk for errors.

# References

1. Joanne Lipman, "Nickelodeon and Pizza Hut Join Forces," *Wall Street Journal,* January 26, 1990, p. B4.
2. Al Urbanski, "The Dawn of Integrated Marketing," *Food & Beverage Marketing,* February 1991, pp. 18–21.
3. "BK Unleashes Mail Effort," *Advertising Age,* April 8, 1991, p. 1.
4. Alison Fahey, "Shops See Surge in Promo Revenues," *Advertising Age,* February 20, 1989, p. 60.
5. Julie Liesse Erickson and Judann Dagnoli, "Food Giants Pull Back on Marketing, but Boost Promotion," *Advertising Age,* February 27, 1989, pp. 1, 78.
6. Marianne M. Jennings, "Kidvid 'Promercials' Raise Hackles of Parents, but Regulations Unlikely," *Marketing News,* February 17, 1984, p. 3.
7. Richard Gibson, "Station Sounds Out a Kid's Wavelength," *Wall Street Journal,* June 18, 1990, p. B1.
8. Robyn Griggs, "Wall Street Junior: Dow Jones May Take Kids Version to School by This Fall," *Mediaweek,* February 25, 1991, pp. 1–2.
9. "Kid Stuff," *PROMO: The International Magazine for Promotion Marketing,* January 25, 1991, pp. 43–43.
10. Joseph Pereira, "Kids' Advertisers Play Hide-and-Seek, Concealing Commercials in Every Cranny," *Wall Street Journal,* April 30, 1990, pp. B1, B6.
11. From an April 1990 advertisement in *Advertising Age.*
12. "Selling to Children," *Consumer Reports,* August 1990, pp.518–521.
13. Ibid.
14. Ibid.
15. Jon Berry, "Kids," *Adweek,* April 15, 1991, pp. 31–35.
16. D. E. Liebert, J. N. Sprafkin, R. M. Liebert, and E. A. Rubinstein, "Effects of Television Commercial Disclaimers on the Product Expectations of Children," *Journal of Communications,* 27 (Winter 1977): 118–124.

# Targeting kids?
# Join the club

*Promoting to Children*

School-based marketing program
makes a 'world' of difference

## Coupons for Kids

**AT&T Pulls Plug on 'Looney' Sweeps**

Company promotes cereal via new children's club

## Children's videos action-packed for promoters

## Forge positive relationships with kids early

## *Mattel sets big coupon effort*

Sunday School Uses
Bus Fleet and Candy
To Win Kids' Souls

Shopping carts for kids

**FIGURE 8–1**

# Targeting Promotion and Publicity to Children

As we look at the headlines in Figure 8–1 taken from various business publications, we may not realize that they would have been uncommon less than a decade ago. Children-targeted marketing communications such as coupons, contests, and sweepstakes simply did not take place to any significant degree until recently. Even premiums for children are much more important than they were in the 1970s when the FTC was attempting to make rules regarding them.

Promotion and public relations aimed at children rapidly gained importance during the last half of the 1980s, and today—in the 1990s—their value in marketing strategy is perhaps greater than that of advertising. To some extent this was indicated in the previous chapter in which it was demonstrated that annual spending on promotion and public relations to children is probably higher than spending on advertising to children. Interestingly, part of the gain in promotion and PR spending by children marketers is in the not-for-profit sector such as museums, zoos, churches, and charities.

The reemergence of kids clubs in the late '80s has provided a new means for conveying promotion and public relations efforts, and simultaneously, these activities have shouldered much of the operations costs of the clubs. Also, the introduction of 800 telephone service has made it possible to create new, personalized promotions to kids such as contests and sampling.

Unlike marketing communications spending in general, advertising dollars for kids are not being converted to promotion and public relations dollars to any great extent. The increases in spending on promotion and PR are mainly new dollars that acknowledge the increasing importance of the kids market and the increasing value of these two activities in marketing to kids. It is no doubt true that the rising costs of television advertising to kids has driven some marketers to consider using more promotion and PR, but marketers now recognize that sales promotion and public relations more than justify their costs by helping make sales to kids, produce brand and seller identity among them, and create loyalties for future marketing.

In this chapter we will examine sales promotion and public relations as they pertain to children. Also, we will take a separate look at kids clubs because they facilitate but also contribute to the costs of these activities.

## Targeting Promotion to the Children's Market

The term "promotion" (sales promotion is the textbook term) embraces a wide range of marketing activities that includes coupons, contests, sweepstakes, premiums, samples, and some 800 telephone services. Estimated spending on promotion to children for 1990 was shown in Chapter 7 as $1,362,214,000. While it is only an estimate, since there is no tracking of this spending, this $1.3 billion is more than is spent on advertising to children, and it appears to be growing at a greater pace.

The classic example of children-targeted promotion is the trinkets found in Cracker Jack boxes since 1912. The idea, of course, is to make the sale—to cause children to buy the product in order to get the premium. A major portion of all promotion efforts similarly intend to *clinch the sale* and to sell additional units of a product.

But there are other purposes of child-oriented promotion. In the fast food industry, for example, promotions have become a very effective way to *compete* for children's business. Many of the firms in this industry feel they can not out-advertise McDonald's, but they can go head-to-head with its promotion programs. So, it may be Flintstones drinking glasses for kids at Pizza Hut, GoBots transformable toys at Wendy's, or a Castle Meal with a surprise for kids at the White Castle restaurants, but they all are intended to get kids to make the fast food meal decision in favor of the respective restaurant chains.

Marketers also have found that promotions can produce *brand and seller identity* in the minds of kids. Free balloons for kids at the opening of a new Wal-Mart store, a school-wide contest among kids to write an essay on "Why I like beef," a new silver dollar to any kid who opens a savings account at a bank—all of these promotion efforts can favorably plant the name of that store, bank, or product in the minds of kids. Such results are the beginnings of seller-buyer relationships.

Carefully developed promotions can *improve the image* of marketers by associating them with a good cause or an important concern of people. McDonald's gave away tree seedlings as part of the environmental protection movement, and White Castle restaurants gave toothpaste to kids with their food and beverage purchases in conjunction with the American Dental Association's National Children's Dental Health Month.

Finally, promotions can build *loyalty* among kids that causes them to consistently want a certain brand of product or buy in a certain store. Indeed, the kids' meals with their premiums, along with playgrounds and other amenities for kids have created a lot of loyal customers for McDonald's. So much so, in fact, that other fast food sellers have turned to similar efforts in an attempt to break that loyalty.

When such evidence of the power of promotions is as strong as it is in the case of McDonald's or Cracker Jacks, it is understandable that kids marketers increasingly are putting more dollars into this marketing activity. Let us look at specific kinds of promotion in order to get a better understanding of the marketing power of promotions overall and the dramatic swing to their use.

### Premiums

The original premium for kids probably was invented by a mom who told her kid, "Eat your vegetables and I'll give you a cookie." Premiums for kids have traditionally been the domain of the food industry. This is still the case, but premiums in the nonfood area are becoming commonplace. Therefore, one way to look at premiums is by product lines. However, it is more useful for this discussion to classify them according to their purposes: (1) premiums for joining clubs, (2) premiums for encouraging the choice of certain retail outlets, and (3) premiums to encourage the purchase of certain products.

*Premiums for joining clubs* are a relatively new, but growing application of premiums simply because the club concept is a relatively new and effective way to target children. The ultimate goal of most kids clubs is the formation of a data base—a mailing list—and most marketers are willing to pay for such a list. Therefore, when children are invited to join a club, attractive premiums may be used as inducements. Some clubs are free, and the premiums offered can be powerful inducements. But even in those clubs that charge a fee ($2–$13), the self-liquidating premiums that are offered are often quite attractive. In a study of what kids want in a club, quality in premiums (gifts) was one of them. The children, for instance, chided the Quaker Oats Popeye Club for the "junk" premiums received for a $2 fee (paper hat, stickers), but applauded the Keebler Fun Club whose fee is $12.95 but included a tee-shirt, some coupons, and a newsletter.[1]

Kraft's Cheese & Macaroni Club has chosen to offer several premiums for its fee of $2.95 and three proofs of purchase—"a wild painter's cap, a fun friendship bracelet, bright shoe laces, plus cool stickers and a fun booklet." The number of premiums alone is likely to be very appealing to a kid; the descriptions should clinch the order.

Two clubs that are free but provide premiums to kids as inducements to join are the Burger King Kids' Club and the Fox Kids' Club. Burger King gives stickers, a mini-poster of comic characters, and a certificate for a child's coach ticket on TWA airline (with the purchase of another TWA ticket), while Fox offers a decal, stickers, and page of puzzles.

Examination of the premium offers by clubs that are national in scope indicates a wide variance in their quality. Some clubs are clearly trying to minimize costs—and seem not to place a very high value on the resulting data bases—by offering paper premiums only, and few of them. At the other end of the continuum are those clubs that charge but seem to acknowledge the value of the data base and are willing to "pay" for it with quality and increased number of premiums.

*Premiums for choosing retail outlets* vary as much as those for joining clubs, and in fact, they often are tied to joining a club sponsored by a retailer (in order to provide the retailer with a data base). Burger King's club, mentioned above, is mainly aimed at attracting repeat customers to its restaurants. This is also usually true of clubs set up by banks and supermarkets. Retailers that do not use the club system may still develop data bases through the use of premiums. Some supermarkets, for example, require children to sign up for a cookie credit card (for free cookies), and build their data bases in this manner. The premium, of course, is the cookie that is given to the child during each visit to the store. Some retailers—supermarkets, department stores, jewelry stores—provide children with premiums such as product samples simply for visiting the stores with their parents. Other stores give children premiums when they make purchases—just because they are kids. Some banks use a similar system. When children open a savings or checking account, and perhaps when they make additional deposits, they receive a gift.

Retail patronage premiums have been around for a long time, but almost always they were targeted to adults. Targeting patronage premiums to kids is relatively novel and acknowledges kids' spending power and their role as future customers. Ironically, and very important to cost-conscious retailers, patronage premiums for kids usually cost much less than those for adults and probably are more effective in the long run.

*Premiums to kids for buying products* or influencing parents to buy a product probably began with Cracker Jacks, and then the cereal industry became famous for the practice. Today it extends to many nonfoods. For example, back in 1985 Family Home Entertainment, a marketer of prerecorded videocassettes, attached a $5 toy to its $29.95 cassettes for kids to induce sales to kids and parents. Even though the characters in the videotapes were often unknown to retailers, and probably to many of the parents who purchased them for their kids, 80,000 cassettes were sold within a few weeks.[2] Another example of premiums to induce the purchase of nonfood products is Galoob toys, which ran an ad in the Sunday comics informing kids that they could receive five gold-finish limited-edition cars free with three proofs of purchase of any Galoob MicroMachine. An order blank was provided. There is no reason why premiums should not have as much appeal in nonfoods as foods when the target is kids who seem to delight in "getting something for nothing." This should particularly be the case with play products.

Use of value-added marketing through premiums for kids, such as that by Family Home Entertainment, is increasingly being targeted to parents by marketers who know that kids influence parents' purchases. The idea, of course, is to attract the parents by allowing them to buy a product or patronize a retail outlet and simultaneously receive something free for their kids. This kind of family appeal is now common in the vacation industry. Howard Johnson, for instance, advertised to parents in *Parade Magazine* (a Sunday newspaper supplement) to "check into any Howard Johnson and your kids will get a vacation to remember—plus KIDS GO HOJO FUNPACKS." The ad went on to say that the funpacks contained games, toys, and surprises. Kid-oriented premiums targeted to parents can meet several needs of the parents. They permit parents to please their children, affirm their status as parents, save money, and cope with economic recession.

### Coupons

In 1990 over 306 billion coupons were issued, with the largest increase in the candy, snacks, and chips categories.[3] A major reason for the increase (actually a doubling) in these categories appears to be the growing potential of the kids market. Couponing to kids is a recent but flourishing idea. In one issue of *Bear Essential News for Kids,* a West Coast regional kids' newspaper, there were 17 coupon offers. The main purpose of coupons targeted to kids, like that of premiums, is to clinch the sale—to the child or to the parent through the child. According to an unpublished report by Frankel and Company, 38 percent of tweens use coupons, but there appears to be no measure of their use among the younger kids.

The appeal of coupons among children is not clear. Studies show only a quarter or so of kids are economic-minded. Perhaps these are the kids who mainly respond to coupons. As for the other 75 percent, they may see coupons as a means to facilitate their purchase requests to their parents. A good bet is that many kids are taking cues from their coupon-using parents as they do in so many other consumer practices.

Coupons that target kids can be found among a range of product lines, although snacks and beverages are the major users. Increasingly, they are combined with other marketing communications to kids. In one issue of the *Houston Chronicle* Sunday comics there were two coupon offers to kids. The first was inside an ad for Major League Baseball Cookies and consisted of a dated 55 cent coupon toward the purchase of one package of cookies. The other coupon was in an ad for SweeTarts combined with an 800 number to call. The emphasis was on free—"The call is FREE and so is Sunny's candy when you use the coupon below." The coupon was a buy-one-get-one-free offer while the 800 number was a chance to wake up Sunny, who, the child was told, was dreaming of SweeTarts. The operator also reminded the young caller to redeem the coupon. Thus, in the SweeTarts case, the coupon was combined with an ad, an 800 number, and the 800 number also provided a personal sales message. That's integrated marketing!

McDonald's used a combination of a contest and coupons that was targeted to all of its customers including kids. In its "Blast Back with Mac" promotion, consumers peeled stickers off soft drink cups to find out if they had won a prize. Often they ended up with coupons that said, "One small fries for 25 cents," or "Big Mac for 59 cents."[4] Sometimes a coupon offer such as this one from McDonald's appeals well to both kids and adults. General Foods ran an ad in newspapers for its new Kool Bursts soft drink that contained a coupon. The announcement format appeared to appeal to children and parents. The ad showed a kid downing a Kool Bursts with the main copy stating, "Save $1.00 on Kool-Aid Kool Bursts. The brand Moms trust . . . the taste kids love." There was a coupon for $1.00 off two six-packs. While kids usually don't look at regular newspapers, and while the primary target for this coupon/ad was parents, it did have some kid appeal and probably caught the attention and interest of kids that looked at the paper.

Sampling Corporation of America, via contracts with schools, distributes coupons in schools to children. Through its system a firm can get coupons for its products to any group of children. Usually it is an integrated promotion program for maximum effectiveness. For instance, Cadbury's Caramello candy bar was the focus of one distribution effort. It consisted of a bag bearing the company's logo, and inside the bag a sample candy bar, a coupon for another free bar, and a booklet of facts about music that also provided a contest for kids to enter.[5]

Some coupons targeted to youngsters (and perhaps also to their parents) by nonfood industries have been showing up with relatively high value. When Live Home Video released *Teenage Mutant Ninja Turtles* on video, it packaged it with $20 in coupons toward purchases at Pizza Hut as part of a tie-in promotion effort. In 1988 Mattel distributed by mail coupons worth up to $5 on purchases of its toys. These coupons, which were a first for the toy industry, were mailed to 70 million families. During the 1990 Christmas selling season, Mattel combined with Coke on another high-value couponing program. Multipacks of Cokes and Coca-Cola brands carried coupons of $1 to $7 for Mattel toys. Coke, in its 1991 summer promotion to the youth market included coupons (it called them certificates) that when redeemed with one dollar could buy an audiocassette. So, it appears that the ice has been broken in targeting coupons to kids that involve nonfoods just as it has for premiums discussed earlier.

## Contests and Sweepstakes

Contests and sweepstakes (contests require a skill) are challenges to children that provide them opportunities to satisfy their achievement need in addition to other needs that are satisfied by the sponsors and their products. While they hold the promise of "something for nothing" like premiums and coupons, they usually involve more participation. Therefore, they may produce more *learning* among the participating children. This learning feature distinguishes contests from other promotion types and may be important to a sponsor who is trying to *build a favorable image* among kids. Pizza Hut has an ongoing contest among school children called "Book It" that rewards children with a free Personal Pan Pizza for reading a certain number of books a month. Some other retail chains have contests in which children are awarded prizes for good grades. School-related contests such as these should not only accomplish the image-building goals of their sponsors because of the high involvement required of children, but also should contribute to a very positive image for these retailers among parents and school officials.

Contests can *create strong brand/seller identity* by requiring children to concentrate on the brand name, store name, or related symbols. In General Foods' magazine, *What's Hot for Kids,* there is a drawing contest sponsored by Super Golden Crisp cereal, one of General Foods' brands. The contest requires kids to draw a picture of any villain who might be "after the honey-sweet Super Golden Crisp cereal Sugar Bear loves." Just going through the exercise of trying to think of who might want to steal Sugar Bear's cereal and then drawing a picture of the character is very likely to indelibly place the concepts of the cereal, its name, and the symbolic representative (Sugar Bear) in the minds of the participants. On the opposite page of this same magazine, there is another contest sponsored by Tang, also a General Foods brand. This one requires kids to take an old pair of sneakers, paint and decorate them, snap a picture of them, and send the picture to the sponsor along with the letters T-A-N-G found on any Tang container. Crayola Products, along with Arista Records recording group Milli Vanilli, also sponsored a skill-based contest in which children were asked to design a Milli Vanilli album cover. The activity and involvement required in all three of these contests are likely to produce much active learning among the kids and give them a chance to satisfy their need for achievement while etching the marketers' symbols in their minds.

Nickelodeon network sponsored a "Nick's Looney Tune Lookout Sweepstake" in which children had to watch the Nickelodeon channel between 5 and 8 PM in order to be on the lookout for certain Looney Tunes characters sneaking across the television screen.[6] If they saw one they were to call an 800 number for a chance to win a prize. Again, active participation was required for what otherwise is a fairly passive activity—TV viewing. In addition to watching for the Looney Tunes characters, the children had to utilize the telephone—which children just love to do. The contest was so successful that AT&T had to ask Nickelodeon officials to cancel it because the children's five million attempted calls per day caused phone line congestion. The addition of the 800 number provided an active, exciting, and personal dimension to this contest. Such involvement not only produced more intensive television viewers but intensive learners of the Nickelodeon logo, the 800 number, and the names of the Looney Tunes characters.

There are a variety of contests and sweepstakes targeted to children (and others) that are intended to be traffic builders for retailers. They may be the game-type contest often found at a fast food restaurant such as McDonald's or a count-the-beans (or whatever) contest sponsored by a supermarket or convenience store. If they require active involvement by children and if the skills required are within their capabilities, children will have fun, learn a lot about the stores, and the retailers can accomplish a number of communications goals.

Well-designed contests and sweepstakes by producers of children's goods can greatly increase sales of their products. The 1991 summertime youth promotion by Coca-Cola placed 5.6 million compact discs inside specially marked multipacks of its drinks. The more packs of Coca-Cola kids purchased, or asked their parents to purchase, the more likely the kids were to get a CD free. The "get-something-for-nothing" aspect of this contest no doubt appealed to kids since they probably perceived the value of the free items as high. If some skill requirement had been added to it, even more involvement could have been obtained.

Contests and sweepstakes are particularly vulnerable to error when targeted to children. It is very easy to design them with a level of complexity beyond children's reach. This is particularly likely to happen where the contest is targeted to a wide range of age groups—a Scrabble contest at McDonald's, for example. At the very least, different learning curves can be expected for kids. Therefore, testing of all features of the program among children is a necessity. The outcomes of a poorly designed contest that does not take into consideration the limited capacities of children can be humiliation, anger, and outright loss of trust among children—just the opposite of the desired effects.

## Children-Targeted Public Relations

In spite of the very commercial reputation of the public relations (PR) person, the PR function probably produces the least commercial and the most credible messages among all the marketing communications. This is very important because there are many people who feel there is too much commercialism in children's marketing.

Public relations is usually an integral part of a marketing communications strategy targeted to children. However, PR may have responsibility for the major thrust of a marketing program when it targets kids as *future* consumers. The three main tools used by public relations when targeting children are *publicity, event marketing,* and *school relations.* Let us consider each of these briefly in terms of their accomplishments and attributes.

## Publicity

In the spring, 1991 issue of *Fantastic Flyer,* a magazine from Delta Airlines for children, there is an article entitled, "The Story of Coca-Cola." The article describes the beginnings of Coca-Cola, its trademarks, advertising, and other interesting facts. It closes with an invitation to the reader to visit "The World of Coca-Cola" in Atlanta. The article is not labeled as an advertisement and it does not have an author. Most likely it was developed by the public relations people at Coca-Cola as a publicity release for publication by such magazines as this one. It is well written, interesting, and it is a very persuasive marketing effort.

Publicity such as this article about Coke has enormous credibility and is particularly useful for *developing favorable attitudes* among young consumers about stores, brands, and services. In the March 1991 issue of *Bear Essential News for Kids,* a regional newspaper for kids, an article entitled, "'Modern Stone-aged Family' Turns 30," notes that the Flintstones are celebrating their 30th anniversary. The article goes on to say that, as part of the celebration, a series of Flintstone classics will be offered on videocassettes. While this information is written as news, it is most likely a publicity release. It is interesting, informative, easy to read, and persuasive. Like the Coca-Cola article, it does a good job of creating interest among children and portraying the enjoyment they would receive from the products discussed.

When publicity such as this appears in news media such as children's magazines and newspapers, it strengthens any advertising and promotion about the products discussed. Not only does the publicity provide additional marketing messages, it also adds credibility to the overall marketing campaign for the products. The older that children get, the more mistrusting they become of advertising; therefore, the credibility of publicity becomes more important for a communications campaign.

Subject matter for publicity aimed at children is usually either the products and services of a company or the company itself. Publicity about products tends to be part of an overall marketing communications program to sell the products, particularly new ones. The articles that result can be much more informative and descriptive than any advertisement, and because they are in news form in a news medium, they are very credible. Items about a company usually have the purpose of casting the company in a good light in order to develop a liking for it among children. This kind of article often talks about a company's involvement in a cause, such as literacy or children's health, or about the company as an employee. Such publicity efforts are effective in building relations with children as future consumers.

There is at least one problem with targeting publicity to children: There are not enough news media outlets to accommodate it. Because television news time to kids is limited, and because there is still very little radio time and newspaper space devoted to kids, the workload appears to fall heavily on kids' magazines. But because there are only a few national magazines targeted to kids, even they have limits as a publicity outlet. Perhaps a public relations agency that handles quite a few projects related to kids marketing would be able to put together a media package that would be effective nationally. As a complement to children-targeted publicity, marketers often utilize a public relations program that sponsors events for children. A discussion of this activity follows.

## Event Marketing

There are many events in which children participate that can be sponsored by a company as a means of conveying marketing communications. Some of the more common ones are Little League athletics, field trips to businesses and other institutions, entertainment events, and scholarly competitions. Many of these events are ongoing, and business firms sponsor them at the request of the event organizers. For instance, Little League teams are always looking for sponsors, annual spelling bees and science fairs often solicit sponsors to provide funds for travel and awards, and teachers frequently seek field trip opportunities for their students as part of their teaching programs.

Generally, events can be more effective marketing efforts when they originate with a firm rather than a school or other children-related organization. Being proactive in event marketing permits a firm to set goals and then pursue them in a formalized manner. By initiating an event, the public relations people can direct the design and location of messages in promotional items such as announcements and brochures, and better control costs of the activity. For example, The Pittsburgh Children's Museum works hand in hand with business firms such as J. C. Penney to plan and execute field trips to the museum for children in the surrounding schools.[7] The museum gets financial support, the children receive an important and beneficial experience, and the sponsoring firm gets a lot of opportunities to present marketing messages about itself to the children, their parents, and their schools. For instance, the firm may be mentioned in press releases and public service announcements, its name may be featured on brochures, posters, and programs, and it may be acknowledged in the announcements at the schools and among the parents.

Events do not have to be part of the children's school program and they do not have to be on school premises. Shopping malls are excellent locations for sponsored events that target children. Companies produce fashion shows, entertainment, and exhibits in malls and shopping centers. In 1990, the ABC television network took its live stage show to twenty-five shopping malls for its sixth year.[8] The show consists of professional routines by comic characters from ABC's Saturday morning lineup for kids. It is targeted to kids aged 2 to 11, and its purpose is to get more viewers for its kidvid programming. The event entertains but it also focuses on issues such as drugs, literacy, and environmental protection. Kids can have their pictures taken with some of the comic characters, and coloring books featuring them also are distributed. ABC is very pleased with the results so far, and it continues to receive a great deal of promotion from its local affiliates.

Many retailers—fast food restaurants, supermarkets, department stores—sponsor field trips for children that are mutually beneficial to everyone involved. These store visits usually are part of the children's educational programs, so the children and the schools benefit. They certainly provide opportunities for retailers and schools to teach consumer education. The stores get the opportunity to help the children become accustomed to visiting them, knowing their layouts and offerings, and they get to meet some of their employees. These in-person relationships with children can be very important: There are opportunities to tell the children about specific offerings of the stores, the philosophies of the stores, and some of the good things the stores are doing in the community. It is also a chance for the promotion department to hand out some coupons and samples for the kids and their parents. All in all, these field trips, when put together properly, are great relationship builders with the stores' future customers.

## School Relations

Properly structured school relations provide opportunities to present marketing messages to school officials, teachers, children, and their parents, while contributing to local and national educational programs. As part of overall marketing goals of a firm, public relations can reach large numbers of children as current, influence, and future consumers through school relations programs. Schools need funds, teacher development, and teaching equipment and aids, and particularly in the area of consumer education. A firm can provide these things as part of its marketing communications efforts. But public relations must put the customer first. That is, a school-based program must be one that truly benefits the children and their schools.

A good example of an innovative and beneficial school-based public relations program is one sponsored by the Citibank Master-Card and Visa Division of Citicorp. It took on the task of dealing with the severe geography illiteracy that exists among our school children. It hired "Mr. World," a former teacher and professional story teller, to show schools how to teach geography in an exciting and effective manner. In 1990 alone, he worked with 300 teachers and principals, taught 8,000 students, and gave out take-home materials to 1,200 parents.[9] All the teaching materials—books, maps, inflatable globes, posters—possessed Citibank's logo. The program received extensive press coverage; there were exhibitions and tie-ins with local Citibank facilities. Citibank was credited as sponsor in all publicity, and a description of the program was inserted in mailings to Citibank's 26 million cardholders.

The demand for useful teaching aids and assistance in the area of consumer education is especially high because children become consumers at an earlier age. Companies have much to contribute to such programs since nobody knows the marketing side of the consuming equation better than the marketer. Innovative, useful, adaptable consumer education programs give a firm many opportunities to present itself and its products in a favorable light to students who will be future consumers. Incidentally, if they have been properly taught about consumerism, the children are more likely to get a lot more satisfaction from the marketplace as future consumers—and from the firms that designed and sponsored the consumer education programs.

So much help is needed by schools that any business firm can contribute a great deal with a relatively small cost. Overcommercializing the program must be avoided, but over a long period of time great relationships with kids can be firmly developed.

## Kids Clubs: A New Channel of Communications

As observed in Chapter 7 on advertising, clubs can provide a single, unified channel for *all* marketing communications to children. While the idea has been around for at least fifty years, kids clubs have risen to prominence again because of their new strategic benefits to marketers. How many clubs there are is anyone's guess, but the number grew dramatically during the last half of the 1980s. Table 8–1 shows two dozen recently formed clubs that are national in scope, and surely there are several hundred local and regional-based clubs. They mainly emanate from retailers, producers, and media, but their popularity is creating interest in them in other quarters such as the financial community. In addition to serving as a channel of communications to children, as discussed here, clubs may also serve as a channel of distribution (as noted in Chapter 5) and as a mechanism for conducting marketing research (discussed in Chapter 8). While usually not associated with any other purposes, clubs could be used by business firms for consumer educa-

**TABLE 8–1**

*Some Well-known Kids Clubs Formed
Between 1985 and 1990*

| Club | Sponsoring Firms |
| --- | --- |
| AT&T Adventurers Club | AT&T |
| Billy the Kid Adventure Club | McGregor Corp. |
| Burger King Kids Clubs | Burger King |
| Children's Book-of-the-Month Club[1] | Time Inc. |
| Doubleday Children's Books Club[1] | Doubleday |
| E. J. Gitano Fashion Club[2] | E. J. Gitano |
| Fantastic Flyer | Delta Airlines |
| Fox Kids Club | Fox Broadcasting |
| Geoffrey's Fun Club | Toys "R" Us |
| Honeycomb Hideout Club | General Foods |
| Household Banker Bear Savings Club | Household International |
| Keebler Elf Fun Club | Keebler |
| Kids' Kitchen Club | Geo. A. Hormel |
| K mart Gym Kids' Club | K mart |
| Kool-Aid Wacky Warehouse | General Foods |
| Kraft Cheese & Macaroni Club | Kraft |
| Lego Builders Club | Lego Systems |
| Mickey Mouse Club[3] | Walt Disney |
| MTB Record Club | MTV Network |
| Nickelodeon Club | Nickelodeon |
| Nintendo's Club | Nintendo |
| Quaker Oats Popeye Club | Quaker Oats |
| Self-Discovery Club | *Family Circle* |
| Sesame Street Kids Club | J. C. Penney |

[1]Negative option club
[2]For girls
[3]First formed in 1955; formalized in 1987

tion, or for many kinds of education, and even for helping children deal with social and environmental problems.

In this age of relationship-oriented marketing, clubs are getting special consideration from children-oriented businesses because they provide *continuity*—an ongoing relationship—with kids. The very nature of clubs causes kids to join them, and in doing so they provide the clubs with their names and addresses. These names and addresses (and often other information) become part of a continually updated data base—the heart of the club—through which relationship marketing takes place. Thus, the club is also *personal,* as are the marketing communications channeled through it. This combination of continuity and personal appeal, often on a mass scale, cannot be duplicated in any other advertising, sales promotion, or publicity medium. This is why the club concept is so attractive for all types of marketing communications and particularly for sales promotion and publicity. Thus, most often the expense of operating a kids club is borne by the firm's marketing communications divisions.

Marketing messages sent through a club not only can be personalized, they can be tailored for kids of a certain age or geographical group because the data base provides information that makes this segmentation possible. Many of the clubs, in fact, are set up with an age group in mind. For instance, Disney Club is for the 8-to-12s, while the Keebler Elf Fun Club is for the under-8 group.

Clubs that are organized on a geographical basis are usually products of local retailers and media. A number of banks are now using the club concept to attract new depositors among youngsters and to build loyalty among them as future depositors. The First National's Kids' Klub, set up by the first National Bank of Pulaski, Tennessee, attracted 424 young depositors with deposits of $33,000 by giving parties for the kids and developing a print ad campaign featuring kids daydreaming about what they would be when they grow up. Each ad had the tagline, "I'm building my future in the First National Bank Kids' Klub."[10] On a more profitable basis, independent television station WNYW-TV in New York set up a kids club that uses frequent contests focusing on popular issues such as environmental quality.[11] It has attracted some major sponsors such as Child World, which put up $700,000 for a year's sponsorship. This one sponsor, incidentally, more than covers the annual expenses of running the 100,000 member club. The payoff for this local media club has been a lot of publicity for the TV station, a profitable group of sponsors who advertise on the station's programs that target kids, and a mailing list of thousands of kids through which relationships can be built for current and future marketing.

A firm that does business with the children's market may elect to market its products and services through a number of kids clubs. The firm knows ahead of time the exact nature of the children in a club—their age, geography, family status—and can refine its marketing communication efforts, such as contests and sampling efforts, accordingly. On a national basis a toy producer or an amusement park, for instance, might distribute coupons through the Burker King Kids Club and the Fox Network Club. Of course, a kids club could seek new members by promoting itself through a noncompeting kids club. Burger King's Kid Club, for example, advertised in the Fox Kids Club magazine.

What's in it for kids? What attracts kids to clubs? On a broad scale, clubs give kids *identity*—they belong to something. Thus they receive a degree of individuality as well as affiliation. They are *elevated in stature* by a club. They can refer to their membership just like Dad can his work or Mom hers. They actually possess identifiers—proof of membership and belonging—such as tee-shirts and caps with the club's logo and they get mail (just like Mom and Dad) with the club's letterhead on it. Children can meet their need for *play* as well as their need for *affiliation* through clubs. Contests, fun reading, games, free or nearly free play items, all contribute to the child's play.

National Creative Marketing, a promotion firm that specializes in premiums for kids, conducted a study to "find out just what kids wanted from kids clubs."[12] As reported in *Food & Beverage Marketing,* it found that kids want quality in their club—in its gifts, the products it sells, and its publications—they want a fun, well done, periodic newsletter, they like the idea of tie-ins with charities to which they can give their money and help, and they generally like the idea of tie-ins with licensed characters, such as Garfield and Snoopy, that are often part of the club culture.

The club notion looks like a winner when it comes to communicating to kids, but not all of them are successful. Kraft General Foods' Honeycomb Hideout Club, for example, didn't make it because it didn't attract enough members, and Nickelodeon network's club was discontinued even though it had three million members because it "didn't offer anything markedly different from what other clubs did."[13] Some firms have considered clubs and backed away from them. General Mills took this path because its executives did not want to make the necessary protracted commitment.

A club that is national in scope may cost several million dollars to operate, require a long-term commitment, and must be put together in quality fashion, perhaps by a specialist in the business. By all means it must have an unique attraction to kids. So, in view of these requirements, the need for a separate organization to run them, clubs are not for every firm that markets to kids. Because the club concept appears to be a beneficial one for both parties, however, a firm that can not meet the requirements of a club may want to join with a noncompeting firm to share some of the responsibility of a club, or it may want to form strategic alliances with several clubs.

## Summary and Suggestions

Of all the marketing communications tools targeted to children, advertising always has received the most attention from marketers as well as those who research and write about the topic. But during the last half of the 1980s, promotion and public relations to children matched advertising in importance. Perhaps more accurately, business firms found that these three communications tools, when integrated and targeted to kids, provided highly effective results. Furthermore, it was found that utilizing kids clubs for channeling integrated marketing communications efforts let marketers reach children with pinpoint accuracy.

It also became apparent that kid-targeted promotion could do more than just clinch the sale. Promotion also could be used for developing brand and seller identity among children and for building preferences and loyalty toward a firm and its products. Likewise, more public relations efforts have been introduced into marketing programs aimed at children. Through publicity, events, and school relations, favorable attitudes among children are being developed. And, both promotion and public relations are effective in reaching children as current, future, and influence markets. The net result has been that the business community which markets to children now spends substantially more on promotion and public relations than on advertising.

A word of caution is in order, however. If children often have trouble understanding some advertising messages, and even are misled by some, how much more will they misunderstand the often more complex promotions and public relations efforts? For example, what does the small print on a coupon mean to them? Or what about the hundreds of words of small print that describe the rules of a contest or sweepstake? Will they understand it when a package says on it "free baseball with five proofs of purchase;" that is, will they perceive the baseball as free? Can they read a publicity release in their newspaper or magazine and understand all the words in it—and its purpose? To deal with these and many more similar questions, give promotion and public relations the three P-tests (see Chapter 7)—pro test, parent test, and pilot test. Few companies have the luxury of wasting money on ineffective marketing communications. These tests will make sure that promotion and public relations are as effective as possible.

**PRO TEST.** Subject all promotion and public relations efforts to examination by someone trained in understanding how kids think. If this person is from the education community or has a background in elementary education, he or she will also be in a position to assess school relations efforts.

**PARENT TEST.** Provide a group of parents with each element of the public relations and promotion effort in order to see what they think about them as marketing messages to children. Parents (with children under 12) have their senses honed regarding what kids like and understand. Also, and equally important, the parents can provide their own perceptions as parents and consumer advocates about marketing communications. Thus, a proper parent test will produce information about the reactions of three groups—kids, parents, advocates.

**PILOT TEST.** On a small scale submit the particular promotion or public relations activity to an appropriate group of children. This is a relatively inexpensive means of getting a good idea of how kids will respond to these marketing communications before spending a lot of money putting them into action.

All three tests can be done by one research shop—in-house or externally. They will pay for themselves many times over in effectiveness and proper behavior.

# References

1. Al Urbanski, "Focus on Clubs," *Foods & Beverage Marketing,* July 1990, p. 35.
2. Michael Kaplan, "Children's Videos Action-packed for Promotors," *Advertising Age,* February 6, 1986, p. 16.
3. Carrie Goerne, "Marketers Using More Coupons to Fight Recession," *Marketing News,* May 13, 1991, p. 6.
4. Scott Hume, "Panic Creeps in Amid More Sluggish Sales," *Advertising Age,* September 11, 1989, p. S-4.
5. "Coupons for Kids," *Food & Beverage Marketing,* September, 1989, p. 37.
6. "AT&T Pulls Plug on Sweeps after Millions of Calls," *PROMO: The International Magazine of Marketing,* March 1991, pp. 1, 55.
7. David A. Adair, "Forge Positive Relationships with Kids Early," *Marketing News,* January 21, 1991, p. 15.
8. Cyndee Miller, "ABC Wants Kids to Bond with Cartoon Characters," *Marketing News,* September 17, 1990, p. 6.
9. David Finn, "School-based Marketing Program Makes a 'World' of Difference," *Marketing News,* January 21, 1991, p. 16.
10. "'Kiddie Banking' 101: The Art of Marketing on a Shoestring," *Marketing Update (Bank Marketing Association),* February 1990, pp. 1–4.
11. Jack Loftus, "No Kidding with Kidvid," *Channels,* June 11, 1990, p. 16.
12. Urbanski, "Focus on Clubs."
13. Joann S. Lublin, "Spread of 'Kids Clubs' Slows Amid Debate," *Wall Street Journal,* January 31, 1991, p. B4.

Kids smell sweet
to fragrance marketers

NEW CHILDREN'S MEALS

Granola, fruit snacks
make play for kids

Lego builds clothing
line for kids

Kids' card
line set

Food makers
microwave
kids' meals

A growth spurt
in kids' music

Children's Jewelry

Kids' Books
Growing Strong

New 'Oat Bran War'
Brewing Over Kids

Kids foods
flood market

cosmetics for babies

FIGURE 9–1

# 9

## Planning and Developing New Products for Children

"If you don't have a kid's product, you better get one," one food company executive jokingly said during a break at an Advertising Research Foundation meeting on researching children as consumers. She was attempting to describe the philosophy behind the rapid-fire appearance of new children's products, particularly by firms not traditionally associated with the kids' business. Her remark is underscored by the headlines in Figure 9–1 that show that children are the target markets of producers in many industries in addition to the traditional sweet things and playthings. The frozen and shelf-stable meals industry discovered kids during the late 1980s, as did toiletries, cosmetics, airlines, banks, and hotels, to name only a few of the new players in this burgeoning new market.

The appearance of so many new products (and services, too) for kids in such a short time may give the impression that it is easy—that creating new kids' products is child's play. And to some extent, it is. (After all, one might ask, how discriminating can a kid be who likes slime and gunk?) But creating *successful* new products for kids is difficult, even bordering on the impossible, according to one published source.[1] Even now, we on the sidelines have already forgotten many of those new products for kids that hit the market in the late '80s because they are no longer around. They failed, as probably a majority of them did—failed in the sense that they did not meet the financial goals of their producers and were pulled from the marketplace. Out of sight, out of mind, but probably not for the firms that did not recoup their costs, or for those that just barely did, but did not get the blockbusters they were expecting.

There was a time, less than forty years ago, when products for kids meant mainly penny candy and dime toys, and all those other items for kids such as jeans, sandwiches, and toy fire trucks were really products-for-parents-for-their-kids. While this type of thinking is still around, particularly in the clothing industry, it is being modified quickly by new social forces that are making kids the decision makers for much of what they consume. In the newer model of marketing thinking—the model for the '90s—successful new products for kids are those that meet parents' approval but are planned for kids, developed for kids, tested on kids, and marketed to kids with kids' needs uppermost in the minds of those that set new product strategies.

In this chapter we want to look at the new product development process that targets kids. We will examine its methods, philosophies, and some of its mistakes. As we consider the creation of new products for kids, we will give special consideration to the packaging that is an integral part of the process.

## Strategies for New Products for Kids

The strategies for new products for children emanate from overall corporate strategy. Product planning and development is a result of corporate strategy and new product strategy with ideas funneled down the corporation as shown in the diagram.

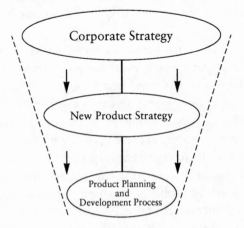

This means that if a firm has new product strategies in place that are related to kids as customers, it should be because top management has decided that children will be part (or all) of the market target for that firm.

The strategies—the goals and philosophies that drive the product planning and development process for kids' products—may differ from company to company, and particularly from industry to industry. Procter and Gamble, for example, only recently began considering children as a market target, and within the scope (no pun intended) of its very wide range of products, children's products are a very minor part. On the other hand, a firm like Fisher-Price has been making kids products "forever," and any changes in its new product strategies tend to reflect how it defines the youth market rather than the extent to which it wishes to be in that market. For example, in recent years Fisher-Price has chosen to extend its name to products for school-age kids in addition to products for preschoolers. The microwavable foods industry has acknowledged children as a market during the past few years, and has produced, for the shelf and freezer, a wide array of products for them. On the other hand, the microwave oven industry appears to be ignoring or avoiding the children's market instead of introducing children-friendly models.

## Product Strategies Based on Importance of Markets

Seeing kids as a *major* market or a *minor* market is one type of new product strategy for firms. Logically, if children are viewed as a major market, as they are at Mattel, rather than as a minor market as they are at Procter and Gamble, the amount of resources and executive attention to children-related product planning and development will be greater. But the main difference is the influence of the child as a consumer that permeates the day-to-day operations of the firm. For example, it was always known that *Sports Illustrated* magazine had some readership among boys. But the staff of *Sports Illustrated* focused on men, the main readers, and boys received only an occasional consideration. At some point, *Sports Illustrated*'s parent company, Time Inc., decided to produce a new product, *Sports Illustrated for Kids,* just for the young set. "The idea: to give kids enticing reading and to turn them into adults who'll buy *SI,*" according to its first publisher, Ann Moore.[2] Time brought together a new staff that "lives and breathes" kids. The research department, for instance, studies kids' lifestyles "around the clock" through what it terms Omnibus Studies. Time Inc. now considers kids an important market as demonstrated by the separate staff and facilities devoted to the magazine. Moreover, in addition to treating kids as a current market for *Sports Illustrated for Kids,* Time Inc. now considers them a future market for the adult *Sports Illustrated.* It is very possible, also, that since Time is in the direct marketing business, it may view the data base of subscribers to *Sports Illustrated for Kids* as market potential for additional products such as videos, clothing, and even other magazines.

When viewed as a minor market, children usually will not receive the attention they do at Time Inc. As noted, Procter and Gamble decided a few years ago to target children, mainly for its Crest for Kids toothpaste and later for its Hawaiian Punch beverage. Among its hundreds of products, many of them number one in their respective markets, there are other properties that Procter and Gamble might target to kids but chooses not to; examples include one of its other beverages, Sunny Delight, or its Duncan Hines cookies. To the extent that Procter and Gamble continues to view kids as a minor market, it is unlikely that very much of its resources and executive time will be invested in the kids market. Consequently, we would not expect much product planning and development effort to focus on kids, either. Any new products for kids are likely to originate as brand extensions and/or imitations of adult products rather than through a long-term innovative process. Both of these strategies are discussed next.

### Product Strategies Based on Originality, Financial Risk, and Returns

Another way of looking at kid-based new product strategies takes into account degree of originality and financial risks and returns. From these standpoints, firms may practice an *innovative* strategy, an *imitative* strategy, or a combination of the two. An innovative strategy dwells on creativeness and attempts to focus on new product ideas that solve major problems and meet needs in new ways. This approach to developing new products for kids demands a commitment to newness and involves a great deal of risk in the sense that often much time and resources are required before a new product results. In addition, special marketing efforts to educate children (and probably parents) about the benefits of the new product may be necessary. However, the financial rewards are usually great for this kind of product. Innovative products do not occur very often in the children's market because innovative product strategies are not the norm for the firms serving this market. Even when they do, we may not know that it was an innovative philosophy that produced them. There seems to be an innovative spirit in some corners of the toy industry. There are independent toy designers, for example, whose livelihood consists of trying to dream up new toys that have unusually high play value—and, of course, unusually high returns. According to one source, a hot new toy can produce $100 million in sales in a single season.[3] Cabbage Patch dolls, for instance, generated around $300 million their first year. What toys qualify as outputs of an innovative product strategy? In the past it may have been the Barbie doll or the Monopoly board game. More recently, perhaps it was Cabbage Patch dolls and the Teenage Mutant Ninja Turtles. At the time of this writing, in-line skates might qualify.

An imitative new product strategy, on the other hand, involves copying, in varying degrees, other products and adding some feature that will be appealing to kids. The product copied may be that of competitors or it may be a product that the company already is marketing to the adult population. To the extent that there is originality, it is related to the modification, and a few of the modifications, such as giving Teddy Ruxpin a vocabulary, deserve much applause for their novelty. The attractiveness of imitating other products in order to produce new ones is the very low risk involved. On the other hand, the returns are unlikely to be anywhere near those of an innovative strategy. Most often the products copied are imitations of adult products, for example, cereals normally eaten by adults that are sweetened to appeal to children's taste such as Kellogg's Frosted Flakes. Sometimes the product itself is hardly altered but changes are made in the marketing communications mix that turn it into a product for kids. This was the case when 7-Up started marketing to kids in the late '80s. More recently it was the case when the Monarch Company decided to reposition its Dad's root beer as a product for youngsters on the basis of marketing research that showed that "60 percent of all root beer drinkers are teens or pre-teens."[4] It created a new theme of "cool cool foam," started downplaying its "old-fashioned" theme, and signed two rap and rock music groups to be its representatives. The result: A new kids' product. For these and many other products, the assumption is that there does not have to be a difference between children's products and adults' products except in the marketing mix.

Since a majority of kids' products are imitations, we might assume that most companies that make products for kids utilize an imitative strategy. That is probably the case, although some toy firms give the impression that they practice a combination of an innovative and imitative strategy with resources available for each.

## Most Common Product Strategy: Kids' Products from Adult Products

We noted above that most new products for kids are imitations of other products, and more specifically, of adult products. If we knew the history of each of the thousands of products that are currently being offered to kids, we would surely discover that most of them started as adult products. Is this the result of imposing our adult culture on kids, of a new product strategy, or simply because adults design and produce kids' products? Probably it is a combination of all three forces.

The significance of this question lies in the fact that, as we have said in every chapter, kids are different from adults. Therefore, we might expect many of these adult-based products to fail. And they do. For example, Fisher-Price introduced its PXL2000 camcorder for kids in 1987 (and relaunched it for 1988 at a lower price), which one toy analyst forecasted to be "one of the most successful product introductions this year."[5] Whether it was its complexity, its relatively high price for a child's toy ($225 for the package), its so-so picture playback quality, or because it was promoted to fathers mainly rather than mothers, it did not do well. Perhaps its lack of success was due to the fact that camcorders were a hot item for adults and someone at Fisher-Price simply decided to sell a scaled-down model to kids believing that its high acceptance at the adult level would translate to kids.

Even though we know that there are basic differences in the thinking of children and adults, we still often ignore this in practice.

So many kids' products are obviously adult products that have been scaled down and "funned up," we might assume that their designers operate on the opposite premise, that is, children and adults are pretty much alike. Dad's root beer would be a good example. In writing about toy designing, one designer was described this way: "Since he can't be sure whether his customers are children or adults, let alone what they consider 'fun' to be, Olney simply tries to please himself."[6] In this designer's case, he seems to believe that if he likes it, children will like it. His premise may in fact have substance, but only if this particular adult possesses that sixth sense about kids that is referred to often in other chapters—that special ability to understand kids.

The prevailing culture certainly offers one basic explanation for kids products being like adult products. Kids are fed ice cream and cake because their parents eat ice cream and cake. Kids may prefer other flavors and shapes of ice cream, but it is still fundamentally an adult product that kids learn to like and desire. We should inject a word of caution here, however, that will be discussed in Chapter 11 on kids as a global market. That is, there appears to be a kids' culture everywhere that transcends sociogeographic cultures. Therefore, until children are taught the cultural values and customs of their society, they are kids first and susceptible to products marketed to their kid-ness. (Kid-ness is a very important concept that is explained in the following section of this chapter.)

The fact that kids' products are made and marketed by adults also explains why kids' products and adult products are similar. Most adults cannot think like a child even though they once were kids themselves. So, they think in adult terms but try hard to consider the likes and dislikes of children. The trouble is, they usually do not understand kids' likes and dislikes very well, either. Then, as if to insure some degree of failure, products that have been designed on the basis of a meager understanding of kids may not be market-tested adequately or at all. (See Chapter 10 for a discussion of market testing of new products for children.)

Believing in a new product strategy that bases kids' products on adult products has a lot of logic to it for at least three reasons. It has worked many times before, it has minimum risks, and it makes sense to other adults who think the same way and may be parents or may be members of the board of directors of a firm. These three reasons seemed to be at work in the case of Dad's root beer, for example. The firm said it took a "cue from the cola giants" (it has worked before), it will continue to try to hold on to its older drinkers (minimum risks), and many of its bottlers have signed on (it makes sense to other adults).[7]

### Most Rewarding Product Strategy: Products Based on Kid-ness

Even though a major portion of products for kids were once products for adults, there are still plenty of products around that are more kid than adult, and may not even have an apparent analog in the adult world. They possess what we might term "kid-ness." In fact, they bring out the kid in adults. Toys, *in general,* are surely the height of kid-ness, and within toys there are those that can be thought of as strictly for kids. Teenage Mutant Ninja Turtles are for kids, as are water-guns, tops, and jacks. Barbie dolls seem to be much more for kids than are baby dolls (which might bring out the mother in adults). In the case of edibles, it would seem that, for example, Popsicle frozen desserts, Fruit Roll-Up snacks, and Kool-Aid Kool Bursts soft drinks are suitable primarily for kids—they exude kid-ness. As for clothing, the culture seems to rule, perhaps because of clothing's conspicuousness, and perhaps because there are no obvious kids-only types. Only color schemes and certain symbols and messages written on the apparel items seem to differentiate them from those of adults.

It is difficult to describe the differences between kids-only and adults-only products, mainly because we can not think in kids' terms very well. The differences do exist, however, and kids seem to sense them. For example, kids seem to know the differences between a scaled-down adult product such as a miniature stove, hand saw, or car that is to be used by the child to imitate grownups, and a set of jacks or a top that is for playing—for being a kid. To the extent a product designer can capture this kid quality and imbue *any* object or service with it, a high degree of satisfaction for kids on a relatively long-term basis is likely to occur. Thus, it is theorized that children's products can be viewed on a continuum ranging from adults-only to kids-only, and that a major portion of products for kids fall in the middle.

Adults Only ⊢—+—+—+—+—+—+—┼—+—+—+—┼—+—+—+—+—⊣ Kids Only

Most Products
for Kids

Further, it is suggested that the more a product can be classified as kids-only (as possessing kid-ness), the more acceptance and liking it will have among children, and the more likely it will be a marketing success. Incidentally, it does not necessarily follow that the more a product is pegged as kids-only the less it is accepted by parents. Kids-only items can provide fond memories for adults (and bring out a feeling of kid-ness in them). In fact, it may be the combined acceptance of kids-only items by kids *and* by parents that keeps such items as stuffed animals, blocks, and jump ropes perennial, year-round sellers.

What is suggested, then, is that new children's products are most successful when based on kid-ness—on that characteristic of kids that separates them from adults. Whatever this ingredient is, it is most apparent in kids' needs and the expression of these needs in the form of wants. As we have suggested in other chapters, there do appear to be people around who have a special ability to understand children. It is probably in the area of children's need expression that this understanding is most critical, so let us give more consideration to it.

## Which Products for Which Needs of Children?

Needs are not for products; products are for needs. There are no products that a child *must* have, and such thinking should never cross the mind of a research and development person or a marketer. Kids do have needs that *must* be satisfied, however. In fact, as far as we know they are the same needs as those of adults. Given the chance, the child will select products and services that best satisfy their needs. The notion that kids can choose the most satisfying products among a set of products has been around for a long time, though this may seem unlikely to most adults. For instance, in the 1930s an experiment allowed children aged 6 months to 5 years to select foods for their meals and eat as much or as little as they desired. The results were very healthy and happy children free from digestive problems of any sort.[8] Today, with the many additional social forces directing children, they often are not given the latitude of acting just for themselves as they were in this study, but are expected to satisfy several other social agents. Still, when given the chance, observations show that they mainly focus on their personal needs.

Even though kid needs are the same as adult needs, their resulting behavior is different. There are two reasons for this. Some needs are more important than others to children. Therefore, they express these needs more. The second reason for the difference is that kids usually translate their needs into wants that differ from those of adults if given the opportunity. Both of these reasons distinguish kids from adults and explain, at least in part, the notion of kid-ness mentioned above.

There is no verified list of the needs that are most important to children. Routine observations, however, indicate that play would be at the top of any such list. What needs follow in importance is guessable, but various research indicates that sentience (the need for sensory expression), affiliation (the need for cooperative relationships with others), and achievement (the need to accomplish something difficult, including becoming adult-like) are the next most important needs for most kids. It appears, also, that kids have a strong need for variety (new experiences), and often fuse this need with the others. Based on what was said earlier, we might hypothesize that there is a need for kids to be kids, whatever we might call it, but it has not been isolated and identified by motivation researchers.

If kids' needs determine their wants, and if kids, when given the chance, can pretty well satisfy their wants, two guidelines for product strategy follow. One, product designers should strive to meet kids' most important needs, and two, the resulting products should be tested on kids. Both of these strategic guidelines border on truisms, but the high failure rate among children's products suggests that they are not applied consistently and/or correctly. For example, if a new product for kids is introduced that does not have play value—children's number one need—it is unlikely to maintain their interest as well as a similar product with play value. Take *Sports Illustrated for Kids*. If it is designed in such a manner as to provide "enticing reading," as its originator said, but *without fun*, it is not likely to be a big favorite in the lives of kids. Therefore, subscriptions are unlikely to be sought or renewed by the children. The fact is that the magazine is filled with fun things along with interesting reading, and therefore is succeeding among children. Suppose now, a firm wishes to introduce a newspaper for kids. Should the newspaper be serious, stuffy, very dull, mostly black and white, and provide only the news because it is a *news*paper? The answer is written in the needs of the children. The newspaper should be fun and should probably only have a little of each of these less desirable characteristics.

There is another guideline for developing new satisfying products for children. That is, try to satisfy a number of needs with one product. This is precisely what children try to do, particularly their most important needs of play, sentience, and affiliation. McDonald's seems to do this very well with all its products for kids by fusing together fun (play), food (sentience), and family (affiliation).

This brings up a serious issue. Should all products for kids be fun? Should food be fun? Medicine? Clothing? Recently, the American Academy of Pediatrics proposed a ban on all food advertising to kids because it "promotes foods that may have an adverse influence on children's health."[9] If companies advertised only healthy foods in accordance with the desires of this group, could the foods have play value? The answer to that question is pretty much the same as the answer to the question, could they be made delicious? Yes and yes, if permitted by the adult world. There is another, perhaps more important question. *Should* these foods be made with play value? There is a basic notion out there that some things should not be fun. Remember how mother used to say, "Stop playing with your food and eat it!" The implication was that food was for eating, not playing. But based on what we have said above, it would seem that kids' foods—meals, beverages, steaks, hot dogs, whatever—should be fun. In fact, it may just be this need for play that most distinguishes children's eating from adults' eating.

## Considering Parents' Wants and Needs
## in New Products for Children

In the introduction to this chapter we noted that successful new products of the '90s are those that *meet parents' approval* while being planned, developed, tested, and marketed with the child in mind. But how often do we actually design children's products with the approval of their parents in mind? A wild guess is 50 percent of the time. For example, at the time of this writing a new magazine for tweens and teens is in the testing stage, and apparently will soon be launched. Parents have not been brought into the decision making at all. How often should we design children's products with consideration of the parents? Answer: always. Perhaps the older the children in the target market (such as those for the new tween and teen magazine), the less parents might have to be considered, but only perhaps. Or said another way: *Certainly, the younger the child, the more consideration must be given the parents in the planning and development of new products.* Below the age of 8 or 9, the parents definitely have veto power. Thus, it is really naive of a producer to attempt to turn a product concept into a successful product for young consumers without researching and assessing parental responses toward it.

Companies may tend to ignore the parents in developing products for kids in the case of product extensions (imitations) because the products and/or brands are already known to adults (e.g., Dad's root beer). In such cases the developers may believe that there would be very few benefits to bringing the parents into the planning and development process. Further, the company might reason, if parental input is wanted, it can use its own employees who are parents as surrogates for the market parents. Perhaps, but it would seem that those people who work in the firm are biased in favor of the firm much more than the parents of children who will consume the product. If there are deadlines to meet, budget limitations to consider, or jobs to be won or lost, the company's goals rather than the parents' goals are likely to rule.

In the case of the development of an innovative product—one that is novel such as Teddy Ruxpin was—the new product personnel can get so excited about it, and at the same time be so secretive, that the parents are left out of the loop. Rarely does a producer of children's products create a blockbuster, and if it appears that it has one on its hands, the economic adrenalin may hurry its development. One way to save time is to avoid obtaining reactions of parents. If management sees research among parents as a chance for the concept to be leaked to competition, they may want to avoid such activity.

Actually, talking to a group of parents about new product ideas for children should benefit the firm as much as the parents. What if the parents see very little redeeming value in the new product, that is, no additional benefits over other similar products? This is quite possible in the case of a product extension, but it may occur, also, in the case of an innovation. This reaction should tell the company either to forget the product in its present form or to modify it. And if parents see the product as too dangerous, too expensive, too unhealthy, too fragile, whatever, there is very little chance that it will sell in quantity. If by chance it does, it may come back to haunt the company in the form of bad publicity, even lawsuits.

Every producer (and hopefully every retailer) has a screening system for new product ideas that evaluates their merits. It will not be flawless. It sometimes rejects good ideas, and accepts bad ones. But its very purpose is to minimize such errors. It is here—in the screening stage of new product planning and development of kids products—that the parents' viewpoints should first be critically considered. If the parents are opposed to the idea, or if representatives of parents such as retailers and consumer advocates believe that parents will be opposed to it in its finished form, this is the time to scrap the idea—before expensive developmental dollars are invested in it. If the product idea is passed on to concept testing, the parents should be involved again. When the product is market-tested and performance-tested, the parents should be a focal point along with the target children. Finally, when the product is introduced, parents' responses to the commercialized product should be assessed once more. It is a responsible way to operate—responsible to the parents and children in the target market, and responsible to the stockholders and investors.

## Remember, the Package Is for Kids, Too

It is hard not to notice the frequent advertising and publicity directed to children by the fresh milk industry, and hard not to notice, also, that the strategy stops at the package. Here is an industry that clearly is targeting the kids market (and rightly so), except when it comes to packaging. The average milk container probably can not be opened by a child, held securely by a child, or drunk out of by a child, and it certainly does not look like it is for a child. And if the child belongs to a large family, the unwieldy size of the gallon container that is probably purchased is practically a guaranteed hazard for the child. Yet, given the thinking of the milk industry, one might expect it soon to be merchandising milk in a *two-gallon* container for the family with a very large number of children. The milk industry and many others that market to children must realize that the package is usually a critical part of the product.

Packaging for kids certainly appears not to be a distinct art form among the companies in the kids' market. On a continuum from adults-only to kids-only, most of the packaging tends to be clustered toward the adult-only end and only occasionally close to the kids-only point. Too often, it appears, we develop new kids' products as spin-offs of adult products and retain the adult packages. Milk cartons, bottles, and jugs are good examples. But so are the typical potato chip bags, candy bar wrappers, and cereal boxes.

A step beyond this adult-only-package-for-children is the adult package with children's visuals. These are the packages that look a lot as if kids designed them. They are imbued with bright colors, words are printed in crayon-like art work, and there often are cartoon characters as spokespersons. Perhaps a good example of this type of children's package would be Kid's Kitchen Mac'N Cheese or Chef Boyardee's canned Dinosaurs. The Kid's Kitchen container carries a warning, "Parental Supervision Advised." One wonders how this message would test out on kids. The preparation directions for Chef Boyardee Dinosaurs start with, "Empty contents . . ." This wording, also, might not test well on literal-minded kids who do not know that the can has to be opened first or how to open it. On Kellogg's Apple Jacks there is the crayon-like art work of a preschooler, suggesting that this is the target market. But beside the large bowl of cereal shown on the package is a statement in small print that says, "Enlarged to show texture." How would this statement test on kids, particularly preschoolers? The ultimate in bad messages for kids' packaging are the necessary hundreds of words small print for contests and sweepstakes, such as those on Banquet's Kid Cuisine frozen meals for its Sticker Stakes game. In contrast, Tyson's Looney Tunes frozen meals choose to offer "free collectibles inside" for the play portion. Also in contrast to Banquet, the directions for preparation are in drawing form (instead of words only). As one writer on packaging notes, "Some marketers think that bright colors, 'dancing' letters, and fanciful characters are all that's involved in designing packaging for children's products."[10] He goes on to point out that systematic thought must be given to all dimensions of the package in order to fully consider children's physical, mental, and emotional states.

The communications function of children's packaging goes beyond identification and directions for use. Even before the product is purchased, the package should clearly communicate certain things from the shelf to the young consumer. Recognizing that children make most of their purchases in a self-service environment, and that they are often reluctant to talk with salespeople (as salespeople are reluctant to talk with them), the package must provide the youngster with an honest visual presentation of product features in a time span of a few seconds. Appropriately called the "silent salesman," the package can do this if it is displayed at children's eye level, and if it employs colors, words, and symbols that match with children's cognitive levels.

Interestingly, the printed communications on a package seem to have some degree of inherent believability among children, perhaps similar to that of print advertising. This can give marketers an unusual opportunity to describe the product and its attributes in a convincing manner. It also means that the package can perform point-of-purchase communications as a continuation of the messages presented in advertising. In fact, with growing limitations on television advertising to children by public policy and by practices such as zapping, and with skepticism among older children about advertising messages, it may be necessary for the package to assume increased communications responsibilities.

It is difficult to identify a truly kids-only package—one that communicates well at their cognitive level, possesses all the utility necessary for their dexterity level, and does not create conflicts between parents and children. They are scarce. Many packages come close, but the designers seem to stop short for some unknown reason. For example, the Sargento cheese people offer Sargento Mootown

Snackers—individually wrapped cheese sticks that are in an ideal form for kids. Yet they do not utilize the resealable container that made them famous, even though cheese products usually require rewrapping. In this case, the resealable feature would keep the sticks together and assure freshness, which in turn would minimize parent-children disagreements about it. The Pringles potato chip package clearly was designed for adults but it is also a desirable design for children because it is easy to handle, easy to open and close. In this case, resealability is provided with a product that, like cheese, requires it. (And with a bit of kid-ness application, the empty package could be turned into a play item for children.) A similar design is being used by Mars Inc.'s Combos and Frito Lay's Doritos. The latter come in a canister that may be a bit big for little hands, but that definitely has reuse value for kids. Maybe one of these days the ready-to-eat cereal industry will adopt the canister-type packaging of these snack foods. It not only would probably please parents and children alike, but would probably increase cereal consumption among kids who often practice "snackage from the package" during after-school television viewing.

A good kids' package, alone, can accomplish some of the major goals in a new product strategy if it is designed with kids in mind. Consider the milk container again. If it were offered in the form of an unbreakable soft drink bottle with a screw-on cap, would kids pick up a chilled one instead of a soft drink during their visits to the nearby convenience store? And if this container came in six-packs, would mom be more inclined to buy them for her brood that constantly experiences spillage and spoilage problems? Would this kind of container cost more if substantially more units of milk were sold? Such questions as these could be asked, also, of the salty snack industry, the cereal industry, and many more. One hopes the answers would not be similar to that given many years ago by an executive in the sliced bread business who was asked why his industry did not sell bread in a reclosable package. He responded that they had experimented with boxes and tins but found them too expensive.

The point is, if we look for *good* examples of kids packaging we can find them. We on the sidelines can even see various features that in combination would make *great* kids packaging. But those on the firing line often do not see these so clearly, perhaps due in great part to their high speed in the race for short-term profits.

## Needed: New, New Product Strategies That Really Target Kids

Most new products for children fail—from 90 to 99 percent of them. In fact, failure is so common that some firms appear to expect it, accept it, and operate on the assumption that the more new products they produce, the more likely they will get a hit. Developing new products for kids seems almost to be viewed as a board game as much as a business undertaking. Worse still, these failure rates often exist for product extensions of successful products, brands, and concepts that should theoretically guarantee at least a modicum of success. All this is reason enough to reevaluate present new product strategies that focus on the children's market.

There are additional factors that require the reappraisal of the planning and development of kids products. A few large retail chains such as Toys "R" Us, K mart, and Wal-Mart that sell these failures as well the successes are becoming increasingly critical of current new product strategies. Toys "R" Us, for example, supposedly vetoed a new product idea at Hasbro in which the producer had already invested $20 million.[11] As the story goes, Toys "R" Us perceived the product—designed to be competition for Nintendo's video game system—as a dud and recommended its scrapping. Even if this incident did not happen in exactly this way, such a thing *could* happen, particularly in the case of Toys "R" Us, which controls around a quarter of all toy sales. These sellers want more successes, more quality items, more responsible products, more sales, and more profit, and they hold some strong views about how to get them.

Also, the cost of doing business with major retailers is going up. Toys "R" Us charges a fee to include a product in its advertisements, for example. Kroger and other supermarkets often will charge a stocking (slotting) fee to take on new foods, beverages, or toiletries for kids. The average producer cannot crank out new products routinely and afford to pay the additional costs of selling them without incurring more losses. More effective product planning and development is necessary.

There are shorter payback periods for new products than before. Most new toys will get only one Christmas selling season to prove themselves. Supermarkets want quicker returns on the new products they stock, and producers demand data to support the desired returns. This may mean higher advertising, promotion, and research budgets for the new products that only large producers may be able to afford.

In addition to the trade, consumers are changing. Parents are demanding more quality in products for their kids, while their kids are increasingly skeptical of advertising that touts new products. Parents are unlikely to be excited by one more cartoon character-based cereal where the only thing that has changed since the last one is the front panel of the box and the shape of the cereal. Even the children may cool down after one box. Me-too products with marginally increased benefits may be viewed as unworthy of changes in hurried consumers' purchase and use habits.

What is needed are new, new product strategies that create excitement among children, their parents, consumer advocates, and sellers. What is needed is to reduce the high failure rate among new products for kids so that their companies will reap more sales and profits, and in turn, invest even more into even better satisfying new products for children. The discussion up to this point has provided some pretty good guidelines for doing this. Let us review and reemphasize them.

1. *Treat children as a major market.* Children are three markets in one and therefore have more potential than any other market group. Treating them as minor—as we have historically treated kids—almost guarantees minor products—products that are at most marginally better than previous ones. This in turn almost guarantees only minor profits. Treat children as they should be treated by marketers: as customers with the most long-term purchasing potential that deserve the most consideration.

2. *Give more attention to innovative than imitative strategies.* Creating novel products for kids requires more risk but it returns more profit. The product planning and development people should live amid kids in order to understand what excites them, pleases

them, makes them happy. In other words, learn the secrets of kid-ness. This kind of investment should produce great ideas that can be translated into great products for kids. Turning Mom's and Dad's products into products for their kids is okay to the extent that the kids want to role-play as adults, but such products will almost always lack the kid-ness ingredient that produces blockbust-ers. Put the people most knowledgeable about kids into planning and developing new products for children.

3. *Put a kids' package on a kids' product.* If a producer really has developed an exciting new product for kids, it ought to show it with an exciting new package for kids. Even though the product has been advertised to kids, and the advertising has brought the kids to the marketplace to consider the product, the attributes of its package can make or break the sale. These attributes should be matched to the cognitive and dexterity levels of the potential young customers. If the package communicates adult-ness, rather than kid-ness, or worse, does not communicate the features of the prod-uct correctly, the children may not understand and may not buy. If the package cannot be managed by little kids, they will tend to avoid it. Once the new product leaves the factory, its best represen-tative may be its package. Make it for kids.

4. *Satisfy kids' most important needs.* It should be unnecessary to have to say this again and again. In fact, it has been said over and over at least since the time of Adam Smith ("The sole purpose of production is consumption"). But we still have too many prod-ucts based on, "Hey, that sounds neat," and "I bet kids will think that's cool." We should not try to define cool; we should try to define and satisfy kids' needs. Almost all products for kids must have play value, but they must satisfy other important needs. A fun cereal is not enough. It must also meet children's need for sentience, and soggy cereal does not meet the sentience need. It is these impor-tant needs and how they are expressed that separate kids from adults. Therefore, focusing on them means focusing on kid-ness, and this will have high payoff for firms and markets.

5. *Always take the parents into consideration.* In all societies parents have the basic role of nurturing and protecting their chil-dren. They are gatekeepers for what the kids consume, at least for the younger children. Producing products for kids without parental approval is the kiss of death. If the kids do obtain a particular prod-

uct that has not met with parental approval, the company is more likely to be the object of word-of-mouth criticism, bad publicity, and even regulatory action.

6. *Test all dimensions of the children's product.* There is a tendency to test the viability of a new children's product along the path of development, but not to test the entire product offering. Perhaps the necessity is not felt since much testing has taken place, or perhaps there is a rush to get to the marketplace for a particular selling season. It is essential to market-test the product along with its complete marketing mix. That is, a test should be conducted of exactly what the young customer and/or his or her parents are being offered. This includes the product, its package, the accompanying promotions, all marketing communications, price, and selling environment. Testing for potential failure is just as important as testing for potential success because the former is more expensive. This topic of market testing is treated in greater detail in the following chapter.

# References

1. Kevin T. Higgins, "Research, Marketing Not Playthings for Toymakers," *Marketing News,* July 5, 1985, p. 1.
2. Ben Allen, "Her Baby Now," *Advertising Age,* September 26, 1988, p. 78.
3. Doug Stewart, "In the Cutthroat World of Toy Sales, Child's Play Is Serious Business," *Smithsonian,* December 1988, pp. 78–83.
4. Allison Fahey, "Dad's Roots for Young Drinkers," *Advertising Age,* May 13, 1991, p. 36.
5. Sara E. Stearn, "Youth Movement: Fisher-Price Turns on Kid Video," *Advertising Age,* October 5, 1987, p. 90.
6. Stewart, "In the Cutthroat World of Toy Sales."
7. Fahey, "Dad's Roots in Young Drinkers."
8. Clara M. Davis, "Self-selection of Diets: An Experiment with Infants," *The Trained Nurse and Hospital Review,* 86, No. 4 (1931): 629–634.
9. "Ad Ban No Cure for Kids' TV," *Advertising Age,* August 5, 1991, p. 14.
10. Sterling Anthony, "Packaging Kids' Products Is Not Child's Play," *Food & Beverage Marketing,* April 1990, pp. 42–43.
11. Amy Dunkin, "How Toys 'R' Us Controls the Game Board," *Business Week,* December 14, 1988, pp. 58–60.

Moderating children poses a challenge

Research With Marketing's Paradoxical Subjects: Children

**Researching children isn't kids' stuff anymore**

Survey box is child's play

Techniques to Obtain Market-related Information from Very Young Children

*'Kids let you know,' so toy marketers listen*

Projective research techniques extract valuable market data from children

Nine Tips For Testing Children's Premiums

*Kids will talk when they're having fun*

**People meters miss kids**

FIGURE 10—1

# 10

# Marketing Research Among Children: Purposes, Procedures, Problems

**A** glance at the business magazine and newspaper headlines displayed in Figure 10–1 will indicate some of the activities and concerns in researching children as consumers. Increasing competition for the children's market requires better pretesting of products and promotions (such as premiums) targeted to kids. The uniqueness of children dictates that special kinds of marketing research procedures and techniques (such as projective techniques) be utilized in order to understand them and successfully market to them. The practice of researching kids for marketing purposes is growing in sophistication and complexity ("Researching children isn't kids' stuff anymore") as marketers strive to reduce mistakes made in past marketing efforts. There are hints that some standardization of procedures in researching child consumers can be expected even though they are "paradoxical subjects." Yet, because of children's limited language abilities and their shyness, conducting research among them is difficult and often produces invalid and unreliable results.

The heightened marketing research activity among children that is indicated in Figure 10–1 is in response to marketers' acknowledging children as three major markets. Yet, in spite of the relatively large amount of research done in this market, one still cannot open a marketing research book and turn to the section on children, although this is sure to change within the decade of the '90s. But we can describe some of the purposes, procedures, and problems of researching kids in the consumer role and provide some directions for dealing with them as immature research subjects.

## Purposes of Researching Young Consumers

As noted above, marketing research among kids is increasing, but the goals have remained the same: (1) to determine children's responses to new products and services; (2) to determine children's reactions to marketing communications—advertising, promotion, packaging; (3) to measure brand/company awareness and affect among children; (4) to assess kids' media habits; (5) to describe kids' influence on parents' purchases; and (6) to measure children's economic behavior.

### Determining Children's Responses to New Products and Services

We are witnessing the introduction of large numbers of new foods and beverages, toys, toiletries and beauty aids, and apparel items developed specifically for kids. These require, although they do not always receive, market testing. There is a tendency not to use traditional market tests for children's products due in part to intense competition and in part to tradition. Both are particularly the case in the toy industry. Instead, in-house testing of new ideas and prototypes is the norm. Some toy producers, for example, test their concepts by showing videotapes made from drawings of the proposed toy to appropriate groups or individual children.[1]

Toy prototypes often are tested in a simulated competitive environment along with other play items to measure children's relative preferences and the play value of new toys. Similar kinds of tests also are commonly used for new kid-targeted foods, beverages, and toiletries. Sometimes the new products are tested in a home setting to provide a more realistic view of their benefits. In this case, extensive interviews with the children, and perhaps their parents, follow, or some kind of diary is kept by the parents.

According to one research house, only around one percent of new toys for children succeed.[2] There does not appear to be a similar measure for kids' foods and beverages—the industries that have the largest numbers of new product introductions to kids—although there are estimates of a success rate of around one-third for supermarket items in general. The very high rate of failure among play items reflects, to some extent, the fact that many toys are not market tested at all. It also suggests that typical in-house market testing may not be realistic enough. Even the play testing of toys among children may not permit enough realism—in terms of children playing together with the toys or in terms of their preferred play environments—and it may be contaminated by the presence of adults. The simulated competition certainly appears not to be realistic enough since the role of the parents, the store setting, and the marketing communications of competitors are usually absent.

## Determining Children's Responses to Marketing Communications

Television advertising to kids appears to be receiving more pretesting than it did just a decade ago. Perhaps this is because it is easier now to develop a high-quality videotape presentation of television ads and programming and to have it tested among a panel of kids. NFO Research, for example, has a program in this form that can test ads for understanding of words and symbols, for recall, and for motivation.[3] It can also provide information about children's reactions to promotions that are part of an ad campaign.

There seems to be little evidence of ad testing in the other media even though the quantity and complexity of print and radio ads targeted to children has increased. For example, the number of print ads in children's newspapers is increasing, and a growing portion of these also contain coupons, contests, and sweepstakes. Also, the increased placement of products and brands in children's movies—a relatively new form of advertising—does not yet seem to be followed up with equal amounts of research that measures its effectiveness or children's responses to it.

Premiums are tested much like new products; namely, by subjecting them to a group of appropriate children in order to assess their play value and perhaps their collectible value.[4] Contests and sweepstakes, in general, seem not to be market-tested among children, perhaps because of their complexity and relatively short-term nature. But because of these characteristics, they beg for prior assessment in order to see if the wording and procedures of the promotion are understood, and to see if children's interest and involvement in them will be sustained during their brief lives. Coupons targeted to children do not seem to be pretested either, unless they are part of an ad campaign. Couponing to children is now done in schools, through the mails, in packaging, and in catalogs and print ads, but it appears we are conducting very little measurement of kids' acceptance and liking of the practice.

New packaging for children's products is cropping up everywhere—microwavable meals, hair care products, premium frozen desserts, video games and software—and with the average cost of developing a new package being around $50,000, there is a need for more package testing. The packages' communications particularly need evaluation. Such aspects of kids' packaging as directions for opening/closing and product use, content descriptions, purchase stimulation, and presentation of brand image require testing for effectiveness. Just what percent of kids' packages are tested is not known, but it does seem to be on the increase. Packagers are finding that children's research firms can subject specific features of a package to groups of kids for evaluation, and do a good job of determining how well the package will communicate the appropriate messages. This kind of testing has not yet been used, however, to evaluate a package's ability to communicate effectively in the competitive environment of a catalog or self-service retailer.

There is little indication that the entire marketing communications mix of a firm that targets kids is being tested as a unit among children. Moreover, evaluating particular elements of a communications campaign, such as the television advertising, coupons, or premiums, may actually detract from testing the entire effort for consistency in image and meaning.

In many cases of children-targeted marketing communications, there does not appear to be systematic testing among children *and* their parents. Marketers to kids still seem to have a questionable tendency to believe that the adult members of a firm who are involved in communications development also can adequately represent the views of parents.

## Determining Brand/Company Awareness

Increasing numbers of retailers and producers are becoming concerned with their images among children as they realize that children are their future consumers. Moreover, these firms understand that proper maintenance of their brands' and companies' images in the minds of children will make it easier to convert the youngsters into customers when they reach market age. Therefore, many more businesses have customer development programs for children, and in turn, they want to know the effects of these programs on kids. Usually they want to know to what extent children are aware of their firms, their firms' brands, and perhaps their missions. Such information is gathered on an annual or semiannual basis in appropriate geographical regions. Typically the information is obtained through personal interviews among children of several ages. It is possible, although difficult, to determine also the firmness of the information in the minds of children of different ages. Focus group interviews and projective techniques may be utilized among children to determine brand/company images in a simulated competitive environment.

It's surprising that only now are significant numbers of firms conducting image research among kids. Since most firms are conspicuous in nature, they are producing images in the minds of people, including kids, whether they like it or not. Appropriate research will let firms know the nature of their images and signal them if they should be modified.

## Determining Children's Influence on Parents' Purchases

The fact that kids probably influence over $130 billion of purchases by their parents is explanation enough for why many business firms research this relationship. Several kinds of firms gather this kind of information—for example, research groups, advertising agencies, retailers, and producers. Procedurally, in-person interviews have usually been conducted among both kids and parents who are asked the degree of influence that the kids have on the parents' purchases of an array of product lines. Some role-playing techniques have been used to gather this data, particularly by individual producers of children's products. Producers tend to share this data with retailers who traditionally have been less likely to gather it.

Needless to say, there are problems with this kind of research. Asking parents to estimate how much influence their children have on their purchases produces some guessing about past behavior of their kids as well as past behavior of the parents themselves. Asking these estimates of children produces even mushier results. In either case, the problems include separating passive and active influence, assessing different degrees of influence for different products within a product line, and accounting for influence that differs in different situations—in-store, in-home, Christmas, vacations, and so on.

To confirm some of the findings obtained from direct inquiries with children and parents, observations may be made of children and parents in the purchase environment. Also, additional inquiries may be conducted with the parents shortly after they make certain purchases for their children, and parents may be asked to keep a diary regarding their kids' influence.

### Measuring Children's Economic Behavior

Children are consumers in their own right. Therefore, measuring their spending and saving behavior is important to a growing number of retailers and producers. Prior to the 1980s, children as a distinct market segment of spenders received little attention from marketers, but today that attention has grown because of the increases in children's economic power. As described in Chapter 2, children have over $8.6 billion a year of their own money to spend, spend around $6.1 billion and save $2.5 billion. Marketers want to know these amounts, but they also want to know when and where the money is spent and saved, and the nature and sources of the income that makes possible this independent consumer behavior.

The magazine *Sports Illustrated for Kids,* for example, conducts a periodic study among children that has as one of its goals assessing some of the economic behavior of children.[5] The magazine determines the amount of savings children have—at home and in an account—and even their knowledge of whose picture is on a one-dollar bill. These measures are sought for children ages 8–12. The study is conducted among children in shopping malls, and mainly among those from middle and upper-middle classes. Therefore, it does not show children's economic behavior in the lower classes. Studies conducted by others, however, do show this behavior and suggest that it is very similar to that of middle- and upper-class children.

Measures of children's spending behavior are also obtained in order to determine how and where the $6.1 billion or more is used.

We know, for instance, that around two-thirds of the money goes for sweet things and playthings, but that the remaining $2 billion is spent on a very wide variety of things—clothing, music, video game parlors, consumer electronics, and more. We do not know much about the allocation process, however. For example, why is one-third of the money spent on play items, one-third on snacks, and the remaining third on a zillion other things? More research of this question is needed and, to some extent, is being done by some retailers. We also do not know much about children's store choices for spending money. We know approximately where they spend it, but we do not know why those particular stores. For example, how much does convenience, location, and shopping with parents have to do with it?

What we do not seem to measure yet is children's economic behavior in response to marketing persuasion. Applying the naive model of children suggests that the most persuasive marketing messages would cause children to spend their money on those products. But is this actually the case? We can only guess. We do know that children save their money, in spite of the many marketing messages targeted to them, although 6-, 7-, and 8-year-olds seem to have more trouble saving than older children. We also know that rich kids and poor kids spend about the same proportion of their money. Finally, it is known from a small unpublished study conducted by the author that children did not hold back on their spending, as their parents did, during the 1990 Christmas season even though there was recession and war in the air. Putting these findings and some others together still tells us little about kids' economic behavior in an atmosphere of marketing influence except, perhaps, that marketing persuasion is not the only determinant of children's spending.

The livelihood of many producers and retailers is dependent on children's spending. Therefore, knowing the amounts spent, where they are spent, and the cues that prompt the spending are very important. Obtaining economic data such as these from children are subject to many errors. These may be minimized by directing more of the research effort to the kids' parents in addition to the kids.

## Techniques and Procedures for Researching Children

Children are a unique set of research subjects, and studying various dimensions of their consumer behavior often requires special techniques and procedures. Applying research tools that are used to study adults' consumer behavior to the study of children's consumer behavior almost always requires some modifications, and even then they may not serve adequately. We will examine the most common research techniques and procedures employed in studying children as consumers in order to highlight their best and worst features. To the extent that it is possible, we will divide them into those for assessing children's *behavior* and those for explaining the *mind world*—the thinking—of children.

## Assessing Children's Consumer Behavior

If we want to know about kids' consumer behaviors, we just ask them or their parents. Not exactly. It is often difficult for children, particularly those under age 8, to make estimates of how much, how many, and in what ways, and to provide much detail to inquiries that begin "Describe . . ." Parents are much better at answering such questions. Most of the economic information about children that was reported in the early chapters of this book was obtained from parents. But for some topics parents may not be reliable. One researcher warns that ". . . parents distort by idealizing, by talking about themselves as children rather than about their own children, by subconsciously presenting themselves as 'good parents,' and by generally being six months to several years behind in their awareness of what the kids are into."[6] There are mainly three techniques for directly assessing children's behavior that avoid most direct questioning. They are (1) observation, (2) laboratory experimentation, and, to some extent, (3) role playing. Often they are used in combination as well as in combination with direct inquiry, and the latter two may be used, also, to understand children's thinking.

**OBSERVATION.** Watching and listening to children avoids the problem of dealing directly with the children and their relative immaturity. It also avoids the reporting of children's behavior by their parents, who are not always aware of some of their behavior and may not be objective about some topics. Observations find their major use in assessing kids' in-store behavior, including their co-shopping behavior with parents, and in describing their use of products. This technique can also produce information about kids' language that is useful in future research. By listening to children's conversations among themselves, the use and meaning of youth-specific jargon can be determined. While the observation technique will not explain children's motives for what they do or say, it will provide descriptions of patterns of behavior in time and space. Reasons for the behavior, if needed, can be obtained through other research means described later in this chapter.

Testing a new board game, for instance, by unobtrusively watching and listening to two or more children play it can provide the game's developers with important information about children's understanding of it (and perhaps of its rules), the time spent in various phases of the game, the sequencing of the events according to the children, the uses of its various parts, its play value, and the degree to which it instigates competitiveness and/or affiliation. Such information, when obtained from children of various age levels and family backgrounds, has enormous value in predicting the success of the game. Much of this information could not be obtained in any other manner.

Unobtrusively watching children in the shopping setting, with and without parents, provides rich insights into child-parent interactions including the type and extent of children's influence on parental consumer behavior—choice of stores, choice of products to consider, evaluative criteria, and actual purchases. Observations directly related to children's own purchases can provide useful information about their comparing of items, time devoted to decisions, extent of browsing, problems encountered with reaching or finding products, impulse purchases, money use, and interactions with store persons. Such information is not only useful in setting marketing strategy, but it can be useful in guiding ethical behavior of merchants. A convenience store chain, for example, conducted observations in some of its stores to determine children's in-store traffic patterns and behavior so that sexually oriented magazines could be displayed out of their reach and line of sight.

The observation technique does not always produce quality data. For example, observations usually can not be obtained in the home setting where many products are actually used and there is no way to adequately simulate the home setting and its atmosphere in a laboratory. Therefore, when observations are made in artificial settings, the results are always somewhat distorted from what would otherwise be a very objective research method. There is a special question of research ethics to be dealt with in the case of the observation technique in terms of its invasion of privacy because the subjects normally do not know they are being studied.

**LABORATORY EXPERIMENTS.** Using laboratory experiments among young consumers provides accounts of their actual behavior under varying conditions. Because the conditions are created by the experimenter, however, there is almost always reduced realism, particularly as compared to the standard observation method (which is often used in tandem with the experimental method). For example, if an experiment is set up to test a new toy's play value compared with that of a competitor's toy, observation will probably provide more accurate information than asking the children to report their preferences between the two products.

Experimenting is a necessary research procedure for testing new products for children. As noted, this technique allows for the creation of various conditions under which a product's use can be examined. Through experimentation variations can be made in the product itself—such as sweetness of a cookie or weight of a toy—and in the product's use environment—for example, in light, temperature, or social setting. The experimental method finds a wide range of uses in marketing research with children in addition to testing new products. It may be used for testing new premiums, packages, and advertising campaigns. Almost always new marketing communications need to be compared with old ones, alternative ones, or those of competitors. This research method is also useful in the store for measuring children's responses to displays, fixtures, facings, and in-store communications. For example, through a series of experiments a bookstore chain was able to meet certain merchandising goals by installing an area with a certain design in each store where children could play with various product offerings while parents shopped. However, in such field experiments there is a loss of control over extraneous influences as compared to laboratory settings.

The inherent disadvantage of the experimental method is that the research conditions are created, rather than real, and therefore may not be representative enough of actual conditions. Testing a new product's play value against one or more competing products, for example, may not produce accurate enough results because the test does not take place in the children's backyard or bedroom where play may have a different meaning.

**ROLE PLAYING.** This technique is a special variation of the experimental method and usually requires the observation technique, also. It circumvents direct questioning by asking children to take the role of someone else while observing the resulting behavior. it usually takes the form of, "Pretend you are . . ." For instance, rather than being asked how a supermarket checkout clerk could be more helpful when the child checks out, the child may be asked to pretend to be a checker. Rather than being asked how his mother might respond to a toy request, the child may be asked to pretend to be his mother.

Role playing is unique in that it provides the child's perspective of others in motor and verbal form. By highlighting this perspective, the actual behavior of the child under regular conditions can be forecasted and explained. For instance, asking a young subject to pretend to be her best friend and respond to her new cosmetics will help explain the subject's use of the cosmetics in the presence of friends.

The obvious shortcomings of role playing is its artificiality through pretending and acting. Also, unless skillfully conducted, children may provide socially desirable behavior (this is how they expect me to behave). But being able to share a child's perspective of another person under certain conditions can have great value to a researcher. This is especially true because children are usually very candid. For example, as part of a study of children's understanding of credit cards, they were asked to pretend to be a banker who is issuing the cards to children. The banker was to tell the children about some of the "dangers" of using credit cards (these had been presented earlier in some reading materials). One child did a good job of explaining that the cards could cause people to spend more than they could afford, and also noted "you can cut your hands on them."

## Explaining the Mind World of Children

Inside the minds of children is a world of attitudes, knowledge, perceptions, and motives that are woven together in ways that we still do not understand very well. Moreover, the deployment of this network of cognitions by children through their thinking and be-havior can be perplexing, also. Nevertheless, marketing researchers strive to explore the mind world of children through a variety of research techniques in order to explain and predict their consumer behavior. Determining what is on the minds of kids through direct questioning is commonplace, but as indicated in the discussion of assessing behavior, the procedure has a lot of shortcomings. Chil-dren lack verbal skills as well as socializing skills, and adults often are intimidating, thus adding to the problem of eliciting meaningful and fruitful dialogue. Therefore, researchers tend to rely on a num-ber of other techniques to study the mind world of youngsters. The techniques most frequently used are (1) attitude scaling, (2) focus groups, and (3) picture-drawing methods. Consideration of each of these three methods will show they can be used to tap different dimensions of children's cognitive world.

**ATTITUDE SCALES.** To get at simple likes–dislikes and action tenden-cies of children, rating scales are useful if the young respondent is already in school and has some formal reading and writing experi-ence (age 7 or 8). In general, the younger the children the fewer the points that can be utilized on scales because of younger children's inability to discriminate. There is probably little need for more than five points regardless of age since most children will not be able to discriminate beyond that level.

Smiley face scales, instead of words (like, dislike), are often used when researching kids, and they make good sense if for no other reason than their play value. Research houses have designed a num-ber of variations of this scale. Scales administered individually may not require the children to do any writing, only pointing. ("Point to the face that shows how much you like or dislike it.") Symbols, such as stars, can be used in different sizes and quantities instead of words. However, a marking system of some kind (check off, underline, circle) usually is necessary if the scale is administered to a group of children.

Where relatively large numbers of children are involved for study, attitude scales have the benefit of being able to be administered in a short amount of time and reveal such attitudinal dimensions as like–dislike, want–don't want, would buy–would not buy. Gener-ally, such scales as these when administered among young children reveal directions of attitudes more accurately than they do intensity of attitudes due to the children's inability to conceptualize their own feelings.

There seems to be a tendency recently for market researchers to use children's jargon for the scale points such as "super," "cool," "great," and "alright" under the assumption that these terms communicate better with the children. This may be true, but a problem is that the researcher may not know the real meaning of these words to children.

**FOCUS GROUPS.** Bringing together six to eight children, perhaps a dozen, to talk about a product, product concept, or other marketing objects is standard fare among marketing researchers. In fact, the focus group method, as this procedure is usually called, appears to be the most popular marketing research technique for exploring the mind world of young consumers. It tends to be a preliminary method that is looked upon not so much for its reliable numbers but more for its reliable ideas.

The sky is the limit on procedure, with as many variations as there are research houses. The number of kids used in a setting may range from a couple of playmates to a dozen or more kids chosen for their verbosity. The setting may be a bare office in downtown Chicago, a research lab beautifully decorated just for this purpose, or an elementary school classroom. In one case, where children were asked to talk about water play items, a kiddies' swimming pool was utilized. Where there is also a need for children to be observed, the physical facilities will be limited to those designed for this purpose. Children may be permitted to lounge on the floor, or they may be seated at a conference table. They may be permitted to be playful, or they may be required to be attentive to a video display. The sessions may be scheduled for as little as fifteen minutes or as long as an hour or more.

This high degree of flexibility is the forte of focus groups. Usually researchers are seeking kids' feelings, perceptions, evaluations, or physical responses to ideas, concepts, new products, packages, ads, or promotions. Generally, there is play involved—trying out a new toy, using play as a format for obtaining evaluations, or just injecting fun into the procedures.

The notions of touch-and-tell and show-and-tell are prevalent in focus groups, and they should be. Kids like to touch things, hold things, particularly in the presence of strangers. These things become "Linus blankets" that provide security, comfort, opportunities to express tactile senses, and play. From the researchers' standpoint, the items held can stimulate discussion from what otherwise may be a shy youngster.

Problems abound with focus groups in spite of their popularity. Getting ten children together, getting permission agreements from parents and / or teachers of ten children, managing ten children who often behave like fish out of water, keeping their attention, and maintaining a friendly and comfortable atmosphere are normal problems in addition to the usual ones of language and shyness. But the large quantity of ideas, words, opinions, perceptions that result seem to outweigh the problems.

There may be a tendency for some marketing executives to get excited by the quantity of output from focus groups and want to make decisions based on it. It is better, however, to view the output as one data point and to test the results through more structured and more reliable methods.

**PICTURE-DRAWING TECHNIQUES.** Obtaining information from children through drawings has been standard practice among psychologists and psychiatrists for a century. It is becoming a standard practice among marketing researchers. The premise of these researchers is that children often cannot or will not articulate what is on their minds, and other procedures must be substituted. Drawings are particularly favored when the goal of the research is to elicit the great amount of nonverbal information or "pictures" that children store in their minds. This visually stored information differs, sometimes totally, from verbally stored thoughts; yet it may be the reason a child likes and selects a certain store, brand, or package. Eliciting visually stored data from children by asking them questions usually will not work well because children do not yet have adequate capacity to transform visual codes into verbal codes.

When asked to draw a picture of something, children usually respond positively, often eagerly, because drawing is an engaging activity to them. Unless specifically requested to draw something they dislike, they usually will draw pictures of things they value. And they draw truthfully—not reproductions, per se, but representations of what is in their minds. The hand that holds the crayon is guided by the mind. Within limits of artistic abilities, the images in the mind of the child—what is real to him or her—are reproduced on paper.

Procedurally, drawings may be made with pen, pencil, crayons, or the many types of color markers. They can be done, also, with fingers and colored fluids. (Finger-drawings tend to be messy and limited to one color, and therefore less commonly used.) Picture-drawing sessions may be conducted one-on-one where several pictures are wanted, or they may be done on a group basis such as in a classroom or as part of a focus group. If done on a group basis, the experimenter must make sure that copying does not take place. The children are given specific instructions and then allowed from fifteen minutes to one hour to complete the task depending on the purposes.

Instructions are the key to obtaining the goals of the picture-drawing research effort. The study reported in Chapter 3 that assessed children's perceptions of the marketplace asked children to "Draw what comes to your mind when you think about going shopping." Through several pilot studies this specific set of directions was found to elicit the widest range of responses—to permit the children the greatest latitude in expressing their perceptions of the marketplace. In effect, each child said with his or her drawing that this is the marketplace, as I see it, in which I go shopping. (Compare this result with asking the children to describe the nature and contents of the marketplace.) Several other statements were used in some earlier studies. For instance, "Draw what you would like to buy when you go shopping" typically elicited drawings of two or three products special to the children. "Draw what comes to your mind when you think about going to the store" usually produced a picture of a toy store, convenience store, or department store. These trial-and-error efforts did demonstrate how much was already stored in the minds of children about consuming and how easy it was to elicit parts of it by choosing specific cue words.

Analyzing the resulting drawings may take several approaches depending on the kinds of information sought. A clinical approach may be taken in which a picture's emphasis (what is placed in the center of the page, for instance), size of objects (all or parts of the objects are larger or smaller than normal), use of color, the width, length, and directions of lines, and distortions are taken into account. For example, in the marketplace study reported in Chapter 3 the children often detailed and overemphasized shopping carts, suggesting that the carts had great importance to them. Subsequent direct questioning indicated this was in fact so. Figure 10–2 shows some of the shopping carts as they were portrayed by the children. Notice, for example, that the children took time to show them with four wheels and wire mesh, even though both are difficult for children to draw. Both of these features appear to be very important to children and to have been firmly planted in their minds during their close-to-the-cart days.

In a more formal manner, content analysis, such as that used in categorizing the contents of advertisements, can be conducted in order to obtain frequencies of the occurrences of possible marketplace objects. A content analysis objectively categorizes the objects in the drawings and thus provides a record of what was contained in the drawings at what frequency. A relatively high frequency is an indicator of high value of that object to the group of children under study, while a low frequency or absence indicates minor importance or perhaps negative feelings toward certain objects. We know that when given the opportunity, children also will omit what they dislike. For instance, in the drawing study reported in Chapter 3, children included all kinds of stores where they would fine children-related items except drug stores. It appears that they do not perceive drug stores as significant places for children to shop.

Once all the contents of the drawings are listed, a variety of other operations can be conducted with the data. Through multidimensional scaling techniques, the listed items can be examined to determine relationships among them. For example, in the previously mentioned study one cluster of drawings was determined to be a name-identity cluster in which children included brand names and store names. This kind of analysis can classify the children into consumer types. In this particular case, we referred to these children as "name-droppers," although more correctly, they are brand-conscious consumers.

Picture-drawing techniques tap information that is unfiltered by socially desirable behavior (Should I answer this way or that?) while retrieving visually stored information. Very few research techniques accomplish both of these objectives. To reduce the questions that

**FIGURE 10-2**

are bound to arise because of the interpretative latitude of the picture-drawing technique, results should be confirmed with more conventional methods.

## Problems in Researching Kids as Customers

There are a lot of problems with researching children as consumers. A recent Advertising Research Foundation workshop, "The Latest in Children's Research and How to Use It More Effectively," was held just to tackle this problem. Experts on the how, when, and where of researching kids presented papers and participated on panels to shed light on the difficulties inherent in effectively eliciting information from children. The workshop produced no magic formula for dealing with the problems associated with research on kids and their consumer behavior, but it was clear that the audience as well as the participants were deeply concerned with discovering solutions.

In order to begin to solve these basic marketing research problems, we must acknowledge the following conditions:

1. We still do not have a good understanding of how children think, and why they behave as they do in the consumer role. Therefore, there is a need for much more basic marketing research among them, and just as important, there is a need for these results to be shared in some noncompetitive way.
2. Our research findings about children's consumer behavior are almost always suspect, so we need to fix our research procedures and reproduce these findings under a new set of theoretical guidelines.
3. Errors made in marketing to children have more downside risk than those made in marketing to others, so it therefore deserves more research underpinnings.
4. There are people who, because of their special training, experience, and perhaps a sixth sense about kids, have a better than average grasp of kids' thinking and behavior, and this type of person should be responsible for much of the marketing research among children.

Let's look at these propositions individually to get an idea of their implications for conducting research among children as consumers.

It is very difficult for a decision maker in a firm that markets to children to admit that *we don't really know why children think and act as they do*. The large number of product failures in the children's market, for example, might be considered testimony to our misunderstanding of kids, but then someone would say that the large number of successes would be testimony to our understanding of them. The point is, though, that children's marketplace desires, and their expression of them, are much more unrestrained than those of adults, and a marketer who understands kids well should be able to sell to them and their parents with relatively consistent success. Said another way, it ought to be easier to sell to children than to adults, but that does not seem to be the case in actuality. The reason, again, is mainly because of our lack of a good understanding of them.

If we in fact do not understand young consumers well, it is research's job to explain them to us. If the decision makers in charge of designing, packaging, advertising, and selling products for kids are expected to know marketing first and markets next—which is typically the case—then someone must be charged with knowing the market. Thus, research should play a more pivotal role in marketing strategy targeted to kids, perhaps even more than that to adults. Consequently, children-oriented business firms need to invest more than usual in research and rely more than usual on research. Yet there are major business firms out there that focus primarily on children and have no research department at all. While this may not prevent them from doing good research (by relying on outside suppliers), it is a deterrent to the way of thinking being suggested here.

Related to the first point listed above, we need to realize that even though we do lots of research among children as consumers, *we can't really trust our findings about their consumer behavior*. For example, writing in a 1990 issue of *Psychology and Marketing,* a children's researcher demonstrates that we often make mistakes in our research with youngsters and will continue to do so unless "the experimental materials and response formats are matched to what the child knows and what the child can do."[7] Other researchers writing in the same issue of the same journal warn us of similar mistakes.[8] These authors are suggesting that even young children may be able to perform better, and may be more sophisticated, than we think, if only we knew how to design our research properly. We make these kinds of mistakes not because we are careless research-ers but because we lack a good understanding of kids.

What I am suggesting here is that the research results on which we base marketing decisions are suspect. Not just the old research, or the research hastily done by inexperienced academicians looking for publications, but possibly much of the research we do and *will* do may be flawed. Again, we produce errors in our research be-cause our thinking about children is too often erroneous. It may be a good idea to retest some of our basic findings about children as consumers if they are to continue to be used to guide our marketing efforts.

All marketers make errors. It's the nature of the beast—the inex-actness of the science. But *errors made in marketing to children probably have the potential to produce more losses than other mar-keting errors*. First of all there are the lost sales because children do not want the goods as we anticipated; there may also be lost sales because our data caused us to underestimate our production. These mistakes could happen in any market, although probably not as frequently as they tend to occur in children's products industries. What if young customers lose faith in a brand, or get angry at a firm ("those people who make it," as one child said about a mal-functioning toy) and vow to never buy its brand again because of some marketing blunder? That can really hurt when the potential buyer is a kid with his entire consumer future ahead of him. Simply put, there is more future business to lose with kids than with adults. Moreover, some types of errors in marketing to children are likely to earn the ire of consumer advocates and regulators because those marketing efforts are monitored more closely than most others. Thus, if a mistake in children's marketing attracts the attention of those concerned with public policy, the losses from the mistake can be devastating.

Finally, we need to acknowledge that *there are people out there who can help us with these problems in marketing to children be-cause of their special background and knowledge*. Throughout this book the idea that adults have trouble truly understanding and ex-plaining children's consumer behavior has been frequently men-tioned. There are exceptions. Some people, for example, in the field of children's education, have a sixth sense about children. These people, with some introduction to the research business, would be very capable of directing research and producing good results from studying children in the consumer role. What is troubling is that they typically are not sought out for positions in marketing research. Fortunately, however, there are a few of these individuals in the field. They often have their own research shops that specialize in children's consumer behavior. They have migrated to it because they seem to recognize that they have special abilities in the area, and to see the need for such specialization. We must rely on this type of person to help us minimize our research errors and maximize our research effectiveness.

## Using Parents as Surrogates for Children in Marketing Research

As we have discussed the purposes for researching children and the various procedures that might be used, we have repeatedly emphasized these problems.

- Adults have trouble talking effectively to kids—adults intimidate, they come across as authority figures with whom children have trouble holding normal conversation, and they use a different language.
- Children have language difficulties—difficulties in expressing themselves, particularly when their knowledge is in visual form, and difficulties with measurements, abstractions, and very personal subjects.

We could add to this list these:

- Children are hard to reach—they are in school, in day care; they are eating, sleeping, and studying.
- Some segments of society see kids as vulnerable and in need of protection from marketing activities including marketing research.

When we realize the severity of the problems in researching kids as consumers, it is understandable that many business firms do minimal research among children and more among parents. In fact, one might ask, why research kids at all? Simply ask the parents about the children. In many ways this is good advice.

Parents can be research surrogates for their children and often are. Let me suggest several areas in which obtaining information about children from their parents is common practice.

1. *Seeking information about children's economic behavior—spending, saving, receiving money.* If a marketing researcher wants to know how much kids get to spend, how often and to what extent it is spent, and how much is saved and in what form, parents are a good resource. Most money that kids spend comes from parents, so parents have good information about it. Kids have some trouble with figures (measures), particularly when talking with adults about it.

2. *Seeking measures of children's influence on parental purchases.* Routinely parents are asked about their children's purchase requests and about their children's direct influence on the parents' purchases. Kids are asked these questions, too, but while the responses of both are very subjective, the recall and judgments of the parents appear to be more trustworthy.

3. *Determining children's media habits.* When and to what extent children watch TV, listen to the radio, read magazines and newspapers, and read billboards can be assessed adequately through research with parents. Most of these activities can be observed and measured (and recorded) by parents, and parents' estimates of time consumed by these activities are usually valid. We often ask children about their media habits, and the results are useful. But estimates of time (two hours, thirty minutes before school) and numbers (pages of reading, stations listened to, programs watched) for children can be problems that may be better estimated by parents.

4. *Estimating product use by children.* When, how, and to what extent certain products are used by children may be better estimated by parents. Children's use of toiletries such as shampoo and toothpaste probably can be more accurately estimated by mom than by the kids. Also problems with the product (bad taste, burns the eyes), or with the package (hard to open/close) are easily remembered and reported by parents. Even the amount of cereal eaten, the number of snacks, and the time spent with certain toys may be better measured by parents. In all cases where the products are expected to be viewed by children as personal or as embarrassing to talk about, research should target the parents.

Since the above four areas potentially embrace a good deal of marketing research that would target parents as surrogates for their children, when should research target children? The answer, in general, is to target kids when their feelings, perceptions, beliefs, and values are sought. Experience with asking parents about the mind world of their kids is not very good. While it is true that parents know their children best, they may not actually know or have given much thought to such matters as their kids' feelings about radio advertising, toy packaging, or in-town billboards. It is best to explore children's cognitions with the children.

Finally, parents (or guardians) should always be informed when market researchers intend to interact with their children. Therefore, for this purpose and for normal information purposes, parents are almost always involved in the marketing research of kids.

# References

1. Timothy Harris, "'Kids Let You Know,' So Toy Marketers Listen," *Advertising Age,* August 24, 1987, p. 19.
2. Kevin T. Higgins, "Research, Marketing Not Playthings for Toymakers," *Marketing News,* July 5, 1985, p. 1.
3. Harris, "'Kids Let You Know.'"
4. Julie D. Taylor, "Nine Tips for Developing and Testing Children's Premiums," *Premium Incentive,* May 1988, p. 30.
5. *Sports Illustrated for Kids Omnibus Study,* Volumes I, II, III (New York: Time Inc., 1989).
6. Gar Roper, "Research with Marketing's Paradoxical Subjects: Children," *Marketing Research,* June 1989, pp. 16–23.
7. Laura A. Peracchio, "Designing Research to Reveal the Young Child's Emerging Competence," *Psychology & Marketing,* Winter 1990, pp. 257–276.
8. Deborah Roedder John and Mita Sujan, "Children's Use of Perceptual Cues in Product Categorization," *Psychology & Marketing,* Winter 1990, pp. 277–294.

# PART FOUR

# Kids as Customers Tomorrow

**FIGURE 11-1**

# 11

# Children as Global Consumers

The world is poised on the threshold of a new era in marketing that is marked by the globalization of products and services. Understanding how consumers around the world respond to global marketing activities has recently emerged as an important topic for consumer research. Practically all of the research about global consumers has focused on adults for very logical reasons. However, within just the past five years, some of this research has begun giving consideration to children. Such questions are being asked as "Are children functioning in the consumer role in other industrialized nations to the extent they are in the United States? and "Is it possible to direct marketing activities to children worldwide much in the same manner as in the States?"

The drawing in Figure 11–1 gives a hint of the answers being found in consumer research that is being directed to children worldwide. It is a drawing by a fourth-grader in Taipei, Taiwan who, along with 90 of his classmates, was asked to "Draw what comes to your mind when you think about going shopping." What we see here is an attempt to describe the marketplace as he experiences it and perceives it—a collection of small stores in the downtown area in which large numbers of people shop at the same time. He shows himself approaching the third store—a toy store—according to his report in a post-performance interview. Thus, he is a shopper. The stores do not have names such as Kroger or K mart. From left to right the wording above each store says: department store; beauty salon; toy store; video game arcade. Also, we can see that the setting is one in which there are many shoppers, and that they walk along the street choosing their places to purchase among these no-name stores. Drawings among similar U.S. children in response to the same directions rarely show a large number of shoppers, almost always show store names, and never show a downtown shopping area. These differences probably reflect, in part, the Confucian culture of togetherness and conformity as compared to the distinctiveness and individuality exhibited in the U.S. culture. The drawing also mirrors the actual shopping environment in Taipei for most families. Most important, this Taiwanese youngster is telling us that there is, indeed, a marketplace in Taiwan and that he participates in it.

In this chapter we want to examine the market potential of children as global consumers. We will look at some reasons for considering children in other nations as consumers, note some recent global marketing efforts toward kids, and look at some actual research results from consumer studies of children in other nations.

## Reasons to Consider Children as Worldwide Consumers

As we have observed in the early chapters of this book, our children were not always considered consumers. It is a phenomenon of the postwar era, and for all practical purposes, of the 1970s and 1980s. Similarly, children of other nations typically have not been considered targets for U.S. marketers. But that is changing, for a number of research-based reasons. Let us consider some of these reasons and note some related myths and mistakes that might result when targeting children of the world as a market.

1. *Over 90 percent of the world's population of families and 75 percent of family personal income are beyond the borders of the United States.* We Americans have good reason to be nationalistic, but it may blind us to the market opportunities that exist beyond our nation. For example, it is probably easy to imagine that the children in Britain might represent a potential market for certain U.S. marketers—and indeed they do—but we could easily overlook the three million kids in Taiwan, for example, who are living in the second-wealthiest country in the Pacific Rim and one with virtually no unemployment.

Table 11–1 shows the estimated population of children for 27

**TABLE 11–1**

*Estimated Youth Population of Industrialized Countries and City States, Ages 5–14*

| Country | Population Ages 5–14 (in thousands) |
|---|---|
| Austria | 878 |
| Australia | 2,371 |
| Belgium | 1,197 |
| Brazil | 52,930 |
| Canada | 3,631 |
| Denmark | 577 |
| Finland | 648 |
| France | 7,479 |
| Hong Kong | 861 |
| India | 311,481 |
| Iran | 24,841 |
| Italy | 7,139 |
| Japan | 15,934 |
| Mexico | 20,893 |
| Netherlands | 1,761 |
| Norway | 515 |
| People's Republic of China | 195,844 |
| Republic of China (Taiwan) | 3,891 |
| Saudi Arabia | 6,430 |
| Singapore | 400 |
| South Korea | 11,549 |
| Spain | 5,974 |
| Sweden | 960 |
| Switzerland | 696 |
| United Kingdom | 7,000 |
| United States | 37,787 |
| West Germany | 5,860 |
| Total | 729,527 |

industrialized nations (including the United States). There are almost three-quarters of a billion children in these countries representing around 23 percent of their total population. Letting one's marketing imagination run wild for a moment, if these children spent only half of what U.S. children spent, their market potential would be equal to around $86.5 billion. (Russia and some other Eastern Block countries are not considered because of their lack of a market-driven economy.) It can be a mistake for a marketer to think that a country like Mexico or Brazil, even though it has a relatively large population of children, is very poor and its people purchase mainly at a subsistence level. While this is relatively true for these two nations, their young consumers may be an exception. The value of the candy and gum market in Mexico alone is estimated at $450 million annually, and PepsiCo's Mexican subsidiary, Sabritas, spends $1 million on advertising to garner an 8 percent share.[1] A marketing error can be made also be perceiving a very small country like Hong Kong as having too small a population of children to support a marketing effort similar to that of PepsiCo in Mexico. Hong Kong's 861,000 kids spend over HK$1 billion yearly ($140 million in U.S. dollars) *of their own money* on snacks and play items and influence many billions more of their parents' spending.[2]

2. *Many countries offer more growth opportunities in children's products than does the United States.* U.S. marketers are finding that children in many other nations do not have available to them the array of snacks, beverages, play items, and clothing that U.S. children have. Further, these marketers' domestic experiences with intense competition, along with research data from overseas, suggest that with appropriate advertising and promotion they could generate additional, profitable business in some other countries with their present product lines. Said simply, U.S. marketers in children goods often are trading market shares here but could be increasing market shares there. For example, General Mills has joined Nestle to go after the ready-to-eat cereal market in Europe.[3] As compared to the 10 pounds per capita of cereal eaten here—at least one-third by kids—Continental Europeans consume only around two pounds. The "Big G" people see this as growth opportunity compared to the United States, where 10 pounds seems to be about the limit and competitors vie for each other's share within this limit.

3. *In many nations the competition for the children's market is*

*not as aggressive as it is here and therefore it may be vulnerable.* It has been said that in the United States when you get a competitor down you kick him; in Asia you help him up. There are different styles and levels of competition, and in those countries where it is milder there is opportunity for U.S. marketers to gain business through U.S.-style competition. McDonald's and Kentucky Fried Chicken both generally have found that it is easy to be competitive in Far East nations with their regular hours of operation, brightly lit and clean interiors, and posted prices—all the things routinely done in the United States. Showing a desire to please customers through these standard merchandising practices of U.S. fast food restaurants automatically places these restaurants a cut above much of the domestic competition. In the case of one McDonald's restaurant in Taipei, for example, young consumers were observed standing outside looking in. Informal interviews with them revealed that they were avoiding the almost constant crush of the crowd inside by sending in one representative with all the orders and then, once the food was obtained, going elsewhere to eat it.

4. *In some countries U.S. goods are favored over domestic goods by families and children.* We hear news reports of some U.S. goods selling for premium prices in the Eastern European countries, suggesting that certain U.S. brands are viewed as having special qualities. This, in fact, may be the case in many nations. Barbie dolls and Cokes, for example, seem to command premium prices in most of the nations in which they are sold. Thus, "Made in America" goods may possess an inherent competitiveness in other countries.

5. *Children's preferences usually are less well defined than those of their parents and therefore susceptible to products from other nations.* "It may play in Peoria but not necessarily in Paris" are the words sometimes used to describe the cultural barriers in other countries. Indeed, cultural differences must be accounted for when seeking markets in other parts of the world, but children—particularly those under age 8—are still learning what is culturally correct and may respond eagerly to novel items from the United States. One might think that toys with a war theme, for instance, would not be acceptable among the relatively docile, peace-loving Chinese families of Hong Kong and Taiwan. G. I. Joe items appear to be an exception, however, and are very appealing to Chinese boys, perhaps in part because they are U.S. made, but also probably in part because of their macho appeal.

## Reasons to Study Children as Global Consumers

In addition to the possible marketing opportunities that exist among children of other nations, there are other reasons to research their consumer behavior development. Let us note four of these.

1. *A body of theory applicable to all nations about how the youngest members of a society become consumers is needed.* Practically all the consumer behavior theory that exists was developed in the United States, and we do not know just how applicable it is to children in other nations. For example, the drawing in Figure 11–1 by a child in Taiwan reminds us, that in the Confucian cultures that emphasize a group orientation, children might develop differently as consumers. Apparently we have only two published studies that address this expected difference, and they found that, indeed, some differences were noticeable, although to some extent predictable, using consumer socialization theory.[4]

2. *Universal guidelines for public policy development are needed.* As global marketing programs are developed, or planned for development, a variety of public policies regarding such efforts are likely to be encountered in the two dozen major industrialized nations. If we had a better understanding of children's consumer behavior worldwide, some universal public policies might be formulated. For instance, as Europe centralizes, there may not be adequate knowledge and agreement about regulating satellite-originated media that will target children as potential markets. Likewise, there may not be an adequate understanding of children globally on which to base a set of self-regulations among the media. A study of the regulation and self-regulation of television advertising in West Germany, for example, showed that there was not sufficient research-based information available to properly develop public policy guidelines.[5]

3. *Universal guidelines for development of consumer education programs are needed.* Just as young people in a society may be educated about the role of worker, marital partner, and faith worshipper, children who are permitted and encouraged to participate in the consumer role need education about it, also. While ordinarily much of this consumer training comes from parents, most states in the United States provide it, also. There appear to be some con-

sumer education efforts in many if not most of the industrialized nations, but there do not seem to be any universal guidelines for these programs. If we had a good understanding of children's consumer socialization and resulting behavior on a global scale, general consumer education programs could be implemented with more confidence in their effectiveness.

4. *Descriptions of the global economy could be enhanced.* There are a number of models of economic structure and development, and essentially none of these account for the nature of consumer behavior among the youngest participants. As we develop understanding of children consumers worldwide, we should be able to improve, and perhaps correct, the descriptions of the world economy that currently exist. For example, one study out of India suggests that consumer socialization differs in countries at different stages of development, and that in fact the standard model of consumer socialization may be reversed.[6] In India, children may introduce mothers to objects and styles of consumer behavior rather than mothers teaching the children these things. This suggests that as children learn more consumer behavior, for example from television, they may influence their parents enough that the consumer behavior of the parents will change. This, in turn, has substantial implications for economic development in that country.

## Children's Consumer Behavior in Other Parts of the World: The Case of the Pacific Rim

I wanted to know the degree of similarity in consumer behavior among children in all the industrialized nations for the purposes mentioned earlier including the assessment of opportunities of a global marketing program directed on them. To accomplish this goal, a research program was established. The background that directed this research will be described briefly followed by actual results from studies of children's consumer behavior in three Pacific Rim countries—Hong Kong, Taiwan, and New Zealand.

### Background

Children's entry into the consumer role, and their subsequently becoming three market segments, is dependent upon childhood consumer socialization that takes place in a particular society. Consumer socialization, as used here, refers to the processes by which the youngest people of a nation acquire skills, knowledge, and attitudes relevant to their functioning in the marketplace.

In the United States learning to be a consumer is expected early in life; therefore, its beginnings can be witnessed at around age 2. Parents take their tots with them to the shopping environment very early in life, perch them high atop a shopping cart, make small talk with them about some of their purchase considerations, and actually buy them things. Such marketplace experiences, along with a great deal of advertising that is targeted to them, soon reveal to the youngsters the desirable things that can be obtained through the purchase process. Two more stages of consumer socialization soon follow. In the next one the child begins making requests for goods and services, and learning tactics that encourage parental acquiescence. By this time marketers may be targeting the children as an influence market. In the final stage the child seeks, is permitted, and even encouraged, to perform independently as a consumer, first by buying something while accompanied by parents, then by performing alone. At this point children are perceived by marketers as a primary market of consumers who buy on their own, an influence market that persuades parents to buy specific kinds and brands of things, and a future market for goods and services that will make independent purchases for many years.

Hence, at the point at which children become independent consumers, they constitute three markets in one: present, influence, and future. Identifying this juncture in the consumer socialization of a nation's children is therefore critical to marketers. Two occurrences mark this point of fruition. One is children possessing money to spend for their own needs and wants; the second is actually spending it—making independent purchases. The money that they spend has most likely been provided by their parents, who as primary socialization agents want the children to practice what they have learned up to that point.

The actual act of independently spending his or her own money for personal needs marks the child as a bona fide consumer. These measures of the nature and extent of children's income and independent purchasing in a particular country can provide both domestic and international marketers with basic indicators of the consumer socialization status of its youngest consumers. When provided on a global basis these measures can aid marketing strategy development for international marketers who seek worldwide expansion.

A basic business question then follows, and that is, are there enough similarities in children worldwide to permit a global marketing strategy? For U.S. marketers such as Toys "R" Us and McDonald's, and European marketers such as Laura Ashley and Benetton, who are already becoming global marketers to children, the answer is apparently yes. However, published measures of similarities and differences in the consumer behavior of children worldwide that would actually answer this question do not exist. That is the purpose of the research efforts being reported here. Even where similarities exist, international marketers must be very alert to cultural differences, although they can take some comfort in knowing that typically children do not yet have well-developed preferences and therefore are susceptible to marketing persuasion. Even if children are not the primary consumers of a firm because of the nature of its offering, they can be cultivated as influence and future markets which may ease the firm's entry into a new culture-specific market.

## The Research Program

In order to determine the extent and nature of children's consumer socialization throughout the industrialized world a three-part, ongoing program was established at Texas A&M University, consisting of the following phases.

**PRELIMINARY PHASE.** This phase consists of contacting by mail three or more individuals, in each of the largest 25 industrial nations, who have been identified as having good knowledge of children's consumer behavior. These experts are asked to complete a pretested questionnaire consisting of eight open-ended questions related to children's age as consumers, their income, purchase behavior, and the influences on their consumer behavior. This phase provides the preliminary assessments of consumer socialization in a country—a first glimpse—that guides researchers in the next two phases. While these data are only rough estimates, they are based on multiple sources of experts and therefore can be informative for potential international marketers.

**ECONOMIC PHASE.** In this part of the research program the data from the preliminary phase are confirmed by visiting the country and, with research assistants selected from its population, surveying parents to determine children's income, saving, spending, and spending patterns. Here, we get specific measures of the extent to which consumer socialization of children is intended by parents and the nature of its development.

**PSYCHOLOGICAL PHASE.** Concurrently with the economic phase, or following shortly after it, we visit selected primary schools and conduct studies among each nation's children in order to assess their perceptions of the marketplace—what it means to them as consumers. This information reveals the psychological dimension of their consumer socialization. It tells us how they feel about being a consumer, what they know about it, and their degree of enthusiasm for it. We obtain the measures of children's perceptions of the marketplace through drawing studies. We have found that drawings not only overcome the difficulties children often have in articulating their feelings, but they also circumvent the language barriers encountered in conducting research among children of many nations.

The measures obtained from all three research phases are compared to similar measures among children in the United States where, as mentioned, children are the focus of both consumer socialization and marketing efforts at a very early age. This relative measure of children's consumer status in a nation provides an additional perspective to international marketers who are familiar with U.S. consumers. We recognize that converting money measures of a nation's children into a common denominator of U.S. dollars does not actually equate them anymore than comparing them on the basis of years of schooling, but it is an acceptable practice of international marketers to look to U.S. consumers as a standard because of the substantial amount of data that exists about U.S. youngsters.

## Methodology

Preliminary data obtained from experts indicated that consumer socialization was occurring among children of the Pacific Rim, and that school-aged children were performing in the consumer role to some extent. Therefore, we decided to undertake our initial research effort in Hong Kong, Taiwan, and New Zealand to determine the nature and extent of children's consumer socialization in these three geographies.

Hong Kong, Taiwan, and New Zealand were the first locations to be researched among the twenty-five to thirty industrialized countries because they were relatively small in population, relatively self-contained, relatively stable, and known to be market driven. Through contact with education officials, an inventory of kindergarten and elementary schools was developed for each nation. A group of public and private schools was selected from major population centers, and clusters of classrooms were randomly chosen from these schools consisting of 500–600 children for each of the three countries.

Children were given a questionnaire that had been developed and tested for each country by researchers recruited and trained for this task. The children were asked to take the questionnaire home to their parents, who were given instructions for completing and returning it. Net sample sizes of 383, 440, and 569 were obtained from Hong Kong (all Chinese), Taiwan, and New Zealand, respectively. Age cells were not equal but adequately matched, and representation of boys and girls was about equal.

## Findings

Table 11–2 summarizes the average income, spending, and savings according to age for children in all three Pacific Rim countries. The existence of these data suggest the existence of a consumer socialization system. To get a comparative picture of these data, Figures 11–2, 11–3, and 11–4 display separate line charts for the children's income, spending, and savings. All the economic data have been converted to U.S. dollars for comparison purposes. Also, in both the table and the charts, similar data for U.S. children are presented in order to provide an additional perspective to the economic information about children in these three countries. Let us consider each economic dimension.

**INCOME.** Children from all three countries receive money to spend by age 4 (which suggests that many may be receiving money to spend before that age). In Hong Kong and Taiwan practically all

**TABLE 11–2**

Income, Spending, and Savings of Children in Hong Kong, Taiwan, and New Zealand, Compared with the United States

| Age | Hong Kong | | | Taiwan | | | New Zealand | | | United States | | |
|---|---|---|---|---|---|---|---|---|---|---|---|---|
| | Income | Spending | Saving | Income | Spending | Saving | Income | Spending | Saving | Income | Spending | Saving |
| 4 | $0.95 | $0.22 | $0.73 | $1.95 | $1.10 | $0.85 | $1.52 | $0.80 | $0.72 | $1.78 | $0.83 | $0.95 |
| 5 | 1.08 | 0.36 | 0.72 | 2.22 | 1.42 | 0.80 | 1.90 | 0.66 | 1.24 | 1.98 | 1.31 | 0.67 |
| 6 | 1.33 | 0.57 | 0.76 | 2.25 | 1.42 | 0.83 | 2.90 | 1.26 | 1.64 | 2.71 | 1.98 | 0.73 |
| 7 | 2.88 | 1.45 | 1.43 | 2.22 | 1.12 | 1.09 | 2.83 | 1.22 | 1.61 | 3.12 | 2.59 | 0.53 |
| 8 | 2.92 | 0.85 | 2.07 | 2.26 | 1.32 | 0.94 | 3.18 | 1.60 | 1.58 | 3.41 | 2.66 | 0.75 |
| 9 | 3.12 | 1.25 | 1.87 | 2.71 | 1.54 | 1.17 | 3.21 | 1.53 | 1.68 | 4.83 | 3.20 | 1.63 |
| 10 | 3.16 | 1.08 | 2.08 | 2.84 | 1.70 | 1.14 | 4.11 | 1.94 | 2.19 | 4.88 | 3.28 | 1.60 |
| 11 | 4.32 | 1.68 | 2.64 | 4.40 | 2.60 | 1.80 | 4.83 | 2.96 | 1.87 | 7.67 | 5.05 | 2.64 |
| 12 | 5.11 | 3.11 | 1.99 | 5.91 | 1.04 | 1.87 | 8.32 | 4.61 | 3.71 | 9.83 | 6.90 | 2.93 |
| Mean | $3.22 | $1.41 | $1.81 | $2.97 | $1.81 | $1.16 | $3.65 | $1.84 | $1.80 | $4.47 | $3.09 | $1.38 |

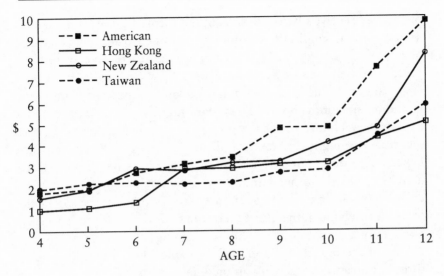

**FIGURE 11–2**

*Income of Children in Hong Kong, Taiwan, and New Zealand Compared with the United States.*

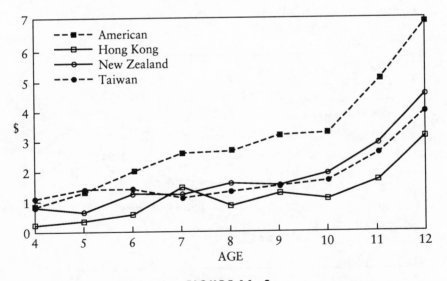

**FIGURE 11–3**

*Spending of Children in Hong Kong, Taiwan, and New Zealand Compared with the United States.*

the money received by children is in the form of allowances. There are occasional small gifts of money but none is the result of work or household chores. In New Zealand, children receive around 28 percent of their income as allowances, 19 percent as gifts from parents, 16 percent as gifts from relatives, and 37 percent from work in and outside of the home. These data suggest that Chinese parents expect their children to have money to spend but to not devote any time earning it. In fact, as indicated in other research, they are expected to devote most of their waking hours to school-related activities. On the other hand, New Zealand parents expect their children (somewhat like U.S. children) to learn about the work ethics from receiving money, and therefore to devote some time to such work efforts as baby-sitting, house cleaning, and milking cows.

One of the first things apparent in Table 11–2 is that kids in all three countries are receiving an income as early as age 4—95 cents for Hong Kong kids, $1.95 for Taiwanese, and $1.52 for New Zealanders—just as they are in the United States. When we realize that average household income for these three nations is substantially below that of the United States, we sense that kids in these three geographies may actually receive a greater proportion of household

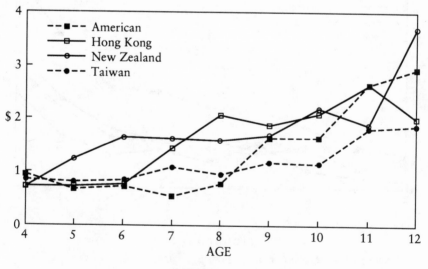

**FIGURE 11–4**

*Saving of Children in Hong Kong, Taiwan, and New Zealand Compared with the United States.*

income to spend than kids in the United States, particularly Taiwanese children. From this single data point one gets the impression that there is a strong desire on the part of parents in the Pacific Rim to get their children indoctrinated into the consumer role.

Another noticeable fact regarding children's income in these three countries is its progressiveness. The chart in Figure 11–2 plots children's income for ages 4–12 for each country as well as the United States and shows a gradual upturn for all. This increase in income that accompanies age suggests that both Chinese and New Zealand parents recognize that their children need more money to spend as they grow older and discover more things to want. Most likely this recognition is prompted in part by the children's requests for more money and more things.

The net results of consumer socialization efforts by parents directed to their children in these three countries is that the children have an average income of $3.22 a week in Hong Kong, $2.97 in Taiwanese, and $3.65 in New Zealand. The higher average income for New Zealand children may be explained in part by the hefty increase in income at age 12 that is a result of these children's working more both in and outside the home.

**SPENDING.** Table 11–2 shows that Hong Kong, Taiwanese, and New Zealand children have money to spend and that they may begin spending some of it as early as age 4. Looking at the line chart in Figure 11–3 we can see a slight increase in children's spending between the ages of 4 and 10 in all countries. At around age 10 their spending behavior becomes much more robust, showing a sharp upturn for all youngsters.

It would appear, then, that by age 10 serious spending by Pacific Rim children has begun. At age 4 the amount of income spent is very small for Hong Kong children (23 percent), but fairly significant for New Zealand (53 percent) and Taiwanese children (56 percent). But by age 7, children from all three places are spending half or more of their money. Overall, children in Hong Kong average spending the least, $1.41 weekly, with children from Taiwan and New Zealand both spending about the same, $1.81 and $1.84, respectively. As might be expected, all three spending levels are less that the $3.09 a week of U.S. kids. Some of the explanation for the level of spending is explained by the level of savings.

**SAVINGS.** Children from all three countries as well as those in the United States save some of their income, but U.S. children save the least—31 percent compared to 49 percent for New Zealand children, 39 percent for Taiwanese, and 56 percent for those in Hong Kong. A look at the line chart in Figure 11–4 shows the generally gradual increase in savings among all the children studied. In no case are children spending all their money as we often characterize them in the United States, although at age 7, U.S. children save relatively little.

Based on the responses of the parents in these studies, there seem to be, at least to some degree, three different philosophies of saving being portrayed here. To oversimplify, U.S. children are expected to save in order to be able to buy higher-ticket items in the near future. New Zealand children are expected to save to insure a bright future for themselves. Chinese children are expected to save in order to help provide eternal prestige (what they call *mien tsu*). Thus, some of the Chinese children's savings are related to the centuries-old value of saving face, while New Zealand children seem to be expected to be frugal, perhaps we would call it conservative, and U.S. children are expected to save for materialistic purposes.

**STORE VISITS.** Pacific Rim parents were asked the extent to which their children get to make independent purchases when they shop together, the extent to which the children make purchase visits to stores on their own, and for both cases, the frequency and the types of stores in which buying takes place. A summary of their responses is displayed in Table 11–3 by country along with similar data on U.S. children for comparison purposes.

It appears that an even larger number of Chinese children at age 4 make independent purchases while accompanying their parents to the marketplace than do children in the United States. For Taiwan this figure is 50 percent; for Hong Kong, 67 percent. The comparable figure for New Zealand is 29 percent; 30 percent for U.S. children. This percentage starts out relatively low for New Zealand children, but increases quickly before leveling off at around 75 percent. It continues in the United States with all children eventually making purchases while shopping with their parents. In Hong Kong and Taiwan the percentage of children who go shopping with parents and make independent purchases actually turns down once the

**TABLE 11–3**

*Shopping Behavior of New Zealand, Taiwanese, and Hong Kong Children Compared to U.S. Children*

| Age | Children (%) | | Average Number of Trips/Week | | Average Number of Different Stores | |
|---|---|---|---|---|---|---|
| | With Parents | Without Parents | With Parents | Without Parents | With Parents | Without Parents |
| | | | Hong Kong | | | |
| 4 | 67 | 2 | 1.2 | 0.7 | 1.0 | 0.0 |
| 5 | 67 | 33 | 1.3 | 1.3 | 1.0 | 1.0 |
| 6 | 70 | 42 | 1.4 | 1.9 | 1.2 | 1.1 |
| 7 | 52 | 53 | 1.4 | 1.8 | 1.3 | 1.4 |
| 8 | 39 | 78 | 1.6 | 2.0 | 1.1 | 1.2 |
| 9 | 42 | 89 | 1.4 | 2.1 | 1.3 | 1.3 |
| 10 | 35 | 99 | 1.5 | 2.9 | 1.3 | 1.7 |
| 11 | 30 | 100 | 1.5 | 3.2 | 1.2 | 1.7 |
| 12 | 34 | 100 | 1.7 | 3.7 | 1.7 | 2.1 |
| | | | Taiwan | | | |
| 4 | 50 | 0 | 1.0 | 0.0 | 1.0 | 0.0 |
| 5 | 80 | 40 | 1.2 | 1.2 | 1.0 | 1.0 |
| 6 | 83 | 50 | 1.0 | 2.0 | 1.3 | 1.3 |
| 7 | 67 | 67 | 1.9 | 1.9 | 1.5 | 1.3 |
| 8 | 72 | 67 | 1.5 | 2.3 | 1.2 | 1.2 |
| 9 | 67 | 100 | 1.5 | 3.1 | 1.3 | 1.6 |
| 10 | 65 | 100 | 1.5 | 2.9 | 1.2 | 1.6 |
| 11 | 54 | 100 | 1.6 | 3.2 | 1.3 | 1.6 |
| 12 | 40 | 100 | 1.6 | 3.4 | 1.4 | 2.3 |
| | | | New Zealand | | | |
| 4 | 29 | 29 | 1.6 | 1.5 | 1.3 | 1.5 |
| 5 | 60 | 35 | 1.6 | 1.6 | 1.7 | 1.4 |
| 6 | 55 | 40 | 1.2 | 1.6 | 1.4 | 1.8 |
| 7 | 76 | 62 | 1.2 | 1.4 | 1.7 | 1.2 |
| 8 | 69 | 64 | 1.1 | 1.5 | 1.9 | 1.5 |
| 9 | 62 | 65 | 1.3 | 1.8 | 1.7 | 1.2 |
| 10 | 64 | 82 | 1.2 | 1.6 | 1.9 | 1.4 |
| 11 | 73 | 80 | 1.2 | 1.8 | 1.9 | 1.4 |
| 12 | 68 | 82 | 1.2 | 1.6 | 1.6 | 1.7 |
| | | | United States | | | |
| 4 | 30 | 6 | 2.0 | 1.0 | 2.0 | 1.0 |
| 5 | 54 | 20 | 2.0 | 1.0 | 2.0 | 1.0 |

**TABLE 11–3 (continued)**

| Age | Children (%) | | Average Number of Trips/Week | | Average Number of Different Stores | |
|---|---|---|---|---|---|---|
| | With Parents | Without Parents | With Parents | Without Parents | With Parents | Without Parents |
| 6 | 65 | 50 | 2.2 | 1.0 | 2.3 | 1.2 |
| 7 | 88 | 71 | 2.8 | 1.6 | 2.5 | 2.0 |
| 8 | 99 | 77 | 2.7 | 1.8 | 2.8 | 2.0 |
| 9 | 99 | 92 | 2.8 | 1.9 | 2.9 | 2.2 |
| 10 | 100 | 99 | 2.9 | 2.3 | 2.9 | 2.2 |
| 11 | 100 | 99 | 2.9 | 2.8 | 2.9 | 2.2 |
| 12 | 100 | 100 | 2.4 | 2.8 | 2.5 | 2.3 |

children are in school. In both of these Chinese cultures, parents (mainly mothers) tend to shop during the time the children are in school, and therefore the youngsters don't accompany them. However, they sometimes shop together at nights (in the "night markets") and on weekends.

The number of trips with parents and the number of types of stores in which purchases are made also are shown in Table 11–3 for children from all four countries. The number of trips and number of different stores tend to be higher for the U.S. children and lowest for New Zealand children. New Zealand mothers often reported that taking children shopping was inconvenient and troublesome; therefore, they tended to minimize shopping trips together, particularly after the children began school. Also, many New Zealand parents live in rural areas (as compared to Hong Kong and Taiwan) and thus try to make fewer shopping trips in general. The result is that a 10-year-old, for example, in New Zealand and Taiwan will go to the store with parents approximately once every three weeks, while a similar youngster in Hong Kong will go slightly more often. In all three cases the youngsters typically will make purchases in a food store (supermarket) and a toy store.

By the time Pacific Rim youngsters are completing the first grade of school, at around age 8, from two-thirds to three-quarters will have made purchase trips on their own, usually to a convenience store. This is similarly true for U.S. kids. While these purchase trips are without parents, they may be with brothers, sisters, and friends. In fact, in New Zealand it is normal for an older sibling to take a younger one to the corner dairy store for a lollie (candy) or a beverage.

The actual number of independent purchase visits to stores increases in number for Taiwanese and Hong Kong children as they tend to make purchases during walks to and from school. The number of different stores in which their independent purchases are made are about the same with or without parents.

Generally speaking, Pacific Rim children show maturity in independent purchases at least as early as American children. They have money of their own to spend, and by the time they are in school they have had some practice in spending it. The frequency of purchase visits increases with age and with income.

**PURCHASE OBJECTS.** What do Pacific Rim children buy with their money? The answer is summarized in Table 11–4 along with comparison data for U.S. children.

A quick glance at the table suggests that children from Hong Kong, Taiwan, and New Zealand differ little from each other or from U.S. kids when it comes to spending money. All of them spend 60 percent or more on things to snack on and things to play with. New Zealanders spend the most on snacks and sweets (53 percent of their money), while Hong Kong and U.S. children spend about the same (38 and 35 percent, respectively) on this category. Tai-

**TABLE 11–4**

*Percent of Income and Spending on Selected Items
by Pacific Rim Children Compared to U.S. Children*

| Product/service Catetory | Hong Kong | Taiwan | New Zealand | United States |
|---|---|---|---|---|
| Snacks/Sweets | 38 | 42 | 53 | 35 |
| Play Items | 25 | 38 | 18 | 31 |
| Clothing | 4 | 2 | 0 | 12 |
| Entertainment | 6 | 5 | 3 | 18 |
| School Supplies | 23 | 12 | 7 | 0 |
| Other | 4 | 1 | 19 | 4 |

wanese kids spend the most on play items (38 percent), followed by U.S. kids (31 percent), Hong Kong kids (25 percent), and New Zealand kids (18 percent).

Regarding snacks, children from all three countries buy both salty and sweet snacks, with a preference for sweets. Noticeably, though, the Chinese children prefer their sweet snacks less sweet than the New Zealand and U.S. children. Also, chewing gum seems popular among Chinese kids as it is among the U.S. kids, but much less so among New Zealand youngsters.

The major differences in purchases among the Pacific Rim children, and between them and U.S. children, are in the other categories shown in Table 11–4. Practically none of the children buy clothes with their own money as compared with U.S. kids who spend at least 12 percent of their money on this category. On the other hand, U.S. kids usually do not buy school-related items with their own money as kids from these Pacific Rim countries do. School items account for almost a quarter of Hong Kong children's spending, 12 percent of Taiwanese spending, and seven percent of New Zealand spending. Also, U.S. kids spend 18 percent of their money on entertainment such as movies and video game parlors while Pacific Rim kids spend 6 percent or less here. Finally, the "other" category is not significant except for New Zealand youngsters who spend about 20 percent of their income on gifts for family members.

## Multinational Marketing Strategy to Kids: Standardize or Localize?

Many business firms in the United States, Great Britain, Japan, and other countries have multinational marketing strategies in place. Some of these firms, such as Mattel, McDonald's, Pepsi, Sony, and Toys "R" Us also target children as one or more markets. Thus, the behavior of these and other firms suggest that a multinational marketing strategy to kids is viable. Let us explore the possibility of this marketing action beyond what a few companies are doing.

Table 11–1 showed that there are at least three-quarters of a billion youngsters in the industrialized world. Further, the study reported above regarding the three Pacific Rim countries of Hong Kong, Taiwan, and New Zealand showed that the minimum average weekly income of children was around $3. There is no reason not to believe that children of European countries would not have at least this much income. In fact, one study of British children shows their income to be close to that of U.S. children.[7] Therefore, if we used $3 weekly as a baseline, we would find that the industrialized world's children have around $117 billion to spend. Thus, producers and sellers of sweet things and playthings, for instance, should be able to sense substantial market opportunities among these 700-plus million kids as primary consumers.

Additionally, kids have even greater market potential as an influence market. In India, for example, many children not only influence the purchases of their parents, but often inform their parents of many other aspects of consumption behavior.[8] A report out of Britain conducted by Market Behavior Limited for The National Consumer Council details how children's influence on parents' purchases of children's athletic shoes is so strong that the children are obtaining a disproportionate share of the family budget.[9] This is in a country where there is still very little television advertising reaching the children. With satellite-based television broadcasting growing rapidly in Europe and Asia, children can be expected to discover many more things to request from their parents.

As U.S. marketers have known for a long time, and as large numbers of them have recently begun to act on, children are a future market that can be cultivated now so that when children reach market age they can more easily be converted into customers—hopefully into more loyal customers. In order to enter new markets overseas it may be necessary for U.S. firms to practice a more than usual amount of customer development. But because the industrialized world's children are already involved in the marketplace—as current and as influence markets—marketing to them as future consumers can be more easily implemented.

Finally, it is logical to ask about the cultural influences on children's consumer behavior around the world. Can U.S. marketers perform effectively in these other cultures, such as the Chinese culture, and can they use standardized (global) marketing strategies or will they have to localize their strategies? The studies in the Pacific Rim indeed did reveal some cultural differences, for example, the emphasis on saving among the Chinese in Hong Kong and Taiwan. Also, there were some subtle differences in the nature of products that Pacific Rim children desired. The Chinese children, for instance, seemed to prefer their sweet snacks less sweet than did American children. So, some localization of marketing strategies may be necessary. Additionally, of course, some language changes would be necessary in marketing communications, although these would not be major matters.

In general, it appears that before there is a geographic culture there is a children's culture; that children are very much alike around the industrialized world. They love to play, first and foremost, they love to snack, mainly on sweets, and they love being children with other children (in contrast to assuming most adult roles). The result is that they very much want the same things, that they generally translate their needs into similar wants that tend to transcend culture. Therefore, it appears that fairly standardized multinational marketing strategies to children around the globe are viable. And they are advisable for those American marketers who are wanting to avoid some of the intense competition domestically and are thinking of seeking market and profit growth across the seas.

# References

1. Stephen Downer, "Mexico Sweet on Pepsi's Candy," *Advertising Age,* October 12, 1987, p. 69.
2. James U. McNeal and Chyon-Hwa Yeh, "A Study of Children's Consumer Socialization in Hong Kong and Its Marketing Implications," in Kin-Chok Mun, ed., *Asia-Pacific Business in the 90's* (Hong Kong: Academy of International Business, Southeast Asia Region, 1990), pp. 322–327.
3. Christopher Knowlton, "Europe Cooks Up a Cereal Brawl," *Fortune,* June 3, 1991, pp. 175–179.
4. McNeal and Yeh, "A Study." See also James U. McNeal and Chyon-Hwa Yeh, "Taiwanese Children as Consumers," *Asia-Pacific International Journal of Marketing,* 2, No. 2 (1990): 32–43.
5. Eduard Stupening, "Detrimental Effects of Television Advertising on Consumer Socialization," *Journal of Business Research,* March 1982, pp. 75–84.
6. Ruby Roy Dholakia, "Intergeneration Differences in Consumer Behavior: Some Evidence from a Developing Country," *Journal of Business Research,* March 1984, pp. 19–34.
7. "Small Change," *The Economist,* December 20, 1986, pp. 63–64.
8. Dholakia, "Intergeneration Differences in Consumer Behavior."
9. *A Qualitative Exploration into Buying Clothes and Shoes* (London: Market Behaviour Limited, 1990).

# Name Index

ABC, 171
Adair, David A., 179
Adams, Muriel J., 129
Advertising Research Foundation, 220
Allen, Ben, 201
Anthony, Sterling, 201
Apple, 72
Arista Records, 167
Arm & Hammer, 97
AT&T, 91, 98, 103

Banquet Kid Cuisine, 194–195
Barbie, 5, 188
*Bear Essential News for Kids,* 140, 164, 169
Berry, Jon, 157
Best, 109
Big Wheel, 5
Binney & Smith, 103
Blockbuster, 76
Bloomingdale's, 123
*Boy's Life,* 71, 137, 140
Bubble Yum, 5
Burger King, 5, 132, 144
Burger King Kids' Club, 6, 132, 162

Cabbage Patch, 185
Cadbury's Caramello, 165
Calvin Klein, 53
Carlson, Les, 87
Caron, Andre, 87
Chef Boyardee's Dinosaurs, 194
Cheetos Paws, 40
Children's Radio Network, 71
Child World, 109, 175
Circle K, 4, 109
Circuit City, 109
Citicorp, 172
*Class Acts,* 71, 140
Coca-Cola, 35, 96, 99, 166, 168, 169

Cracker Jacks, 160, 161
Crayola, 96, 167

Dad's root beer, 185
Dagnoli, Judann, 157
Davis, Clara, 201
Delta Airlines, 71
Dennis, W., 61
Dholokia, Ruby Roy, 250
DiLeo, Joseph H., 61
Dillard's, 53
Disney Land, 125
Disney World, 125
Domino's Pizza, 138
Downer, Stephen, 250
Dunkin, Amy, 201

Electronic Sketch Pad, 82
Erickson, Julie L., 157
Esprit, 41, 53, 117

Fahey, Alison, 157, 201
Family Circle, 123
Family Home Entertainment, 163
*Fantastic Flyer,* 71, 169
Fidelity Investments, 101
Finn, David, 179
First Children's Bank, 6, 31
First National Bank Kids' Klub, 125, 175
Fisher-Price, 103, 183, 186
Flintstones, 160, 169
Foley's, 53
Foote, Cone & Belding, 149
Forcade, Karen, 149, 157
*Fort Worth Star Telegram,* 140
Fox Kids' Club, 6, 132, 162
Frankel and Company, 164
Freeman, Laurie, 129
Frito Lay Doritos, 196
Frosted Flakes, 5, 185
Fruit Roll-ups, 188

Galoob MicroMachines, 163
Galst, Joann Paley, 87
Gap, 41
Gap Kids, 6
General Foods' Honeycomb Hideout Club,
    176
General Mills, 91, 176
Geoffrey, 5
Gibson, Richard, 157
Gitano, 41, 82
Gobots, 160
Goerne, Carrie, 179
Graham, Ellen, 61, 87
Green Mountain Express, 123
Griggs, Robyn, 157
Grossbart, Sanford, 87
Guber, Selina S., 65
Guess, 53
Guest, Lester P., 104

Hall, Jim, 20
Hammacher Schlemmer, 72
Harris, Timothy, 225
Hershey, 35
Higgins, Kevin T., 201, 225
*Houston Chronicle*, 165
Howard Johnson, 164
Hume, Scott, 179
Hyatt, 98

Imperial, 100

Jacoby, Jacob, 104
J. C. Penney, 123, 171
Jennings, Marianne M., 157
John, Deborah R., 225

Kansas Beef Council, 102
Kaplan, Michael, 179
Kathleen Harrington Communications,
    132
Kaybee, 39
Keebler, 123
Keebler Fan Club, 162
Kellogg, 91
Kellogg's Apple Jacks, 194
Kentucky Fried Chicken, 233
Kids Choice Broadcasting Network, 6
Kid's Kitchen Mac 'N Cheese, 194
K-Mart, 4, 13, 39, 48, 53, 82, 91, 109,
    117, 123, 197
Knowlton, Christopher, 250

Kool-Aid, 83, 123
Kool Bursts, 165, 188
Kraft, 6, 98
Kraft Cheese and Macaroni Club, 6, 162
Kroger, 13, 39, 44
Kyner, David B., 104

Lego, 123
Leo, Dr. Joseph H., 61
Levi's, 82
Levi Strauss, 149
Liebert, D. E., 157
Liebert, R. M., 157
The Limited, 110
Lipman, Joanne, 157
Live Home Video, 166
Liz Claiborne, 117
Loftus, Jack, 179
Looney Tunes, 168
Lublin, Joann S. 179

Magiera, Marcy, 129
Magnet, Myron, 37
Major League Basball Cookies, 165
Market Behavior Limited, 249
Mars Inc. Combos, 196
MasterCard, 172
Mattel, 166
McDaniel, S. W., 104
McDonald, Ronald, 5
McDonald's, 76, 92, 101, 138, 160, 161,
    165, 166, 233
McNeal, James U., 20, 37, 61, 87, 104,
    129, 250
Miller, Cyndee, 87, 179
Milli Vanilli, 167
*Milwaukee Journal*, 140
Minute Maid, 72
*Money*, 29
Moser, Penny, 104
Mun, Kin-Chok, 250
Murphy, Patrick, 104
Murray, Henry A., 104
My First Sony, 82
*My Weekly Reader*, 139

National Creative Marketing, 176
*New York Times*, 140
NFO Research, 205
Nickelodeon, 6, 123, 131, 137, 167
Nike, 83, 101
Nintendo, 83, 123, 149
Nordstrom's, 110

*Parade Magazine,* 164
*Parents,* 29
Peracchio, Laura A., 225
Pereira, Joseph, 87, 157
Pittsburgh Children's Museum, 171
Pizza Hut, 76, 99, 131, 160, 166
Polaroid Cool Cam, 150
Popsicle, 188
Polo, 41
Porter, Donald, 129
Price, Tim, 149
Pringles, 196

Quaker Oats Popeye Club, 162

Revco, 109
Richard, Betsy, 65
Roper, Gar, 225
Rosenberg, Merri, 129, 179
Rozek, Michael, 37
Rubenstein, E. A., 157

Safeway, 109
Sakowitz, 109
Sampling Corporation of America, 165
Sargent's Mootown Snackers, 195–196
Sasson, 41
Sears, 82, 91, 109
7-Eleven, 4, 109
7th Heaven, 123
7-up, 91, 101, 185
Shepherdon, Nancy, 37
Sight and Sound Entertainment, 143
Smart, Denise, 104
Sony, 82
South Hills Mall, 89
*Sports Illustrated for Kids,* 6, 29, 30, 37, 142, 183, 208
Sprafken, J. N., 157

Stearn, Sara E., 201
Stern Walters, 132
Stewart, Doug, 201
Stipp, Horst, 65
Stupening, Edward, 250
Sugar Bear, 167
Sugar Pops, 5
Sujan, Mita, 225
*Sunday Journal,* 140
Super Golden Crisp, 167
Sweetarts, 165

Tang, 167
Taylor, Julie, D., 225
Teddy Ruxpin, 185
Teenage Mutant Ninja Turtles, 166, 188
Toys "R" Us, 5, 39, 53, 110
Twiglet Bank, 125
Tyson's Looney Tunes Meals, 132, 195

United Artists, 125
Urbanski, Al, 129, 157

Visa, 172

Waldon Kids, 6
Wallack, Janet, 129
*Wall Street Journal,* 142
Wal-Mart, 4, 48, 53, 91, 109, 110, 161, 197
Ward, Scott, 87
*What's Hot for Kids,* 71, 167
White, Mary Alice, 87
White Castle, 160
Whittle Communications, 143

Yeh, Chyon-Hwa, 250
Young Americans Bank, 31, 140
Youth Research, 149

# Subject Index

Advertising to children, 131–157
  ban, 5
  effects, 144–147
  encoding/decoding problems, 147–153
  expenditures, 133–136
  in-school, 142, 143
  in-store, 142
  by mail, 143
  model of, 144–145
  point-of-purchase, 143
  second generation, 131–132
  solipsism in, 4
Advocates (consumer), 5
Allowances, 26
  purposes, 28
Anti-shoppers, 13
Attitude-behavior relationships, 144–146

Baby boom, 4, 7
Banks for kids, 30–31
  practices toward children, 31, 125
Brand awareness among children, 54, 55,
  206–207
Brand loyalty among children, 92–101
Brands, 41
  designer, 41
  licensed, 41

Catalogs for children, 72, 76
  convenience of, 72
  influence on purchases in, 76
  in the home, 72
  purchases from, 76
  that target children, 123
Children as consumers, 3–20
  adults' understanding of, 149
  age of understanding, 150–152
  as a bona fide market, 5
  development among, 8–13, 104
  expenditures by, 4–5
  globally, 229–250

  mindset of, 151–152
  as multi-dimensional market, 14–17
  population of, 4, 5, 7, 230
  publications about, 6
  thinking pattern of, 148–149, 151, 154
  understanding of marketplace, 36
Children's market, 3–20
  benefit segments, 16–17
  demographic segments, 16
  diagram of, 14
  future dimension of, 14, 15, 16, 89–104
  global competition for, 232–233
  from a global perspective, 229–250
  in Hong Kong, 232, 238–250
  in India, 249
  influencer dimension of, 14, 15, 16,
    63–86
  lifestyle segments, 16
  measurements of, 207–209
  in Mexico, 232
  in New Zealand, 238–250
  in the Pacific Rim, 235–250
  primary dimensions of, 14–15, 23–37,
    39–58
  product usage-rate segment, 17
  size, 14–15
  in Taiwan, 229, 238–250
  in the UK, 248–249
Clubs (kids), 132, 173–178
  attractiveness to kids, 176–177
  as channel of distribution, 123–124
  for consumer education, 173–174
  by convenience stores, 117–118
  list of, 174
  and mail advertising, 143
  personal nature, 175
  and premiums, 162
  and relationship marketing, 173–175
  and sales promotion, 131–132
  as single communications channel, 132,
    173

Comic books, 141
Consumer education of children, 5, 89,
  98, 112
  by restaurants, 119–120
  in retailing, 127–128
  by supermarkets, 121–122
  universal guidelines for, 234–235
Consumer socialization, 8
  agents, 8
  marketer's role in, 8, 113–114
  and values, 153
Contests, 166–168
  "Book It," 166
  and brand/seller identity, 167
  children's need met by, 166
  problems, 168
  from retailers, 168
  school-related, 166–167
Coupons, 164–166
  appeal to children, 164–165
  kids' use of, 164–165
  product-targeted, 164–165
  purposes, 164–165

Ethics in marketing to children, 20
Event marketing to children, 170–172
  effectiveness of, 171
  locations, 171–172
  by retailers, 171–172
  types, 170–171
Evoked set, 146
Experts on childrens' consumer behavior,
  103, 187, 222–223

Federal Trade Commission, 5

Global market of children, 229–250
  characteristics, 238–250
  cultural influences in, 249–250
  enhancing descriptions of, 235
  growth opportunities in, 232
  marketing strategies directed to, 248
  preferences among, 233
  reasons to consider, 230–233
  reasons to study, 234–235
  research program in, 237–238
  for U.S. goods, 233

Hong Kong children as consumers, 230–
  232, 238–250
Hotels, 6

Income (children's), 23–27
  by age, 24, 26
  through allowance, 26
  annual, 24, 25
  evaluation of, 28, 29
  through gifts, 27
  from grandparents, 28
  for household chores, 27
  in the Pacific Rim countries, 242–244
  from part-time work, 27, 28
  sources, 26–30
  weekly, 24
Influence (childrens'), 63–71
  by age, 65, 66
  extent of, 65–70
  measurement of, 207–208
  on parental choice of stores, 76
  on parental purchases, 10
  on product types, 64, 67–70
  reasons for, 64–65
  in store, 10

Kid Kustomer, 18
Kid-ness, 187, 188–189

Loyalty among children, 92–101
  and the communications mix, 103–104
  contributing factors, 94, 95
  and likes, 146
  model, 95–101
  through participation, 100
  product-related, 96–98
  proneness, 92, 93
  in retailing, 110–111
  strategies to develop, 92–101

Magazines for children, 140–142
  advertising in, 141
  as credible media, 99–100, 140–142
  as gifts, 141
  pop-up art in, 142
  problems with, 141–142
Marketing communications to children,
  103–104
  expenditures for, 133–136
  joint efforts in, 131
  one channel for, 131, 132
  one source of, 132
  testing, 150–151, 205–206
Marketing research (among children),
  203–225
  for assessing childrens' behavior, 210

Marketing research, *cont.*
  through attitude scales, 214–215
  to measure children's influence, 207–208, 224
  through concept testing, 204–205
  for explaining children's mindworld, 209–210, 213–214
  through focus groups, 215–216
  through laboratory experiments, 212–213
  by market testing, 204
  to measure childrens' economic behavior, 165–209, 224
  mistakes in, 221
  through the observation technique, 210–212
  via parents as surrogates, 223
  through picture drawing, 46–61, 216–220
  problems, 220–223
  purposes of, 204–209
  in restaurants, 119–120
  through role playing, 213
  techniques and procedures for, 210–220
  for testing marketing communications, 205–206, 224
Marketing to children globally, 229–250
  history of, 4
  integrated, 3, 90–91
  using a multidimensional segmentation strategy for, 101–104
  perception of kids' influence, 81–84
  responses to children, 34, 35
  with strategies that target them as future customers, 89–90
  top management involvement in, 103–104
Mental scripts, 10
*Mien Tsu,* 244
Money, children's understanding of, 11, 12

Needs, 189–191
  affiliation, 191
  belonging, 92, 93
  children vs. adult, 190
  fusion of, 191
  for order, 93
  play, 190
  for products, 189–191
  sentience, 190
  variety, 190

Newspapers, 139–140
  advertising to children, 139–140
  influence on reading habits, 140
  and promotion to children, 140–141
New Zealand children as consumers, 238–250

Out-of-stocks, 94
Overprivileged children, 32–34
  demographics for, 33, 34
  household behavior of, 34
  income of, 32–34
  parents of, 33
  purchases by, 33–34
  savings of, 32–34
  spending by, 32–34

P-tests of marketing strategies to children, 147–156, 177–179
Packaging for children, 194–197
  as communications, 150–151, 195
  kids-only, 195–196
  kids vs. adults, 194, 195
  in product development, 193–197
  in purchase environment, 147–148
  as silent salesmen, 132
  in shopping stages, 10
  testing of, 206
Parent test of marketing strategies to children, 154, 155, 178
Perceptions (children's)
  obtained through drawings, 47–61
  regarding fitness, 40
  of retail environments, 47–50, 55–58
  of shopping experience, 46, 47
Pilot tests of marketing strategies to children, 154, 155, 178
Premiums for children, 161–164
  for buying products, 163–164
  for choosing retail outlets, 163
  for joining clubs, 162
  purposes, 161–164
  testing, 205–206
Price consciousness of children, 54, 61
Product placement, 72, 142, 143–144
Products for children, 18, 20, 182–200
  from adult products, 186–188
  based on kid-ness, 188–189
  derived from culture, 186
  development strategies for, 182–189
  evoked by the word "shopping," 50–53
  failures among, 197

food, 51, 52
  guidelines for, developing, 198–200
  imitative strategy for, 184
  innovative strategy for, 184
  kid-only vs. adult-only, 188–189
  most favored by children, 39, 40
  and needs, 189–191
  nonfood, 53
  and packaging, 193–197
  and parental needs, 192
  and play, 191
  toys, 185, 188
  trends in children's purchases of, 40–42
Publicity targeted to children, 131–132,
    159, 168–170
  and advertising, 169–170
  to develop favorable attitudes, 169
  in magazines, 169–170
  media outlets for, 169–170
Public policy, 234
Public relations targeted to children, 132,
    147, 159, 168–177
  credibility of, 168–169
  three main tools of, 169
Purchase requests (by children), 70–86
  information used in, 70
  locations of, 74–75
  marketers' influence on, 74–75, 81–85
  marketing strategies toward, 84–87
  parental responses to, 77–81
  and parental style, 80–81
  in shopping stages, 9–12
  in store, 9–10
  styles of, 72–74
Purchases (children's), 44–46
  by age, 44–46
  independent, 4, 44
  in the Pacific Rim, 247–248
  of products: *see* products
  rate of, 44–46
  in stores types, 43, 44

Radio (children's), 138–139
  advertising, 138–139
  problems in, 138–139
  programming, 138–139
  rating system for, 139
Retailing to kids, 107–129
  by apparel stores, 117
  through catalogs, 123
  with a children orientation, 113–114
  without a children orientation, 115–116
  through consumer education, 114–115
  by convenience stores, 117–118
  through clubs, 123–124
  by department stores, 118
  by drug stores, 119
  ethical practices in, 114–115
  by hotels/motels, 120
  as a future market, 110
  historical comparison of, 111–129
  by mass merchandisers, 118–119
  by movie theaters, 125
  through promotions, 114
  recommendations for, 127–129
  by restaurants, 119–120
  by service retailers, 124–125
  through shopping facilitators, 114
  by specialty stores, 121
  through store personnel, 114
  by supermarkets, 121–122
  through telephones, 122–123
  by variety stores, 122
  through vending machines, 122

Sales promotion (to kids), 131–133, 147,
    159–161
  and brand and seller identity, 161
  expenditures, 160
  and image, 160–161
  and loyalty, 161
  purposes of, 160–161
  as a way to compete, 160–161
Savings (children's), 23–29
  by age, 24
  annual, 24
  means of, 30
  in Pacific Rim countries, 244–247
  popularity of, 29, 30
  practices, 15
  purposes, 30
  rate of, 29, 30, 31
  weekly, 24
School relations, 172–173
  as a part of marketing goals, 172–173
Schools as sources of children's product in-
    formation, 72
Shopping behavior (of children), 9–13
  facilitators of, 114–115
  independent/dependent of parental be-
    havior, 59
  in the Pacific Rim, 244–247
  children's perceptions of: *see* Perceptions
  products obtained through: *see* Products

Shopping behavior (of children), *cont.*
  solo in, 12
  stages in development of, 9–13, 50
  TV advertising and, 9
Shopping carts, 57, 61, 114, 218
Signs in stores, 58
Sociological changes in families, 6, 7, 8
  and children's economic status, 6, 7
  and divorces, 7
  dual careers, 7–8
  and postponement of children, 7
  single-parent homes, 7
Sources of new customers, 91
Spending (children's), 26–31
  by age, 26, 31–32
  annual, 24, 31–32, 35–36
  at Christmas, 30
  by overprivileged children, 32–35
  by Pacific Rim children, 243
  trends in, 32
  weekly, 24, 31, 32, 35
Stores that target children, 43–61
  arcades, 49
  computer, 49
  convenience, 12, 49
  department, 44, 49
  discount, 43, 44

  drug, 49
  fast food, 49
  fixtures in, 58
  images of, 61
  mall, 49
  music in, 58
  and patronage, 44–46
  personnel in, 59, 60
  preferences for, 11, 42–44
  tactics, 35–36
  shoe, 49
  specialty, 43, 44, 48
  supermarkets, 43, 47, 48, 61
  variety, 49
  visits by Pacific Rim children to, 244–246
Sweepstakes for children, 166–168

Taiwanese children as consumers, 64, 229, 233, 235–250
Telephone marketing to children, 165, 167–168
Television marketing to children, 133–135
  expenditures on, 137
  and shopping stages, 9

Video advertising to children, 142

# About the Author

**Dr. James U. McNeal** is professor of marketing at Texas A&M University, where he teaches courses in marketing and consumer behavior. His primary research interests focus on the consumer behavior of children and include tracking the income, savings, and spending patterns of four- to twelve-year-olds. His measures of their expenditures include the amount spent, where they spent it, the products and services purchased, and the frequency of purchase. Dr. McNeal also utilizes a picture-drawing technique to assay the perceptions children hold of the shopping setting, i.e., its stores and their layout, interior/exterior characteristics, and product/brand offerings. Recently, he began extending his research to overseas economies. Dr. McNeal has consulted in the area of children's consumer behavior with such major firms as AT&T, Binney and Smith, Campbell Soup, Procter & Gamble, Sears, and Walt Disney. He is author of seven books and fifty articles, including *Children as Consumers* (Lexington Books, 1987) and *A Bibliography of Research and Writings on Marketing and Advertising to Children* (Lexington Books, 1991).